Afro-Latinos
in the U.S. Economy

A gift from the AEA Summer
Training Program/IPODS
2021 Cohort

Afro-Latinos in the U.S. Economy

Michelle Holder and Alan A. Aja

LEXINGTON BOOKS
Lanham • Boulder • New York • London

Published by Lexington Books
An imprint of The Rowman & Littlefield Publishing Group, Inc.
4501 Forbes Boulevard, Suite 200, Lanham, Maryland 20706
www.rowman.com

6 Tinworth Street, London SE11 5AL, United Kingdom

British Library Cataloguing in Publication Information Available

Library of Congress Cataloging-in-Publication Data
Names: Holder, Michelle, author. | Aja, Alan A., author.
Title: Afro-Latinos in the U.S. economy / Michelle Holder and Alan A. Aja.
Description: Lanham, Maryland : Lexington Books, [2021] | Includes
  bibliographical references and index.
Identifiers: LCCN 2021006394 (print) | LCCN 2021006395 (ebook) | ISBN
  9781498546249 (cloth) | ISBN 9781498546256 (epub)
Subjects: LCSH: African Americans—Economic conditions. | Hispanic
  Americans—Economic conditions. | African Americans—Social conditions.
  | Hispanic Americans—Social conditions. | African Americans—Race
  identity. | Hispanic Americans—Race identity.
Classification: LCC E185.8 .H697 2021 (print) | LCC E185.8 (ebook) | DDC
  305.896/073—dc23
LC record available at https://lccn.loc.gov/2021006394
LC ebook record available at https://lccn.loc.gov/2021006395

Michelle and Alan would jointly like to dedicate the book to the late, great Miriam Jiménez Román. We are forever grateful for her immense intellectual influence on our lives. Rest in power.

I dedicate this book to the most important Afro-Latinas in my life—my mother Daphne Elsada, my daughters Dream Milagros and Damaris Wanjiku, Yvonne, Imani, Desiree, and Nilda. I love you all "to infinity and beyond." *Michelle*

This book is dedicated to my parents, Loyda Puig Aja and Antonio Juan Aja, whose unconditional support during our upbringing allowed us to center social justice in all we do. *Alan*

PRAISE FOR *AFRO-LATINOS IN THE U.S. ECONOMY*

"Providing crucial quantitative evidence and insightful economics-based analyses, Michelle Holder and Alan A. Aja unpack how and why Blackness matters for people self-identifying as both Black and Latinx in the United States."

—**Monika Gosin**, College of William & Mary

Contents

List of Tables and Figures

TABLES

FIGURES

Preface

As we, the co-authors, delved into the final edits of our book, the COVID-19 epidemic hit. As scholars of racial inequality in our respective fields, we are versed in the literature that examines the intersections of racism and health disparities, but few could have been prepared for the trauma and economic effects of COVID-19. Our own positions as City University of New York (CUNY) professors accentuated the growing reality: many of our students and colleagues are "essential" workers, laboring in multiple part-time jobs in local industries that placed them in harm's way, including our own institutions. Our systems, as the literature teaches us, directly place Black Americans in harm's way at all levels—environmentally, socially, and economically. Thus, almost immediately, it became clear that the wave of epidemic illnesses had a disproportionate effect on Black and brown communities. Media reports began to appear that positive COVID cases, as well as deaths due to the illness, from New York City to Chicago to Miami were predominantly "Hispanic" and "Black," with little attention paid to the fact that the two groups aren't mutually exclusive. Save for a few scholars on social media who called out the apparent oversights and erasure, our own scanning couldn't find a single mainstream news article that mentioned the epidemic's impact on the Afro-Latinx community.

And yet, as we practiced physical distancing, and worked in social isolation either with, and even from, our families, another wave of profound and pronounced inequality surfaced. As the police killings of Breonna Taylor and George Floyd began to dominate the airwaves, and a Black-centered, multicultural and youth-led yet intergenerational coalition of people began to take to the streets, calls for "Black Lives Matter" were heard once again. COVID-19 had thrust into view and exacerbated the deep and systemic racial wounds of American society, and the subsequent wave of protests and actions sought to directly confront everyday threats to Black communities.

While this book serves as a portrait of the U.S. Afro-Latinx community using recent data, it was written almost entirely prior to the COVID-19 pandemic and wave of uprisings against police violence. We therefore remain hopeful that the current wave of multiracial protest further shapes not only how we collect data, but also informs social movements of the larger, expansive meaning of "Black" in the United States. Through this increased understanding, our further hope is that this book can be useful for transformative action and policy change.

Acknowledgments

Both Alan and Michelle would like to jointly thank and humbly honor Miriam Jiménez Román, without whom this book would not be possible—you were a shining, beautiful light that was taken from us all too soon. We would also like to thank Joseph Parry of Lexington Books for his infinite patience and persistence in bringing this book to the public, Alison Keefner, Karim Adnane for his expert research assistance, Miriam Jiménez Román and Juan Flores for co-editing the fantastic book *The Afro-Latin@ Reader*, Darrick Hamilton, William "Sandy" Darity Jr., Stephan Lefebvre, Patrick Mason, Monika Gosin, and Brandon Martínez for expert methodological and analytical assistance. We would also like to thank the New School for Social Research, our training ground for many things intellectual and activist-oriented, the City University of New York (CUNY), the National Economic Association (NEA), the American Society for Hispanic Economists (ASHE), the Union of Radical Political Economists (URPE), and the International Association for Feminist Economics (IAFFE). Rest in peace Mr. George Floyd and Ms. Breonna Taylor, among many, many other souls taken from us tragically and too soon.

Michelle Holder would like to thank her mom, Daphne Elsada—Ma, you are the original Afro-Latina role model for me! I'd also like to thank my daughters Dream Milagros and Damaris Wanjiku, whom I'm sure I neglected too often in trying to complete this book. I'd like to thank my awesome brothers Alberto and Michael, always protective, and always supportive of everything I do. I'd like to thank my beautiful niece Imani Meade, sister-in-law Nilda Meade, nephew Ian Meade, my cousins Yvonne Clare, Desiree Holder-Walker, Norma Holder, and Gordon Clare, my sisters-from-other-mothers Agnes Callamard, Jai Landau, Rose Golden, Regina Eaton and Helen Yosef, my brothers-from-other-mothers Adrian Techeira, Robert Jones, and Bobo

Diallo, my godson Khaya Adams, my niece Stella Golden, Tony Medina, Tazewell V. Hurst III, Dr. Melvin Thornton, Joan Williams, Aissatou Barry, Denise Eaton and C. & S. Rush, my friends and colleagues at John Jay College, including Joan Hoffman, Jay Hamilton, Rita Taveras, Geert Dhondt, Christian Parenti, Josh Hamilton, Cathy Mulder, Sara Bernardo, Jessica Gordon-Nembhard, Amy Adamczyk, Alison Pease, Samantha Majic, Daniel Stageman, Elizabeth Nisbet, Shonna Trinch and Lila Kazemian, with a special shout-out to Ian Seda-Irizarry, who told me I had to read Miriam Jiménez Román and Juan Flores's *The Afro-Latin@ Reader*, and he couldn't have been more right since Alan and I cite this text liberally throughout this book. I'd also like to thank my dear friends and colleagues John Sarich, Scott Carter, Steve Carbo, Sarah Tobias, Dana (Dane) Schechtman, Nina Banks, Rhonda Sharpe, Janelle Jones, Kate Bahn, Bill Spriggs, Cruz Bueno, Cary Bueno, Teresa Ghilarducci, Stephanie Seguino, Elissa Braunstein, Randy Albelda, Thomas Masterson, Nell Abernathy, Radhika Balakrishnan, Heidi Hartmann, Valerie Wilson, John Schmitt, Caroline Hossein, Rakeen Mabud, Yana van der Meulen Rodgers, Matt Hughes, Kendra Bozarth, Jocelyn C. Frye, Mona Ali, Sirisha Naidu, and Smita Ramnarain. I'd also like to give an institutional shout-out to John Jay College, my academic home. My sincerest apologies to anyone I've very likely forgotten to mention herein. Special shout-outs to Tone Loc (again—so nice, had to say it twice!), Naomi Minkoff of Rowman & Littlefield, and our highly-skilled but anonymous proofreader. I couldn't have done this without your collective and steadfast guidance—gracias!

Alan Aja would like to thank his family, from Brooklyn to Oakland to Orlando to Loveland to Philadelphia, for their unconditional support as this book was under development. Especially my parents, Loyda Puig and Antonio Aja, whose life dedication to social justice forever shaped our own. To Wendy and Liam Elian, whose patience and love are forever appreciated amid the stress of teaching and book deadlines. With thanks to Vane, David, Jesse Miguel, and Lucas Joaquin for their familial support. Special thanks to colleagues and friends of the Department of Puerto Rican & Latino Studies and interdisciplinary allies at Brooklyn College (CUNY), María Pérez y González, Reynaldo Ortiz-Minaya, Vanessa Pérez Rosario, Carla Santamaria, Matilda Nistal, Roberto Martinez, Irene Sosa, Gaston Alonso, Carolina Bank Muñoz, Tamara Mose, Jeanne Theoharis, Joseph Entin, Prudence Cumberbatch, Jocelyn Wills, Alex Vitale, María Scharrón-del Río, Mike Menser, Lawrence Johnson, Ken Gould, Rojo Robles, James Davis, and many others who supported me amid the forces of austerity to be a part of this project. I would like to thank the Chairs at Brooklyn College who voted favorably on my sabbatical fellowship as I desperately needed relief from the persistent austerity and ongoing struggle to keep ethnic studies alive and resourced at CUNY, and I am grateful for our union's support (PSC-CUNY) in this regard. At times, external advice from Miriam Jiménez Román, Danielle Clealand, Sandy Darity Jr., Nancy López, Antwuan Wallace, and Darrick Hamilton was sought when methodologies and analysis provided the typical roadblock, to which I am grateful. E-mail exchanges with Louise Seamster, Fenaba Addo, Victor Ray, and Stephan Lefebvre over larger sociological content in this book were extremely helpful. This includes work conducted on the "Color of Wealth in Miami," a collaboration with Anne Price, Darrick Hamilton, Sandy Darity Jr., Mark Paul, Danielle Clealand, Gretchen Beesing, Daniel Bustillo, Jhumpa Bhattacharya, and Khai Zaw. I am so grateful for that experience as it informed one of our chapters and provided a model for needed, larger-scale to localized studies on the Afro-Latinx "wealth" experience. This also goes to the amazing folks at the *Modern Monetary Network* and *National Jobs for All Coalition*, whose work and advocacy for a federal job guarantee are embedded within. Special thanks to doctoral candidate Brandon Martínez at the University of Miami who came in at the last minute with his burgeoning expertise. Finally, merci/gracias to the welcoming folks in the Facultad de Geografía e Historia at the Universitat de Barcelona who provided a temporary home and space during my semester sabbatical to work on early stages of this project, especially Meritxell Tous Mata and Pilar Jordan for hosting me with such open arms. Apologies to anyone I have likely forgotten.

Chapter One

Demographic and Historical Context

According to the U.S. Census Bureau, there are well over 1 million Afro-Latinxs estimated to be living in the United States.[1] While this group constitutes a comparatively small segment of the U.S. population, it is often viewed as the nexus between this country's two largest minority groups—African Americans and Latinxs, who comprise 13 percent and 17 percent, respectively, of the U.S. population. When one thinks of great Afro-Latinxs in recent history, individuals such as Arturo Schomburg, Celia Cruz, and Roberto Clemente may come to mind. Conventional narrative holds that Latinxs and African Americans, when studied as distinct groups, have long histories of battling similar forms of discrimination and disenfranchisement in the U.S., and therefore share socioeconomic characteristics in common such as lower average wages and higher unemployment and poverty rates when compared to non-Latinx whites. But compared to the Latinx community overall, Afro-Latinxs in the U.S. are much more likely to be born in the country, and many native-born Afro-Latinxs have an African American parent. Indeed, it has been estimated that nearly half of Afro-Latinxs under the age of 18 in the U.S. have one parent who is African American.[2] U.S. Census data supports the significant place of African Americans in the Afro-Latinx community; *just over 20 percent of all Afro-Latinxs in the U.S., regardless of nativity, indicate African American as their primary ancestry, and nearly a third of all U.S. born (including Puerto Ricans) Afro-Latinxs indicate their primary ancestry as African American*—see figure 1.1.

The aim of this book is to outline the current position and status of Afro-Latinxs in the economy of the United States as well as uncover their specific racialized material experiences. By their unique positioning as both "Black" and "Hispanic/Latinx," the Afro-Latinx community, regardless of national origin, is virtually overlooked in the economics discipline. Little research has been

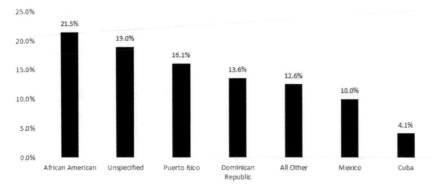

Figure 1.1.   **Reported Primary Ancestry of Afro-Latinxs in the U.S., 2011–2015.** *Data Source*: Author analysis of 2011–2015 American Community Survey 5-year data obtained from Steven Ruggles, Katie Genadek, Ronald Goeken, Josiah Grover, and Matthew Sobek. Integrated Public Use Microdata Series, Version 6.0 [dataset]. Minneapolis, University of Minnesota, 2015. http://doi.org/1018128/D010.V6.0.

disseminated in the field of economics on the contributions of Afro-Latinxs to the American economy with regard to income and wealth generation, labor market status, occupational mobility, and educational attainment. On the other hand, the fields of anthropology, history, sociology, political science, legal studies, and ethnic studies, broadly speaking, continue to produce more research on U.S. Afro-Latinxs, as have overlapping fields from the humanities, cultural studies, and literary criticism.[3] The discipline of economics is, thus, behind the curve in exploring the dimensions of this demographic group. As such, this book will serve as the first of its kind in the field of economics. We hope this book, written in an accessible way, will provide in-depth analyses on the economic position of Afro-Latinxs in the U.S. which can be used to both complement and supplement interdisciplinary research conducted on this group in other major social science disciplines as well as in the humanities.

In this text we utilize U.S. Census Bureau data from the American Community Survey (ACS) to provide a vivid statistical portrait of the U.S. Afro-Latinx community. We complement and strengthen this portrait with qualitative and other forms of research to address limitations posed by data analysis alone. The quantitative analyses in this book underscore existing economic research on Afro-Latinxs which shows that this group appears to share more in common with African Americans than with other major Latinx groups, particularly white-identified Latinxs, with respect to income, wealth, poverty, education, and labor market status. Like African Americans, whom we define as those whose ancestors were enslaved in the U.S., who were born in the U.S. though their parent(s) may not have been, or non-Latinx Blacks who are foreign-born but are now citizens or residents of the U.S., Afro-Latinxs experience higher rates of poverty and unemployment than either non-Latinx whites as well as Latinxs of all backgrounds. Afro-Latinxs also have higher educational attainment levels, on average, than the Latinx community in general, but, counterintuitively, this does not yield expected economic returns when measured by income, occupational status, or other indicators of economic well-being. [4] This is a *crucial* finding, especially as it joins a burgeoning set of literature that challenges prevailing economic theory which posits that education alone is the panacea for economic stability and mobility.[5] In fact, Census data has shown that educational attainment for Latinxs overall is lower when compared to African Americans, and there is a similar pattern for African Americans vis-à-vis non-Latinx whites, but rarely has the Afro-Latinx community been included in these kinds of comparisons.[6] In chapter 3, we present hypotheses regarding why higher relative educational attainment among Afro-Latinxs has not resulted in a better labor market status for this demographic.

The main thesis we posit in this book is that "Blackness matters" for Afro-Latinxs in the U.S. By "Blackness," we mean the state of being from African descent. Afro-Latinxs have economic outcomes that closely resemble those of African Americans primarily due to five reasons:

1. As already noted, over 20 percent of Afro-Latinxs in the U.S., irrespective of nativity, report African American ancestry (see figure 1.1).
2. Many, if not most, Afro-Latinxs likely possess Black phenotypical characteristics (discussed further in this chapter), and rather than deny their African ancestry, Afro-Latinxs who "check both" likely *embrace* their "Blackness," and may do so to tie themselves directly to the Black experience, whether in the U.S. or in their Latin American/Caribbean countries of origin. *This choice is of incredible significance, given the potential material ramifications of "choosing Blackness" along with the understanding that Afro-Latinxs could simply choose "not to choose" (a racial affiliation).*
3. Those Afro-Latinxs who possess Black phenotypical characteristics are vulnerable to anti-Black bias in market activities, leading economic outcomes for Afro-Latinxs to bear similarities to economic outcomes of African Americans. In addition, economic disparities persist even in the presence of higher relative educational attainment levels of Afro-Latinxs.
4. The large estimated share of Afro-Latinx youth who have an African American parent serves to bring the African American experience and the Afro-Latinx experience in the U.S. closer.
5. Seventeen percent and 14 percent, respectively, of Afro-Latinxs report Puerto Rican and Dominican ancestries—see figure 1.1; these are communities where many members have historically been "racialized" economically, socially, and spatially in the U.S., often alongside Black Americans.

In an illuminating commentary for *HipLatina*, Dr. Alai Reyes-Santos, a Puerto Rican professor of Ethnic Studies and Conflict Resolution, captures what's at stake in choosing Blackness:

> . . . I have to assert my blackness every day. This is the life of Black Latinxs. We are questioned. Why not just claim to be Latinos? Why not claim whiteness when racial ambiguity leaves people wondering? Doctors mark the white category for us on their data figures because they think it will please us; at the same time treating us in racist ways, asking us: "Racism is not that bad here, right?" while doing a Pap smear.[7]

Dr. Reyes-Santos's quote speaks to the complex nature of living both as *Latina* and *Black*, pointedly noting the anti-Black racism she's encountered. It isn't just a matter that Afro-Latinxs may have dark skin or kinky hair or other (superficial) features that are phenotypically associated with African ancestry, and thus have no choice but to acknowledge their Blackness. Indeed, research exists which shows that many dark-skinned Latinxs, if asked, will self-identify as white.[8] Other research on the Latinx community in the U.S. shows economic penalties associated with darker skin tones.[9] In the face of this, as we discuss below, there is evidence that Afro-Latinxs in the U.S. have sought as well as received refuge, and experienced rapprochement, in African American communities. At the same time, economic research on African Americans clearly shows that, for a host of indicators, outcomes for Blacks are worse than those for non-Latinx whites, and this is critical in helping us understand the typical Afro-Latinx economic experience. Therefore, whether or not one "chooses Blackness," Afro-Latinxs face obstacles in the American economy, including inequities in access to health care, credit, jobs, decent housing, and good schools. Put differently, Blackness (or anti-Blackness) not only matters, but is constant, persistent, and determinant in economic outcomes for Afro-descendant groups, whether native or foreign-born.

Before we delve into our statistical portrait, let us first explain how we chose our terminology, especially as we define "Afro-Latinx" in this book.

TERMINOLOGY—DEFINING "AFRO-LATINX"

The title of this book includes the term "Afro-Latinos" that we, the co-authors, use to describe persons who identify as of both Black/African descent and Latinx/Latin@. The research in this book covers this demographic group in the U.S. only, though the majority of Afro-Latinxs live outside the U.S. However, because little attention has been paid in the economics literature to this group, we felt it was imperative to undertake research that outlines the position of this demographic within the American economy. But to talk about this group, we needed to carefully choose the terminology used to describe this demographic's racial and ethnic composition. While we use the term "Afro-Latinos" in the book title, throughout the text we use the terms "Afro-Latinx," "Afro-Latinas," "Afro-Latinos," "Black Latinos," or "Black Latinx" so as to include different intra-group measures and identities; we also use these terms when referencing or quoting interdisciplinary sources. Below we discuss why we chose these terms for this text.

In the economics field, the terminology most frequently used to describe persons who are both Black and Latinx/Latin@ has been Afro-Latinos; in some studies the terms "Black Latinos" or "Hispanic Black/Black Hispanics" have also been used. In order to make this publication accessible to scholars in the field of economics, therefore, we made the decision to use "Afro-Latino" in the title of this book. However, the term "Latino" has been criticized as lacking gender-neutrality, given the masculine-centered "o." As an alternative, "Latin@" has been used in academic as well as popular publications instead of Latino since the former takes into account both the "a" and "o" together as gender-inclusive. Unfortunately, however, Latin@ also operates from a binary space of gender normativity. The term "Latinx" has gained wider acceptance to describe persons of Latin American ancestry because of its gender-neutrality; this term also takes into account gender fluidity and non-binary notions of gender. As such, we decided to use this term most frequently. However, the use of "Latinx" itself has also come under critique precisely because of its gender-neutrality, since much of the existing academic literature on women who are both Black and of Latin American ancestry uses the term "Latina."[10] Because we recognize and acknowledge the importance of inclusive language for identity, we therefore collectively used the terminologies we felt were most appropriate and respectful, in our subjective opinion, to the context of the topic being discussed. Thus, in our "Afro-Latinas in the U.S." analysis (chapter 4) we exclusively use the term "Latina" since we are specifically examining the economic position of those who identify and experience racialized material realities as femme/women. In most other sections we predominantly use the term "Latinx" and, in some contexts, "Latino" and/or "Hispanic" will appear when citing studies and quoting sources. We also predominantly use the descriptor "Afro" in conjunction with "Latinx," and "Latina," but this is mostly due to convention rather than a strong preference for using that term instead of "Black."

We also want to make a point about how we define "Afro-Latinx" relative to the work of our colleagues across interdisciplinary spheres.[11] Afro-Latinxs, for the most part, have been defined as people of African origin whose roots are situated in Latin America, a definition that distinguishes them from African Americans (discussed more below). But as the reader may have noticed, we stress the finding that a sizable percentage of U.S. Afro-Latinxs, regardless of nativity, have mixed parentage from Latin American and African American backgrounds. This does not mean, however, that we view all cultural expressions of Blackness as the same; we are aware that different social dynamics can be at play regarding the degree to which an individual *embraces Blackness*.

AFRO-LATINX ORIGINS IN THE U.S.

According to 2010 U.S. Census data, just over half of Latinxs in the U.S. identified as white, while just under half identified as neither white nor Black.[12] Also according to that data, approximately 2 percent of Latinxs in the U.S. identified as Black. As noted throughout this book, there are consistent similarities between the economic experiences of Afro-Latinxs and African Americans. Along with a significant share of Afro-Latinxs identifying as having African American ancestry, nativity could also play a role here; 73 percent of Afro-Latinxs in the U.S. indicate they were born in the U.S. while 64 percent of Latinxs in general in the U.S. report being born here—see figure 1.2.[13] In addition, 88 percent of Afro-Latinxs in the U.S. indicate American citizenship compared to 78 percent of Latinxs in general in the U.S.—see figure 1.3.[14] These findings, which distinguish the U.S. Afro-Latinx community from the more general Latinx experience, also come with caveats.

As noted, nativity may play a role in an Afro-Latinx's own identity formation, with implications for their lived realities. While most Latinxs were born in the United States—see figure 1.2—this is even truer for Afro-Latinxs. This adds another layer to the predominant narrative that views Latinxs as "newer" to the U.S., products of more recent (im)migrations and henceforth subject to the typical discriminatory immigrant experience (especially in a hostile, putative "post-racial" era). While this is true for many recent Afro-Latinx immigrants, there is a more complex historical picture that needs to be illustrated.

Conventional narrative holds that the Afro-Latinx experience extends to the occupation of indigenous lands during early periods of European settler-colonialism of the Americas.[15] It has been estimated that 10 to 15 times as many Africans from various societies, ethnic groups, and sovereign arrangements were violently kidnapped and enslaved into Spanish and Portuguese colonial systems relative to what would become the United States.[16] This tends to invoke a dichotomous narrative about Afro-descendants in the

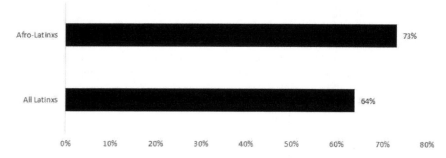

Figure 1.2. Percent of Group Born in the U.S. & Territories, 2011–2015. *Data Source*: Author analysis of 2011–2015 American Community Survey 5-year data obtained from Steven Ruggles, Katie Genadek, Ronald Goeken, Josiah Grover, and Matthew Sobek. Integrated Public Use Microdata Series, Version 6.0 [dataset]. Minneapolis, University of Minnesota, 2015. http://doi.org/1018128/D010.V6.0.

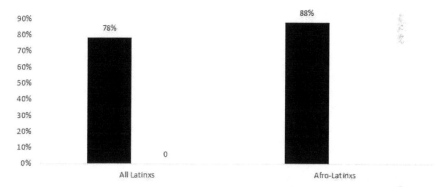

Figure 1.3. Percent of Latinxs & Afro-Latinxs in the U.S. Who Are Citizens, 2011–2015. *Data Source*: Author analysis of 2011–2015 American Community Survey 5-year data obtained from Steven Ruggles, Katie Genadek, Ronald Goeken, Josiah Grover, and Matthew Sobek. Integrated Public Use Microdata Series, Version 6.0 [dataset]. Minneapolis, University of Minnesota, 2015. http://doi.org/1018128/D010.V6.0.

Americas based on geographic origin and settler-colonial constructs, one that distinguishes groups by "Afro-Hispanics/Latinxs" and "African Americans" (as well as Afro-Caribbean/"West Indians").

But the Afro-Latinx presence in the United States isn't simply a by-product of more recent south to north immigration as put forth in the dominant frame; Afro-Latinxs are also bound up in, and were central to, the inception and expansion of slave and subsequent economic constructs in what would become the United States. Groundbreaking pieces by Peter H. Wood, Virginia Meacham Gould and Jack D. Forbes provide windows into the economic

roles and conditions of the first Africans in the earliest expeditions by Spanish *conquistadores* from Florida to the Southwest in the mid-1500s to 1600s,
as well as the ways in which Spanish and French colonists attempted to control enslaved and mixed-race groups through brutality and legal techniques in
what later became the American state of Louisiana.[17] In fact, early evidence
of Afro-Latinx origins in African American communities, and vice versa, has
been uncovered. Refugio I. Rochin, writing in the *Professional Agricultural
Workers Journal*, noted:

> Some Afro-Latinos derive from African Americans who escaped the English
> and sought refuge in the territory of Spain. . . . Beginning in 1688, Negro slaves
> who escaped the English colonies, came to this Spanish territory, were not re-
> turned to their English masters.[18]

As the U.S. geographically expanded and extended its hegemony throughout
Mexico, Central America, and the Caribbean in the mid to late 19th century,
annexing parts of former Spanish colonies turned independent countries,
this further tied economies and fueled disruption and northward migration.[19]
Hence, as the U.S. Latinx experience itself became more stratified, the economic stories of Afro-Latinxs remained largely untold. Some Latinxs, like
Mexicans and Puerto Ricans, were recruited for low-wage labor in various
burgeoning sectors of the U.S. economy, while others (like post-1959 Cuban
exiles and South American professionals) occupied a more favorable position.[20] These stratified histories are central in understanding a complex group
whose labor market experiences are not uniform, varying by the intersecting
forces of ancestry, language, race, gender, locality, and if applicable, immigration status and context of arrival.[21]

Given this complex sociohistorical backdrop, where exactly do Afro-
Latinxs come from? What can Census data tell us about their origins? As we
emphasized, millions of Latinxs (regardless of race) in the U.S. were born
in this country, and millions were born in several other countries, primarily
Mexico or countries in the Caribbean or Central and South America. Indeed,
there are over thirty countries (and many territories, including Puerto Rico) in
the Caribbean as well as Central and South America, with diverse populations
descending from indigenous groups, people of African descent, Europeans,
and Asians. Over 60 percent of Latinxs in the U.S. are of Mexican ancestry,
approximately 35 million persons according to 2015 data from the U.S. Census Bureau.[22] Also according to that data, another 5.3 million Latinxs in this
country are Puerto Rican, 2.1 million are of Cuban descent, and 1.9 million
are of Dominican descent. The remaining 11 million U.S. Latinxs are from
Central American countries (5.2 million), primarily El Salvador (2.2 million),
and South American countries (3.4 million), primarily Colombia (1 million), and 2.7 million have their ancestry indicated as "other," including over

700,000 "Spaniards."[23] But what if we sought to count where Afro-Latinxs fit within these larger "ancestry-based" distributions?

Let's revisit figure 1.1 for context. It shows that 17 percent of Afro-Latinxs indicate their ancestry as Puerto Rican, 14 percent indicate the Dominican Republic, 10 percent indicate Mexican ancestry, and 4 percent note Cuban ancestry.[24] In addition, as previously indicated, an important finding regarding the reported ancestries of Afro-Latinxs in the U.S. is that over 20 percent indicate African American as their primary ancestry. However, looking at the ancestry of Afro-Latinxs in the U.S. from the perspective of which Latinx subgroups are most likely to indicate Black/African ancestry, we can see from figure 1.4 that Latinxs from the country of Panama are the most likely to indicate they are Black—34.3 percent—followed by persons with origins in Belize (28.4 percent), the Dominican Republic (11.4 percent), Costa Rica (6.3 percent), and, finally, Puerto Rico, where 5.6 percent identify as Black. This may seem counterintuitive, since the largest share of Afro-Latinxs in the U.S. indicate their *place* of ancestry as being Puerto Rico. However, the latter statement is simply a function of the sheer size of the Puerto Rican community in the U.S.; according to the Census Bureau, Puerto Ricans constitute the second largest subgroup (by ancestry) of Latinxs in the U.S.

Consistent with our figures, a recent report noted that U.S. Latinxs with Caribbean roots are the most likely to report being Afro-Latinx compared to Latinxs from other regions. But one notable exception has consistently been found in the literature: Cubans.[25] Cubans in the U.S. present a peculiar case

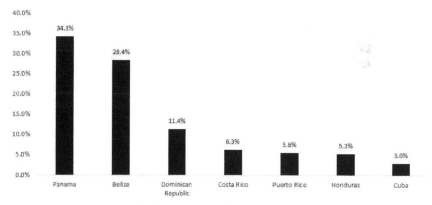

Figure 1.4. Proportion of Select Latinx Subgroups in the U.S. That Are Afro-Latinx, 2011–2015. Data Source: Author analysis of 2011–2015 American Community Survey 5-year data obtained from Steven Ruggles, Katie Genadek, Ronald Goeken, Josiah Grover, and Matthew Sobek. Integrated Public Use Microdata Series, Version 6.0 [dataset]. Minneapolis, University of Minnesota, 2015. http://doi.org/1018128/D010.V6.0. *Note that the data in this chart is only for Latinxs in the U.S. that are citizens.

with regard to racial self-identification. While it is estimated that more than 50 percent of the resident Cuban population is of African descent (likely an underestimate), only 7 percent of Latinxs of Cuban descent in the U.S. identify as Black.[26] Indeed, the majority of Latinxs of Cuban descent in the U.S. identify as white when asked about their race.[27] After the Cuban revolution, hundreds of thousands of Cubans immigrated to the U.S. voluntarily or involuntarily; many upper middle class Cubans left due to the new socioeconomic and political order in Cuba. Given the systemic racism and colorism that existed in Cuba during and after the revolution, it is likely many upper middle class Cubans who left after the revolution identified as white, or were white-passing.[28] Sixty-five percent of the over 2 million Latinxs of Cuban descent in the U.S. reside in Florida, and the largest Latinx subgroup in Florida is comprised of people of Cuban descent (about one in three Latinxs in Florida are of Cuban origin). However, 85 percent of Latinxs in Florida identify as white, and only 2.7 percent identify as Black.

But amid the "whiteness" of the numbers, it's clear that Afro-Cuban migrants and their children, even if they see themselves as belonging to the same ethnic group (Cubans, or even "Hispanic/Latinx"), do not have the same everyday economic experiences as white Cubans and other Latinxs. Monika Gosin found, in interviewing post-1980 (Mariel boatlift and subsequent years) Afro-Cubans in Miami and Los Angeles, that many felt other white and Mexican-American Latinxs questioned their multiple identities, and rejected them (Afro-Latinxs) from the larger shared Latinx affiliation because of their Blackness.[29] Gosin also documented how these Afro-Latinxs used "resistance strategies" whenever they felt others were rejecting their agency, especially in asserting and claiming their Blackness. In Gosin's research on Miami specifically, which involved text analyses and in-depth interviews, the central ideologies of Black exclusion as "upheld by white supremacy" were evident regardless of one's ancestral origins. In other words, African Americans and Black Cuban Americans may originate from different geographic spaces but experience anti-Black discrimination in ways that lead to shared identities and cross-group rapprochement.[30]

AFRO-LATINXS AND AFRICAN AMERICANS

Findings from research on Afro-Latinxs in the U.S. instigate the following question: why are many economic indicators for Afro-Latinxs in the U.S. more similar to economic indicators for African Americans than to other Latinxs? A few theories have been espoused. In their study of Latinx racial identity and wage differentials across national subgroups, William Darity Jr., Jason Dietrich, and Darrick Hamilton note:

Indeed, because of the widespread Latina and Latino resistance to embracing a Black identity, those Latin@s who self-report their race as Black in the censuses are very likely to have phenotypical attributes that would lead them to be perceived as Black by others—and therefore subject to the economic penalties associated with Blackness in a racist society.[31]

These authors contextualize a set of key issues we will explore further in this book, including the apparent likelihood that a large number of Afro-descendant Latinxs in the U.S. do not identify as "Black/African American," which would contribute to an underreporting and underdocumenting of anti-Black discrimination. These researchers also go on to point out that evidence from several surveys on Latinxs and skin shade suggest that Latinxs who do identify as Black tend to have darker complexions.[32] "Colorism," typically recognized as discrimination based on complexion operating across and within groups, with people of darker complexions on the receiving end of discrimination, is a phenomenon that has a long-standing and ugly history in the U.S.[33] Interdisciplinary social science evidence finds "colorism penalties" operating among Latinxs across and within ancestry groups.[34] Latinxs who self-report, or who have been historically racialized or appear as "white," including many native-born Cubans, Colombians, Venezuelans, and other South American groups, tend to have more favorable socioeconomic outcomes compared to those from other ancestry groups, like Puerto Ricans, Dominicans and Panamanians, who have experienced different types of racialization.[35]

The "coloristic" material reality by ancestry group is profound when phenotype discrimination is measured in political and economic spheres. Latinxs who possess white or (northern) European phenotypical characteristics are found to be less likely to experience voting, housing, criminal justice, and health-related discrimination compared to their darker-skinned peers.[36] With respect to economic outcomes, research conducted by Arthur H. Goldsmith, William Darity Jr. and Darrick Hamilton found a 7 percent wage advantage for lighter-complexioned Black men compared to Black men who did not have a light complexion.[37] Thus, having dark skin appears to pose a disadvantage with regard to wages in the U.S. labor market, and if, as Darity Jr. and Hamilton have posited, Afro-Latinxs tend to have darker complexions, then Goldsmith et al.'s findings suggest that Afro-Latinxs will encounter labor market discrimination in the U.S. As this book will underscore, the implications are profound across all spheres—income, wealth, poverty, health, and general social well-being.[38]

Another reason why Afro-Latinxs in the U.S. may share more in common with African Americans is the size of the Afro-Latinx youth demographic in the U.S. and this group's parentage; a slightly higher share (34 percent) of Afro-Latinxs in the U.S. are under 18 years of age than Latinxs in general

(31 percent).[39] In addition, as noted earlier, it's been estimated that nearly half of Afro-Latinx youth in the U.S. have one parent who is non-Latinx Black.[40] Indeed, John Logan posits that marriages/relationships between Latinxs and African Americans who have children together are the most important reason for the *contemporary* presence of Afro-Latinxs in the United States.[41] Moreover, these Afro-Latinx children may be living with a non-Latinx Black parent, and, as such, may be subject to the economic conditions their African American/non-Latinx Black parent faces. This has implications for the communities Afro-Latinx children live in, the schools they attend, the networks they have access to, their paths for human capital acquisition, and their access to well-paying jobs when they reach adult age.

Finally, as also noted earlier, quantitative analysis from our research shows that over 20 percent of Afro-Latinxs in the U.S., regardless of nativity, indicate African American as their primary ancestry (see figure 1.1). Indeed, this is the most frequently reported category of ancestry for Afro-Latinxs, whether they are native born or not, while the remainder identify their Hispanic/Latinx ancestral (national) origins. Afro-Latinxs thus exhibit strong affinity with the African American community.

Along with intermarriage, to identify other factors one must delve into the literature on the relationship between geography and identity-formation, or the larger socio-spatial realities in which African Americans and many Latinx groups share racialized histories. In general, the Black/African American community, along with Native American/Tribal communities, have been consistently found to be the most spatially isolated group. Latinxs usually occupy a middle or "buffer-ground" as a collectivity, yet separate from the former, while many Asian-Pacific Islanders (a diverse and complex group unto itself) are thought to hug-up spatially against non-Latinx white localities.[42] From this purview, it is little wonder that African Americans and Latinxs are often mentioned in concordance with each other on measures of spatial distribution, segregation, and intergroup contact.

While much hasn't been published on the geographic distribution of the Afro-Latinx community, Logan's analysis of census 1980, 1990, and 2000 data provides a window into the spatial parameters U.S. Afro-Latinxs occupy, or better put, where they reside.[43] As expected, the New York City metropolitan area is where the largest concentration of Afro-Latinxs reside, followed by the Miami and Chicago metro areas.[44] In hindsight, this is not a surprise: these localities are where Caribbean Latinxs, including Puerto Ricans and Dominicans (who possess large documented shares of Afro-descendancy, however underreported), have long settled during various waves of (im)migration.[45]

But there's more to the story. Logan found that in geographic localities where there are fewer African Americans, there are also lower percentages of

"Hispanic Blacks."[46] However, in cities with a large share of African Americans (over 10 percent of the population), Afro-Latinxs tend to be located.[47]

That Afro-Latinxs are more likely to live in metro areas where there are more African Americans cannot be overstated for its role in shared racialized experiences. Racism and residential segregation have been long documented as central features of the American economy, specifically as key variables in forces that perpetuate economic disparities, especially the racial wealth gap.[48] Studies that examine Latinx residential patterns by *within-group* variables, particularly race and ancestry, are instructive.[49] Douglas Massey and Nancy Denton used 1970 and 1980 census data to find that Caribbean Latinxs (called "Caribbean Hispanics" in their study), which included many who identified *outside* the Black/white frame, had a high degree of segregation from both "Black Hispanics" and "non-Hispanic Blacks."[50] Similarly, Logan found that levels of segregation of Afro-Latinxs from white and "other" Latinxs mirror those of African Americans relative to the (non-Latinx) white population.[51]

In essence, the scholarly evidence speaks volumes about how expansive anti-Blackness has become, including being practiced by those who may be viewed as Black but do not want to identify as such. This leads to further unpacking an important methodological challenge, one that could help us understand why Afro-Latinxs are often left out of economics research that focuses on the larger Latinx community. The majority of the Latinx community in the U.S., which includes many who are of mixed-race and Afro-descendant backgrounds, have been found to assert a white or non-racial identity that, in itself, can be reflective of anti-Blackness.[52] Meanwhile, as Darity Jr. et al. posit, this is analogous to the "passing" phenomenon in the African American community during the pre–civil rights era.[53] This is imperative to unpack since our goal is to understand the material well-being of Afro-Latinxs in the U.S, regardless of whether they identify as Black. The next section tackles this methodological quandary.

LATINXS AND A "PREFERENCE FOR WHITENESS?"

In the U.S. Census Bureau's 2017 American Community Survey (ACS) two of the earliest questions ask a respondent first about Hispanic/Latino/Spanish origin, and then about race.[54] Immediately preceding the question about Hispanic/Latino origin is a statement which read as follows:

NOTE: Please answer BOTH Question 5 about Hispanic origin and Question 6 about race. For this survey, Hispanic origins are not races.[55] (*emphasis not ours*)

When a national census was first conducted in the U.S. in 1790 there were no questions asking about race or ethnicity; persons were classified as "white," "free," or "slave."[56] Indeed, the term "white" itself was not routinely used to describe early colonists in the New World, but rather the terms "Christians" or "Englishmen."[57] It wasn't until Bacon's Rebellion of 1676 in Virginia in which indentured European servants and enslaved Blacks participated with English colonials to resist British rule that the terms white and Black were thenceforth associated with Europeans (free or indentured) and slaves, respectively, in order to promote and solidify racial stratification. By the middle of the nineteenth-century racial categorizations began to appear on decennial censuses, but no term existed to describe persons of Hispanic/ Latinx ancestry. It wasn't until censuses in the early twentieth century that the category "Mexican" was added as a separate racial classification, only to be subsequently folded into the white category.[58] Separate Hispanic/Latino categories were not added until the 1970 census.

With regard to racial identification, according to recent U.S. Census Bureau's ACS data for the period 2011–2015, approximately 31 percent of Latinxs classify themselves as "some other race" or "two or more races," while the majority of Latinxs, 66 percent, classify themselves as white (note that a higher percentage of Latinxs identified as white in the 2011–2015 period when compared to 2010 decennial census data).[59] Comparatively, only 2 percent of Latinxs indicate their race as Black in the ACS.[60] Economists William Darity Jr., Jason Dietrich, and Darrick Hamilton have labeled census data that shows a majority of Latinxs in the U.S. identifying as white as evidence of "Latinos' preference for whiteness" in the U. S., or "bleach in the rainbow," challenging the prevailing notion that Latinx communities derive from "racial democracies."[61] In a different publication, one which measured earnings of Latinx men by race, and which found considerable intra-group disparities regardless of national origin, the same authors called it "passing on blackness."[62] Indeed, these researchers actively dispute the notion that Latinxs in America have a "neutral" view toward race.

That there exists a politics in asserting a racial identity which may be incongruent to one's actual material-level treatment has been met by calls from researchers and policy advocates to create methodologies that reflect these complexities in self-identification.[63] For instance, studies that question measurements of race and ethnicity, and how Latinxs view themselves within this framework, have argued for a combined census question where "Hispanic/Latino" is considered alongside typical racial categories.[64] However, this has been met with resistance (see discussion in chapter 6) which ignores the historical and present contours that inform the "flight to whiteness" or an intermediary "otherness," one grounded in the concept of *mestizaje*.[65]

Afro-Latina scholar and longtime anti-Black racism activist Miriam Jiménez Róman helps us define this:

> Latin@s may well be the only social group in the world who so emphatically insist on their ethno-racial mixture. But even as mestizo, or mixed identity— expressed variably as raza, "rainbow people," or "mutts"—is a commonplace collective designation, Latin@s are also understood to be "of any race." This apparent contradiction can be traced to the convergence of two seemingly distinct racial formations. On the one hand, the national ideologies of our countries of origin emphasize racial mixture and equate it with racial democracy—even as whiteness continues to be privileged, and indigenous and African ancestry are viewed as something to be overcome or ignored. On the other hand, in the United States Latin@s have been allocated an ambiguous racial middle ground that makes invisible those too dark to conform to the mestizo ideal, while simultaneously distancing them from other communities of color, particularly African Americans.[66]

Jiménez Román's critical observation speaks to the commonplace view that Latinxs occupy this non-Black and non-white middle space as "mestizos." Thus, *mestizaje* is ostensibly the result of hundreds of years of racial mixing among diverse populaces into a, purportedly, "post-racial" space. From Caribbean countries like Cuba, Puerto Rico, and the Dominican Republic to South American countries including Argentina, *mestizaje* was actually promoted as public policy at different times under nationalist contours, in that a middle-space identity was encouraged through intermarriage so as to move "beyond" race.[67] The outcome, as Jiménez Román observed, overlooked the "bottom caste" experience of Afro-Latinxs. In fact, sociologist Eduardo Bonilla-Silva has argued the "Latin Americanization" thesis as central to the emerging racial order in the United States.[68] By his analysis, a racial hierarchy has formed where whites are at the top, followed by "honorary whites," then a collective Black formation. This formulation includes assimilated white Latinxs in the privileged white frame, light-skinned Latinxs amid "honorary whites," and dark-skinned Latinxs (Afro-Latinxs) in the "collective Black" frame alongside African Americans and other U.S. Afro-descendant groups (like Caribbean Blacks). This also suggests that for Afro-Latinxs and others in the "collective Black" formulation there is the simultaneity of confronting anti-Black racism among non-Latinx white Americans as well as among non-Black Latinxs and other subaltern, differentially racialized groups.

This reinforces one of the methodological challenges in collecting demographic data we've already noted—controlling for the intra-group phenomenon of preferencing a white or mixed (or non-Black) identity given coloristic, anti-Black treatment at the everyday level. A study by economist Patrick Mason found that for Latinxs of color across different ancestry groups, hiding behind numerous identities, whether "white" or Hispanic, did not shield them from wage discrimination.[69] This echoes previously noted findings by Darity Jr. et al. and others.[70] Other nuanced methodologies have emerged, however, both on the quantitative and qualitative sides. Surveys that ask both respondents as well as observers to assess the respondent's skin shade (dark, medium, light), and, on the observer side, provided a scale, have helped capture the breadth of anti-Black discrimination.[71] Integrating the qualitative side, Nancy López and colleagues' mixed-method approach of asking people not just how they self-identify, but how they believe others view or identify them (called "street race-gender") has been able to uncover various economic inequalities rooted in overt and covert forms of anti-Black discrimination. Taken together, these approaches underscore the differences between how individuals or group members may self-identify versus their social classification, the latter a more potent and reliable predictor of outcomes.[72]

It is important to stress that Latinxs in the U.S. don't have a monolithic identity. The construction of race can be different among Latinxs compared to how it is generally interpreted in the U.S. Although race is a social construction, in the U.S. race is largely tied to genealogy and ancestry, while race among Latinxs is typically codified by phenotype and ancestry. Just as race is not a straightforward matter in the U.S. it is also not a straightforward matter for the Latinx community. For example, for the first author of this book, Michelle Holder, self-identified Afro-Latinxs in her own family arrived at this identification in many ways.[73] She explains:

> My mother is an Afro-Latina born in Panama whose black grandfather emigrated from Barbados to work on the Panama Canal; my father is an African American born in Georgia, so I identify as both an African American and an Afro-Latina; my daughters' father is Mexican American; my older brother's father was Afro-Latinx from Panama with a similar familial background as my mother; my sister-in-law is Puerto Rican and my nephews are black Puerto Ricans.
>
> Many Afro-Latinxs in the U.S. with family members born and raised in the country of Panama have stories very similar to my own; a typically male relative emigrated from various parts of the Caribbean in the early twentieth century for employment opportunities that building the Panama Canal offered, and remained to build their lives in the country. Their children and grandchildren were then sent to America in the 1950s and 1960s for the next level of economic opportunity.

For the second author, Alan Aja, who comes from a white Cuban American family, his experience was more similar to that documented in the vast post-1959 (post-revolution) Cuban immigration literature which, by default, centers the white-Cuban experience. This literature often overlooks the presence and contributions of Afro-Latinxs (especially Afro-Cubans) who were migrating over a century earlier and building transnational ties with African Americans.[74] It also ignores Afro-Cubans who either arrived or were born in the U.S. during the predominantly white-Cuban waves of immigration post-revolution (1959–present), yet experienced segmented spatial and economic trajectories as opposed to their white or lighter-skinned peers.[75]

> My parents are Cuban refugees who arrived in the U.S. in the mid to late 1960s, and I grew up and spent my early years in Miami, Florida, then later in Louisville, Kentucky. It wasn't until I was conducting doctoral work that I learned about bifurcated racialized migrations where government (Cold War) policy invested in predominantly white/white-passing political exiles during the early stages of the Cuban revolution (1959–1979) with regard to our settlement development, a type of investment that was not extended to African Americans, other black/ Latinx immigrant groups, or our Puerto Rican hermanxs. At the same time, any relation to Afro-descendant ancestry through lineage, intermarriage/partnerships, or friendships was virtually swept under the rug, erased, and/or evaded in ways that would stress whiteness and promote anti-blackness. Today, in conjunction with my Cuban American or Latinx identity, I self-identify as "white," aware of the numerous sociopolitical forces that construct whiteness and the incessant privileges it yields relative to the majority of my Latinx hermanxs.

Both of our lived experiences of identity formation speak to the sometimes profound differences in the ways Latinxs are racialized in the U.S. We tend to view racial inequality in America in white/non-white terms, one that presumes "non-white" economic experiences as being uniform across groups.[76] Within this frame, Latinxs and Asians are viewed as distinct, emerging groups that, by their "multi-racial-ness" and "other"-based identities, bend the boundaries of the prevailing Black/white dichotomous frame. The problem with this perspective is that it ignores the historic and present role of Afro-Latinxs, and it views all Latinx economic experiences as uniform, as products of more recent immigration, although many have roots that stem prior to and during the country's inception, including Afro-Latinxs. This suggests that conventional theories which scholars (including economists) have used to explain the economic position of Latinxs, such as assimilation theory and its extensions, are as inadequate for most Afro-Latinxs as they would be for explaining African American and Native American social positions.[77] Furthermore, beneath "other"-based identities, there is coloristic evidence operating from larger local and national levels that crosses over into market-based spheres.[78] Thus, the predominant narrative, one that obfuscates "Latinx Blackness," undoubtedly challenges ours, and other researchers', abilities to more precisely document the Afro-Latinx economic condition in the U.S.

ARE AFRO-LATINXS MORE "AFRO"
(i.e., BLACK) THAN LATINX?

The title of this section is, of course, a *rhetorical* question. Obviously, one cannot measure how "Black" or how "Latinx" someone is—as we've emphasized in this text, race is not biological, and neither is ethnicity. But it's a rhetorical question we wanted to pose in the context of identity politics. Our research, along with other scholarship, shows the economic experiences of Afro-Latinxs in the U.S. more closely resembles the economic experiences of African Americans than it does Latinxs in general. Thus, the question arises, does race "supersede" ethnicity in the economic status of American Afro-Latinxs, and, if so, why? Afro-Latinxs who identify as such claim both a Black and a Latinx identity. African American is the most cited primary ancestry among Afro-Latinxs in the U.S., followed closely by Puerto Rico, with 16.1 percent of Afro-Latinxs reporting Puerto Rican ancestry. If ancestral analysis is restricted only to Afro-Latinxs born in the U.S. or its territories, nearly a third report African American ancestry. Many Afro-Latinxs, therefore, clearly identify with African Americans.

What factors, other than economic similarities between Afro-Latinxs in the U.S. and African Americans, might explain this? Along with those Afro-Latinxs who have an African American parent, there could be several other contributing factors, outlined in an extensive literature that measures racial identification among Latinxs by ancestry, longevity in the U.S. (e.g., first or second generation), locality, socioeconomic background, social context, and other factors.[79] First, though Afro-Latinx survey respondents report over 20 different countries of origin, only a handful of countries or territories dominate this group's ancestral distribution, including Puerto Rico as the second most cited area/category of ancestry, followed by the Dominican Republic, Mexico, Cuba, and then widely distributed across other ancestral origins (see figure 1.1). Thus, the countries that predominate among the ancestral origins of Afro-Latinxs in the U.S. are Caribbean, where large Black populations exist.

There is also literature that examines processes of racialization occurring among Latinxs as a collectivity, pointing to the range of forces that determine identity, including whom one may partner with or marry.[80] Recent research on "Hispanic" intermarriage in the U.S. shows divergent race-based patterns operating within the group.[81] Take, for example, that "non-white" Puerto Ricans, as Zhenchao Qian, Daniel T. Lichter, and Dmitry Tumin note in their recent study of Latinx intermarriage in the U.S., "may follow the color line and marry Blacks more often than self-identified white Puerto Ricans, especially if the former are segregated from non-Hispanic whites in neighborhoods or occupational niches."[82]

The authors' reference to group intermarriage along "color lines" in the context of socio-spatial segregation is instructive, especially as we explore (in subsequent chapters) matters of wealth, occupational status, and income of U.S. Afro-Latinxs. It also adds to the intergroup relations literature that examines the political and economic confluences between African Americans and Puerto Ricans, especially in shared localities in the Northeastern country.[83]

In addition, African American culture in the United States has developed over a period of four centuries, and for much of that time African Americans were considered the largest minority group in the country. While of course still evolving, often argued is that the African American culture is fairly well-defined, with uniform and identifiable elements extending back to, and well beyond and outside of, the U.S. slave experience. On the other hand, the Latinx community in the U.S. is viewed as more heterogenous, with many influences from different pre- and post-colonized countries and regions. In the case of Puerto Ricans as well as Dominicans, localized proximity to African American culture during earlier stages of migration to the U.S. could have had a racialized effect—especially across generations. There is scholarly literature that finds correlations between longevity in the U.S. and racial identity falling along conventional Black/white frames.[84] This has also been found among Cubans in late nineteenth- to early twentieth-century economic migrations from Florida to New York.[85]

Lastly, and relatedly, Afro-Latinxs who demonstrate a preference for self-identifying as Black or "*also* African American" could be asserting an identity based on shared anti-Black discrimination. Colorism has been found to correlate with how one racially identifies.[86] This process of identity formation, however, is complex: it can be intergenerational, vary by group and sociopolitical context, and isn't always uniform. At different points in their lives, Afro-Latinxs (or their children) may "choose Blackness" which affirms agency and rapprochement with Black Americans at large, whether or not they previously identified with or sought common cause economically or politically with African Americans. As an intergroup comparative example, Anglophone Caribbean and African continent immigrant communities have often been viewed by economists and other scholars as possessing human capital endowments and a work ethic that African Americans supposedly lack, hence racism is viewed as less determinant in economic disparities.[87] This not only provides cover for the ways in which white supremacy relies on inter- and intra-group hierarchies so as to ensure its maintenance, but also suppresses the crucial role of African American cultural identity (as a set of historical institutions and structures that affirms Blackness) for Black ethnic groups, including Afro-Latinxs.[88]

Within the context of the data and its admitted limitations, what else can we demographically learn about the Afro-Latinx community in the United States? What does the community look like based on gender, educational attainment, median age, household size, and marital status? The remainder of the chapter provides descriptive data to inform these inquiries. We, the authors, would like to point out at this juncture in the text that, to our extreme dismay, we were unable to examine issues related to the economic state of Afro-Latinx LGBTQ+, nonbinary, and gender-nonconforming communities given the limitations of the U.S. Census data we used, and it is our sincere hope that in the immediate future the U.S. Census Bureau will implement the collection of data that is inclusive of the identities of these communities.

DEMOGRAPHICS

Gender

Utilizing the U.S. Census Bureau's ACS 5-year sample for 2011–2015, we find that Afro-Latinxs have a slightly higher percentage of women than men compared to Latinxs overall, 50.7 percent versus 50.1 percent, a statistically significant difference (at the 10 percent level)—see table 1.1.[89] The higher proportion of women among Afro-Latinxs compared to all Latinxs follows a pattern similar to that for African Americans compared to non-Latinx whites. In addition, the divergence in the one-to-one proportion of African American

Table 1.1.   Percent Female by Select Demographic Groups in the U.S., 2011–2015

White Non-Latinx	51.2%
African American	52.6%
Asian	52.7%
Native American & Alaskan Native	51.0%
All Latinxs	50.1%
Latinxs Who Identify as Black	50.7%
Latinxs Who Identify as White	50.5%
All Latinxs Citizens	50.8%
Latinxs Citizens Who Identify as Black	51.2%
Latinxs Citizens Who Identify as White	51.1%

Data Source: Author analysis of 2011–2015 American Community Survey 5-Year data obtained from Steven Ruggles, Katie Genadek, Ronald Goeken, Josiah Grover, and Matthew Sobek. Integrated Public Use Microdata Series, Version 6.0 [dataset]. Minneapolis, University of Minnesota, 2015. http://doi.org/10.18128/D010.V6.0.
NOTE: The categories "white non-latinx" and "Asian" are restricted to U.S. citizens.

men to women starts in the age group 25–29.[90] Researchers Justin Wolfers, David Leonhardt, and Kevin Quealy, using 2010 Census data, estimated that a million and a half "prime age" (defined as 25–54 years old) Black men were absent from the everyday lives of the African American community, with an estimated 600,000 absent due to incarceration, and the remaining 900,000 absent due primarily to mortality-related issues, most notably the cumulative impact of homicide, which the researchers estimated resulted in the reduction of 200,000 Black men in the prime-age group.[91] Despite this, however, the demographic that appears to have the highest proportion of females in the U.S. are Asians: 52.7 percent of Asians in the U.S. are female, compared to 52.6 percent female in the African American population.[92]

Another similar pattern emerges when examining intra-group gender composition among Afro-Latinxs by nativity. Afro-Latinxs who are U.S. citizens have a higher proportion of women when compared to Afro-Latinxs regardless of citizenship status: 51.2 percent of Afro-Latinx citizens are Afro-Latina compared to 50.7 percent of Afro-Latinxs regardless of citizenship status, a statistically significant difference (at the 10 percent level).

Educational Attainment

Educational attainment in the Afro-Latinx community in the U.S. presents a *profound* area for research; as can be seen in table 1.2, Afro-Latinxs possess a higher median level of educational attainment when compared to all Latinxs as well as white Latinxs. However, as will become evident throughout this book, the economic rewards normally associated with more education do not appear to be accruing to Afro-Latinxs in the forms of lower unemployment and poverty rates, higher income, or more wealth. We discuss these counterintuitive findings more in depth in chapters 2 and 3.

Table 1.2. Median Educational Attainment Level for Select Demographic Groups 25+ Years Old in the U.S., 2011–2015

All Persons 25+ Years of Age	1 but Less than 2 Years of College
White Non-Latinx	1 but Less than 2 Years of College
African American	H.S. Graduate or Equivalent
Asian	Associate's Degree
Native American & Alaskan Native	H.S. Graduate or Equivalent
All Latinxs	H.S. Graduate or Equivalent
Afro-Latinxs	Some College, but Less than 1 Year
Latinxs Who Identify as White	H.S. Graduate or Equivalent

Data Source: Author analysis of 2011–2015 American Community Survey 5-Year data obtained from Steven Ruggles, Katie Genadek, Ronald Goeken, Josiah Grover, and Matthew Sobek. Integrated Public Use Microdata Series, Version 6.0 [dataset]. Minneapolis, University of Minnesota, 2015. http://doi.org /10.18128/D010.V6.0.
NOTE: The categories "white non-Latinx" and "Asian" are restricted to U.S. citizens.

Median Age

Table 1.3 shows the median age of Afro-Latinxs in the U.S., comparing non-Latinx whites, non-Latinx Blacks (African Americans), Asians, Native Americans, and the Latinx community at large. It also includes Latinx respondents by race and all groups by citizenship status. Unsurprisingly, the oldest group is white non-Latinxs, followed closely by Asians and African Americans, and then Latinxs.

As a group, Afro-Latinxs are young (25 years median age) compared to other groups in the distribution, especially when we look at groups by nativity status. This is noteworthy; while Latinxs as a collectivity are typically younger than other major groups in the U.S., there is a recent upward trend from a median age of 25 in 2000 to 28 in 2015.[93] The role of white Latinxs in the statistics is important here, in that, compared to Afro-Latinxs and the community as a whole, they tend to have a median age that skews upward.

Table 1.3. Median Age by Select Demographic Groups in the U.S., 2011–2015

White Non-Latinx	47
African American	39
Asian	39
Native American & Alaskan Native	35
All Latinxs	30
Latinxs Who Identify as Black	25
Latinxs Who Identify as White	31
All Latinx Citizens	25
Latinxs Citizens Who Identify as Black	23
Latinxs Citizens Who Identify as White	26

Data Source: Author analysis of 2011–2015 American Community Survey 5-Year data obtained from Steven Ruggles, Katie Genadek, Ronald Goeken, Josiah Grover, and Matthew Sobek. Integrated Public Use Microdata Series, Version 6.0 [dataset]. Minneapolis, University of Minnesota, 2015. http://doi.org/10.18128/D010.V6.0.
NOTE: The categories "white non-Latinx" and "Asian" are restricted to U.S. citizens.

Mean/Median Family Size

Table 1.4 provides a comparative analysis of all family members occupying a housing unit related to the householder by marriage, birth, or adoption. Among the U.S. Latinx community, Afro-Latinxs report a median "family size" (three) smaller than white Latinxs (four) and the Latinx community in general (four). Compared to other groups in the U.S., Afro-Latinxs look similar to the larger African American community (three), as well as Asians (three) and Native Americans (three).[94]

Table 1.4. **Mean and Median Family Size by Select Demographic Groups**

Groups	Mean	Median
Non-Latinx		
Whites	2.84	2.00
African Americans/Blacks	2.91	3.00
Asians	3.46	3.00
Native Americans	3.71	3.00
Latinx		
All Latinx	3.80	4.00
White Latinx	3.76	4.00
Afro-Latinx	3.41	3.00

Note: Mean values between one group and white non-Latinx are all significant at the 0.001 level.
Source: Author Analysis of American Community Survey, 2017 via Steven Ruggles, Sarah Flood, Ronald Goeken, Josiah Grover, Erin Meyer, Jose Pacas, and Matthew Sobek. IPUMS USA: Version 9.0 [dataset]. Minneapolis, MN: IPUMS, 2019. https://doi.org/10.18128/D010.V9.0.

Marital Status

Table 1.5 outlines the marital status of Afro-Latinxs relative to other Latinxs and comparative demographic groups, measuring those 18 years and older who reported ever being married. The patterns reveal a profound picture: Afro-Latinxs, regardless of citizenship status, are the least likely to have been married relative to every other demographic group. Reporting at a 50 percent ever-married rate (51 percent taking into account citizenship), the only group they come close to in comparison is African Americans (non-Latinx), who report a 57 percent marital rate. White Latinxs, we must point out, are much more likely to be married compared to Afro-Latinxs, and tend to skew the overall Latinx marital rate upward (67 percent marital rate for white Latinxs compared to 65 percent for Latinxs overall). At the same time, Latinxs as a group, regardless of citizenship status, fall somewhere in the middle of distribution alongside Native Americans, with Asians and non-Latinx whites the most likely to be married.[95]

In our attempt to examine general demographic patterns of U.S. Afro-Latinxs, including age, gender, marital status, and family size, we want to point out that these are stand-alone, brief analyses meant to generate a larger representative picture of the group and provide context for the rest of the book, where we cover some topics much more in depth.

**Table 1.5. Percent Married (with Spouse
Present in Household) by Ethnic/Racial Group**

Groups	Married, Spouse Present (%) Mean
Non-Latinx	
Whites	46%
African Americans	23%
Asians	47%
Native Americans	26%
Latinx	
All Latinx	32%
White Latinx	33%
Afro-Latinx	21%

Note: Mean values between one group and white non-
Latinx are all significant at the 0.001 level.
Source: Author Analysis of American Community Survey,
2017 via Steven Ruggles, Sarah Flood, Ronald Goeken,
Josiah Grover, Erin Meyer, Jose Pacas, and Matthew
Sobek. IPUMS USA: Version 9.0 [dataset]. Minneapolis,
MN: IPUMS, 2019. https://doi.org/10.18128/D010.V9.0.

ORDER OF BOOK

In the following pages, we continue our exploratory look at Afro-Latinxs in the U.S. economy. Now that the demographic context has been set in this chapter, with a general understanding of the U.S. Afro-Latinx's geographic dispersion, median age, family size, marital status, ancestral distribution, and gender composition, we continue with our study.

Chapter 2 examines the socioeconomic position of U.S. Afro-Latinxs through the lenses of education, income, wealth, and poverty. In a larger context, educational attainment for Latinxs is found to be lower at all levels when compared to African Americans and white non-Hispanics. [96] Data from the Census Bureau[97] as well as the Urban Institute[98] also show that Latinxs and African Americans have lower median income and household wealth levels, and higher poverty rates, than non-Latinx whites. In addition, one-quarter of African Americans live in poverty, while 24 percent of Latinxs in the U.S, are poor; this is in stark contrast to an 11 percent poverty rate for white non-Hispanics.[99] However, similar data shows that when African Americans have similar or equal educational levels as (non-Latinx) whites, their economic returns are significantly lower. Using original quantitative analysis, this chapter examines whether education, income, wealth, and poverty rates among Latinxs as well as African Americans intersect to form related levels of educational attainment, income, and poverty among Afro-Latinxs, and whether asset holding (using homeownership as proxy) and poverty rates among the latter group fall within or outside the range of analogous levels for African Americans and Latinxs. We assess whether determining factors specific to Afro-Latinx wealth and poverty may be unrelated to factors that determine either Latinx or African American wealth and poverty. We also juxtapose our findings against existing literature, including recent localized studies of the "racial wealth gap" for white non-Latinxs, African Americans, and Latinxs, as well as across Latinx ancestry groups.

Chapter 3 continues with an examination of the labor market status of Afro-Latinxs. We provide an exploratory look at the occupational distribution of Afro-Latinxs in the U.S. as well as major labor force indicators for the group, including unemployment and labor force participation rates.[100] We also examine the role of networks as well as employer discrimination in disparate labor market outcomes for Afro-Latinxs.

Chapter 4 considers Afro-Latinas and their economic condition through the lens of "intersectionality." African American female scholar and critical race theorist Kimberlé Crenshaw was part of a vanguard of scholars in the 1990s proposing "intersectional theory," which posits that while marginalized groups can share disenfranchisement in common, forms of discrimination and marginalization differ depending on race, class, ethnicity, gender, sexual orientation, ancestry, and so on.[101] In addition, the overlapping of various forms of exclusion and bias creates distinctive and new forms of oppression and marginalization, sometimes compounded for particular groups. Intersectional theory therefore posits that in order to combat discrimination and exclusion, strategies must be specific to the marginalized group. This chapter will explore the scope of oppression Afro-Latinas face in the U.S. given this group's race, ethnicity, ancestry, immigrant status, and gender.

Chapter 5 provides a nuanced, introductory analysis of Afro-Latinxs in the criminal justice system, with an eye on the economic effects of mass incarceration on the group. Conventional narrative holds that the two demographic groups most likely to be victims of mass incarceration are African Americans and Latinxs, but very little has been published on the Afro-Latinx community in this regard. Given that the post-incarceration experience is met with economic as well as political disenfranchisement (poor wages, denial of voting rights), and that there are no national statistics which could help us understand the rate of incarceration among the U.S. Afro-Latinx community, this chapter provides an exploratory analysis using proxy representative data of groups with a relatively large share of Afro-Latinx members (such as Puerto Ricans). We also cite a recent study covering Miami-Dade County in Florida that finds, as we suspect exists at the national level, that Afro-Latinx individuals (alongside non-Latinx Blacks) are disproportionately subject to punitive treatment at all levels of the justice system, from arrests to sentencing.[102]

Finally, economists typically address the topic of discrimination in the context of markets and market transactions, including the labor, housing, and capital/credit markets. Discrimination in markets usually takes the form of excluding a group or groups from equitable access to a market, and can occur for reasons such as: simple bigotry, what economists classify as exhibiting a "taste" or "preference" for discrimination; assumptions about the productive ability, employability, or credit-worthiness of certain groups given average group characteristics, what economists classify as "statistical discrimination"; collusive behavior on the part of employers or unions. Our final chapter, chapter 6, written within the context of resurgent movements that center Black lives, will outline the ways in which African Americans and Latinxs experience discrimination in markets in the U.S., highlight what other social science literature indicates about discrimination against Afro-Latinxs, and draw comparisons about the kinds of discrimination Afro-Latinxs face as a group in the U.S. economy when compared to other Latinxs and African Americans. We end the chapter by highlighting recent bold policy recommendations to improve the position of the Afro-Latinx community in the U.S. economy, some of which have now made it into the policy agenda thanks to pressure and organizing by subaltern groups, even in the midst of a currently hostile federal administration. We also draw upon our respective experiences working for grassroots labor, advocacy, and public policy organizations to discuss how bold policy solutions can hold universal merits and intentions, but address specific barriers faced by Afro-Latinxs in the United States.

NOTES

1. U.S. Census Bureau American Community Survey data for 2015. Also see Sharon R. Ennis, Merarys Ríos-Vargas, and Nora G. Albert, "The Hispanic Population: 2010" (U.S. Census Bureau, May 1, 2011) for an examination of the 2010 Census which reports that 1.2 million people identified as "Hispanic" and "Black or African American" when given the "One Race" option. In addition, according to a Pew Research Center 2014 survey one-quarter of Latinxs in the U.S. self-identify as Afro-Latino. However, in the same survey 39 percent of Afro-Latinos report their race as white while only 18 percent report their race as Black. See Gustavo López and Ana Gonzalez-Barrera, "Afro-Latino: A deeply rooted identity among U.S. Hispanics," *Pew Research Center's Hispanic Trends Project* (blog), 2016, http://www.pewresearch.org /fact-tank/2016/03/01/afro-latino-a-deeply-rooted-identity-among-u-s-hispanics/.

2. John R. Logan, "How Race Counts for Hispanic Americans," in *The Afro-Latin@ Reader: History and Culture in the United States*, ed. Miriam Jiménez Román and Juan Flores (Durham, NC: Duke University Press, 2010), 475–84.

3. See for example Miriam Jiménez Román and Juan Flores, *The Afro-Latin@ Reader: History and Culture in the United States* (Duke University Press, 2010); Antonio Lopez, *Unbecoming Blackness: The Diaspora Cultures of Afro-Cuban America* (NYU Press, 2012); Suzanne Oboler and A. Dzidzienyo, eds., *Neither Enemies nor Friends: Latinos, Blacks, Afro-Latinos* (Palgrave Macmillan, 2005); Monika Gosin, *The Racial Politics of Division: Interethnic Struggles for Legitimacy in Multicultural Miami* (Cornell University Press, 2019); Susan Greenbaum, *More than Black: Afro-Cubans in Tampa* (University of Florida Press, 2002); Petra R. Rivera-Rideau, Jennifer A. Jones, and Tianna Paschel, eds., *Afro-Latin@s in Movement: Critical Approaches to Blackness and Transnationalism in the Americas*, Afro-Latin@ Diasporas (Palgrave Macmillan US, 2016); Vanessa K. Valdés, *Diasporic Blackness: The Life and Times of Arturo Schomberg* (SUNY Press, 2017).

4. While education is often viewed as a "great equalizer," as a key vehicle toward socioeconomic mobility for subaltern groups like African Americans and Latinxs, a number of recent studies place this view in a more nuanced, critical context that centers structural forces that also affect the Afro-Latinx community. See William Darity Jr. et al., "What We Get Wrong about Closing the Racial Wealth Gap" (Samuel DuBois Cook Center on Social Equity, Insight Center for Community Economic Development, 2018), https://socialequity.duke.edu/portfolioitem/whatwe-get-wrong-about-closing-the-racial-wealth-gap/; Darrick Hamilton, "The Federal Job Guarantee: A Step Toward Racial Justice," *Dissent Magazine*, November 9, 2015, www.dissentmagazine.org/online_articles/federal-job-guarantee-racial-justicedarrick-hamilton; Janelle Jones and John Schmitt, "A College Degree Is No Guarantee" (Washington, DC: Center for Economic and Policy Research, May 2014), http://cepr.net/documents/black-coll-grads-2014-05.pdf; Yunju Nam, Darrick Hamilton, William A. Darity Jr. and Anne E. Price, "Bootstraps Are for Black Kids: Race, Wealth, and the Impact of Intergenerational Transfers on Adult Outcomes" (Insight Center for Community Economic Development, September 2015), https://sanford.duke.edu/articles/bootstraps-are-black-kids, among others. See chapters 2 and 3 for further discussion.

5. See for example Alan A. Aja et al., "The Color of Wealth in Miami" (A Joint Publication of the Kirwan Center on the Study of Race and Ethnicity (Ohio State University), Samuel DuBois Cook Center on Social Equity (Duke University), Insight Center for Community Economic Development (Oakland, California), 2019, http://kirwaninstitute.osu.edu/wp-content/uploads/2019/02/The-Color-of-Wealth-in-Miami-Metro.pdf; Darity Jr. et al., "What We Get Wrong"; Jones and Schmitt, "A College Degree Is No Guarantee"; William Darity Jr., Jason Dietrich, and Darrick Hamilton, "Bleach in the Rainbow: Latin Ethnicity and Preference for Whiteness," in *The Afro-Latin@ Reader: History and Culture in the United States*, ed. Miriam Jiménez Román and Juan Flores (Durham, NC: Duke University Press, 2010), 485–98; Darrick Hamilton et al., "Umbrellas Don't Make It Rain: Why Studying and Working Hard Isn't Enough for Black Americans" (New York: Samuel DuBois Cook Center on Social Equity at Duke University, the New School, and Insight Center for Community Economic Development, 2015), http://www.insightcced.org/uploads/CRWG/Umbrellas-Dont-Make-It-Rain8.pdf; Logan, "How Race Counts."

6. Camille L. Ryan and Kurt Bauman, "Educational Attainment in the United States, 2015" (Washington, DC: U.S. Census Bureau, March 2016), https://www.census.gov/content/dam/Census/library/publications/2016/demo/p20-578.pdf.

7. Alai Reyes-Santos, 2018, "What It Means to Be a Black Latina in Higher Education," *HipLatina* (blog), October 20, 2018, https://hiplatina.com/what-it-means-to-be-a-black-latina-in-higher-education/.

8. Darity Jr., Dietrich, and Hamilton, "Bleach in the Rainbow."

9. Alberto Davila, Marie T. Mora, and Sue K. Stockly, "Does Mestizaje Matter in the U.S.? Economic Stratification of Mexican Immigrants," *American Economic Review* 101, 3 (May 2011): 593–97, doi: 10.1257/aer.101.3.593.

10. For a recent scholarly piece about the politics and linguistic meanings of the term "Latinx," see for example Catalina (Kathleen) de Onís, 2017, "What's in an 'x'? An Exchange about the Politics of 'Latinx,'" *Chiricú Journal: Latina/o Literatures, Arts, and Cultures* 1, no. 2 (Spring 2017): 78–91, doi: 10.2979/chiricu.1.2.07.

11. Petra R. Rivera-Rideau, Jennifer A. Jones, and Tianna Paschel, eds., *Afro-Latin@s in Movement: Critical Approaches to Blackness and Transnationalism in the Americas*, Afro-Latin@ Diasporas (Palgrave Macmillan US, 2016); Suzanne Oboler and A. Dzidzienyo, eds., *Neither Enemies nor Friends: Latinos, Blacks, Afro-Latinos* (Palgrave Macmillan, 2005); Miriam Jiménez Román and Juan Flores, *The Afro-Latin@ Reader: History and Culture in the United States* (Durham, NC: Duke University Press, 2010).

12. U.S. Census Bureau 2010 Decennial census data.

13. Author analysis of American Community Survey data for 2011–2015 from IPUMS.

14. Author analysis of American Community Survey data for 2011–2015 from IPUMS.

15. More precisely, the island of Quisqueya (indigenous name), then renamed Santo Domingo (La Española) and now Haiti and the Dominican Republic, has been chronically overlooked in the literature for its historical significance in Afro-Latinx origins. *The CUNY Dominican Studies Institute* has provided an online educational tool ("First Blacks in the Americas") for these reasons, pointing out that "the Trans-Atlantic slave trade and New World Black slavery in general, as conventionally understood, begin in this first European settlement of the Americas, expanding from there as a fundamental feature of the society based on domination and colonization that was subsequently imposed on most of the continent." CUNY Dominican Studies Institute, "A Silenced History | First Blacks in the Americas," n.d., http://www.firstblacks.org/en/summaries/about-03-silence/.

16. See Gustavo López and Ana Gonzalez-Barrera, "Afro-Latino: A Deeply Rooted Identity among U.S. Hispanics," *Pew Research Center's Hispanic Trends Project* (blog), 2016, https://www.pewresearch.org/hispanic/2016/03/01/afro-latino-a-deeply-rooted-identity-among-u-s-hispanics/; George Reid Andrews, "Afro-Latin America by the Numbers: The Politics of the Census," *ReVista: Harvard Review of Latin America* (blog), Winter 2018, https://revista.drclas.harvard.edu/book/afro-latin-america-numbers-politics-census; also see Román and Flores, *The Afro-Latin@ Reader*.

17. In Román and Flores, *The Afro-Latin@ Reader*.

18. Refugio I. Rochin, "Latinos and Afro-Latino Legacy in the United States: History, Culture and Issues of Identity," *Professional Agricultural Workers Journal* 3, no. 2 (2016): 10, https://econpapers.repec.org/article/agspawjal/236907.htm.

19. Juan Gonzalez, *Harvest of Empire: A History of Latinos in America* (New York: Penguin Books, 2001).

20. Among Latinx subgroups, generalized evidence points to select South Americans and Cubans generally doing socioeconomically better than Mexicans, Central Americans, and other Caribbean Latinx groups. See Seth Motel and Eileen Patten, "Hispanics of Puerto Rican Origin in the United States, 2010 (statistical profile)," Pew Research Center, Pew Research Hispanic Trends Project, 2012. http://www.pewhispanic.org/2012/06/27/hispanics-of-puerto-rican-origin-in-the-united-states-2010/. As we discuss throughout the book, this also varies considerably by nativity, waves of arrival (if applicable), self-reported race, gender, political context of absorption into the economy, and other inter- and intra-group factors.

21. In the subsequent chapter, we discuss numerous variables that may affect Afro-Latino wealth and poverty specifically. For instance, the extent of pre-migration resources, and level of state support, as underscored by William Darity Jr. et al., "What We Get Wrong about Closing the Racial Wealth Gap" (Samuel DuBois Cook Center on Social Equity, Insight Center for Community Economic Development, 2018) in a recent report on the racial wealth gap, further provides layers for understanding the economic reality of the Latinx community. For a local level example, see Alan A. Aja et al., "The Color of Wealth in Miami" (A Joint Publication of the Kirwan Center on the Study of Race and Ethnicity (Ohio State University), Samuel DuBois Cook Center on Social Equity (Duke University), Insight Center for Community Economic Development (Oakland, California), 2019), http://kirwaninstitute.osu.edu/wp-content/uploads/2019/02/The-Color-of-Wealth-in-Miami-Metro.pdf.

22. U.S. Census Bureau American Community Survey data for 2015.

23. Author analysis of 2011–2015 ACS data from IPUMS as well as American Community Survey data for 2011–2015 from the U.S. Census Bureau.

24. Author analysis of American Community Survey data for 2011–2015 from IPUMS.

25. Gustavo López and Ana Gonzalez-Barrera, "Afro-Latino: A Deeply Rooted Identity among U.S. Hispanics," *Pew Research Center's Hispanic Trends Project* (blog), 2016, http://www.pewresearch.org/fact-tank/2016/03/01/afro-latino-a-deeply-rooted-identity-among-u-s-hispanics/.

26. There is discrepancy in the figures for the Afro-descendant population in Cuba from different sources. Lowest estimate is at 33 percent and highest is 75—this despite the latest Cuban Census (2012) with 9.3 percent self-reporting as Black, 26.6 percent as mulatto/mestizo (mixed-race), and the rest declaring themselves white. See for example B. Denise Hawkins, "In Cuba, African Roots Run Deep, but It's a Lesson Students Aren't Learning in the Classroom," *NBC News*, September 1, 2017, https://www.nbcnews.com/news/nbcblk/cuba-african-roots-run-deep-it-s-lesson-students-aren-n767616. For academic literature, see Lisandro Pérez, "Racialization among Cubans and Cuban Americans," in *How the United States Racializes Latinos: White Hegemony and Its Consequences*, ed. José A. Cobas, Jorge

Duany, and Joe R. Feagin (Boulder: Paradigm, 2009); also see Danielle Clealand, *The Power of Race in Cuba: Racial Ideology and Black Consciousness during the Revolution* (Oxford: Oxford University Press, 2017); Devyn Spence Benson, *Antiracism in Cuba: The Unfinished Revolution*, Envisioning Cuba (Chapel Hill: University of North Carolina Press, 2016); Alan A. Aja, *Miami's Forgotten Cubans: Race, Racialization and the Local Afro-Cuban Experience* (London, United Kingdom: Palgrave Macmillan, 2016).

27. There are several studies that underscore the apparent overwhelming white identity among Cubans in the United States, especially in South Florida. For instance, a 2006 Pew Research Center Fact Sheet noted that an astonishing 86 percent of Cubans in the U.S. (using 2004 figures) considered themselves white, this compared to 60 percent of Mexicans and just above 50 percent of Central Americans and Puerto Ricans respectively declaring themselves as white. Important to note that while around a third of other Latinx groups chose the "some other race" option, Cubans did not follow suit, with only 8 percent declaring themselves as such. Fact sheet can be accessed here: https://www.pewhispanic.org/2006/08/25/cubans-in-the-united-states/.

28. See Danielle Clealand, *The Power of Race in Cuba: Racial Ideology and Black Consciousness during the Revolution* (Oxford: Oxford University Press, 2017); Mark Q. Sawyer, *Racial Politics in Post-Revolutionary Cuba* (New York, NY: Cambridge University Press, 2005).

29. Monika Gosin, "'A Bitter Diversion': Afro-Cuban Immigrants, Race, and Everyday-Life Resistance," *Latino Studies* 15, no. 1 (April 1, 2017): 4–28, https://link.springer.com/article/10.1057/s41276-017-0046-2.

30. For more on intra-Cuban racism, see also Alan A. Aja, *Miami's Forgotten Cubans: Race, Racialization and the Local Afro-Cuban Experience* (London, United Kingdom: Palgrave Macmillan, 2016); Julie A. Dowling and C. Alison Newby, "So Far from Miami: Afro-Cuban Encounters with Mexicans in the US Southwest," *Latino Studies* 8, no. 2 (June 1, 2010): 176–94, https://doi.org/10.1057/lst.2010.19; Monika Gosin, *The Racial Politics of Division: Interethnic Struggles for Legitimacy in Multicultural Miami* (Cornell University Press, 2019); C. Alison Newby and Julie A. Dowling, "Black and Hispanic: The Racial Identification of Afro-Cuban Immigrants in the Southwest," *Sociological Perspectives* 50, no. 3 (2007): 343–66, doi:10.1525/sop.2007.50.3.343; Susan Greenbaum, *More than Black: Afro-Cubans in Tampa* (Gainesville: University of Florida Press, 2002).

31. William A. Darity Jr., Jason Dietrich, and Darrick Hamilton, 2010, "Bleach in the Rainbow: Latino Ethnicity and Preference for Whiteness," in *The Afro-Latin@ Reader: History and Culture in the United States*, edited by Miriam Jiménez Román and Juan Flores (Durham: Duke University Press), 500. Note: In this study, skin color was assessed by the interviewer and measured on a five-point scale: very dark, dark, medium, light, very light.

32. Darity Jr., Dietrich, and Hamilton, "Bleach in the Rainbow."

33. Numerous earlier studies have documented the role of skin color-based (colorism) stratification in the Black American community. See for example Verna M. Keith and Cedric Herring, "Skin Tone and Stratification in the Black Community," *American Journal of Sociology* 97, no. 3 (1991): 760–78, an original work using the

National Survey of Black Americans (1979–1980) by demographic variables including native-born status and gender. For a succinct, historical view, Margaret Hunter, "The Persistent Problem of Colorism: Skin Tone, Status, and Inequality," *Sociology Compass* 1, no. 1 (September 2007): 237–54, https://doi.org/10.1111/j.1751-9020 .2007.00006.x; Eduardo Bonilla-Silva, *Racism without Racists: Color-Blind Racism and the Persistence of Racial Inequality in the United States* (Boulder: Rowman & Littlefield, 2nd edition, 2009).

34. Several studies reinforce each other's findings, albeit applying different indicators of measure. Logan's study: John R. Logan, "How Race Counts for Hispanic Americans" (Albany, NY: Lewis Mumford Center for Comparative Urban and Regional Research, University at Albany, July 14, 2003), doi: 10.1177 /0307920104040799; John R. Logan, "How Race Counts for Hispanic Americans," in *The Afro-Latin@ Reader: History and Culture in the United States*, ed. Miriam Jiménez Román and Juan Flores (Durham, NC: Duke University Press, 2010), 475–84, looks at several socioeconomic variables by national origin groups, including wages, poverty status, and years of schooling. Rogelio Sáenz and Maria Cristina Morales, *Latinos in the United States: Diversity and Change* (Cambridge, UK: John Wiley & Sons, 2015), using ACS data, demonstrate that native-born Latinx origin groups that have the most individuals identifying themselves as white in the census (e.g., Cuban, Colombian, and other South Americans) also report higher wages when compared to other national origin groups with lower numbers of individuals identifying as white, notably Mexicans, Salvadorans, and Guatemalans. Howard Hogan, "Reporting of Race Among Hispanics: Analysis of ACS Data," in *The Frontiers of Applied Demography*, ed. David A. Swanson, vol. 9, Applied Demography Series (Cham: Springer International Publishing, 2017), 169–91, COI 10 (2017).1007/978-3-319-43329-5_9) also found that Latinx groups that self-report as white yield lower poverty rates than those who identify their race as "some other race" or "Black."

35. By "racialization," we borrow Burton et al.'s (Linda M. Burton et al., "Critical Race Theories, Colorism, and the Decade's Research on Families of Color," *Journal of Marriage and Family* 72, no. 3 (2010): 440–59, doi:10.1111/j.1741 -3737.2010.00712.x) summary definition, in which they explain it as when "the assignment of racial meaning to real, perceived or ascribed differences among individuals or groups, produces hierarchies of power and privilege among races." For more on racialization processes among and within Latinx groups, see Douglas S. Massey, "The Racialization of Latinos in the United States," in *The Oxford Handbook of Ethnicity, Crime, and Immigration*, by Sandra Bucerius and Michael Tonry (Oxford, UK: Oxford University Press, 2014). Also see José A. Cobas, Jorge Duany, and Joe R. Feagin, *How the United States Racializes Latinos: White Hegemony and Its Consequences* (London: Routledge Press, 2009); Eduardo Bonilla-Silva, "We Are All Americans! The Latin Americanization of Racial Stratification in the USA," *Race and Society*, Symposium on the Latin Americanization of Race Relations in the United States, 5, no. 1 (2002): 3–16, https://doi.org/10.1016/j.racsoc.2003.12.008; Eduardo Bonilla-Silva, "From Bi-Racial to Tri-Racial: Towards a New System of Racial Stratification in the USA," *Ethnic and Racial Studies* 27, no. 6 (November 1, 2004): 931–50, doi:10.1080/0141987042000268530; Ramón Grosfoguel, *Colonial*

Subjects: Puerto Ricans in a Global Perspective (University of California Press, 2003). For more on socioeconomic disparities by race see John R. Logan, "How Race Counts for Hispanic Americans," in *The Afro-Latin@ Reader: History and Culture in the United States*, ed. Miriam Jiménez Román and Juan Flores (Durham, NC: Duke University Press, 2010), 475–84; also see Tanya Golash-Boza and William Darity Jr., "Latino Racial Choices: The Effects of Skin Colour and Discrimination on Latinos' and Latinas' Racial Self-Identifications," *Ethnic and Racial Studies* 31, no. 5 (July 1, 2008): 899–934, doi: 10.1080/01419870701568858; Howard Hogan, "Reporting of Race Among Hispanics: Analysis of ACS Data," in *The Frontiers of Applied Demography*, ed. David A. Swanson, vol. 9, Applied Demography Series (Cham: Springer International Publishing, 2017), 169–91, doi: 10(2017)1007/978-3-319-43329-5_9; Rogelio Sáenz and Maria Cristina Morales, *Latinos in the United States: Diversity and Change* (Cambridge, UK: John Wiley & Sons, 2015).

36. See for instance M. A. Turner, R. Santos, D. Levy, D. Wissoker, C. Arandia, R. Pitingolo, "Housing Discrimination Against Racial and Ethnic Minorities 2012," Executive Summary (June), prepared for the U.S. Department of Housing and Urban Development, Washington DC, 2013. http://www.huduser.org/portal/Publications/pdf /HUD-514_HDS2012_execsumm.pdf.; Clara E. Rodriguez, Michael H. Miyawaki, and Grigoris Argeros, "Latino Racial Reporting in the US: To Be or Not to Be," *Sociology Compass* 7, no. 6 (2013): (390–403), https://doi.org/10.1111/soc4.12032; Jessica G. Finkeldey and Stephen Demuth, "Race/Ethnicity, Perceived Skin Color, and the Likelihood of Adult Arrest," *Race and Justice*, February 4, 2019, https://jour nals.sagepub.com/doi/10.1177/2153368719826269; Howard Hogan, "Reporting of Race Among Hispanics: Analysis of ACS Data," in *The Frontiers of Applied Demography*, ed. David A. Swanson, vol. 9, Applied Demography Series (Cham: Springer International Publishing, 2017), 169–91; Thomas Alexis LaVeist-Ramos et al., "Are Black Hispanics Black or Hispanic? Exploring Disparities at the Intersection of Race and Ethnicity," *Journal of Epidemiol Community Health* 66, no. 7 (July 1, 2012): 11–15, http://dx.doi.org.proxyau.wrlc.org/10.1136/jech.2009.103879.

Note: These coloristic penalties are also found for dark-skinned Latinxs when educational levels are equal to their white Latinx peers (findings we will underscore throughout the book) and groups are of similar ethnic (ancestral) backgrounds. See Rogelío Sáenz and Maria Cristina Morales, *Latinos in the United States: Diversity and Change* (Cambridge, UK: John Wiley & Sons, 2015). Also, for a synopsis on the relationship between skin shade and political party affiliation among all groups (including empirical evidence that light-skinned Latinxs are more likely to support the Republican Party), see Spencer Piston, "Lighter-Skinned Minorities Are More Likely to Support Republicans," *Washington Post*, 2014, https://www.washingtonpost .com/news/monkey-cage/wp/2014/09/17/lighter-skinned minorities-are-more-likely -to-support-republicans/.

37. Arthur H. Goldsmith, Darrick Hamilton, and William A. Darity Jr., "Shades of Discrimination: Skin Tone and Wages," *American Economic Review* 96, no. 2 (2006): 245, https://doi.org/10.1007/s41996-018-0012-x. Note: the study echoes similar findings as conducted by economist Patrick Mason. See Patrick L. Mason, "Annual

Income, Hourly Wages, and Identity Among Mexican-Americans and Other Latinos," *Industrial Relations: A Journal of Economy and Society* 43, no. 4 (2004): 817–34, https://ssrn.com/abstract=591471.

38. Beverly Araujo Dawson and Laura Quiros, "The Effects of Racial Socialization on the Racial and Ethnic Identity Development of Latinas," *Journal of Latina/o Psychology* 2, no. 4 (2014): 200–203, https://doi.org/10.1080/10911359.2012.740342, provides a well-researched qualitative intersectional examination (in-depth interviews of Latinx women) of intra-Latinx colorism and its effects on identity formation. For more on colorism and health, see Adolfo G. Cuevas, Beverly Araujo Dawson, and David R. Williams, "Race and Skin Color in Latino Health: An Analytic Review," *American Journal of Public Health* 106, no. 12 (December 2016): 2131–36, https://www.ncbi.nlm.nih.gov/pmc/articles/PMC5104999/; also see Nancy López, "Contextualizing Lived Race-Gender and the Racialized-Gendered Social Determinants of Health," in *Mapping "Race": Critical Approaches to Health Disparities Research*, ed. Laura E. Gómez and Nancy López (New Brunswick, NJ: Rutgers University Press, 2013), 179–211.

39. Author analysis of 2015 American Community Survey data from IPUMS.

40. Logan, "How Race Counts."

41. Logan, "How Race Counts."

42. See Douglas S. Massey and Nancy A. Denton, *American Apartheid: Segregation and the Making of the Underclass* (Cambridge, MA: Harvard University Press, 1993); also see nuanced updates in Douglas S. Massey, "Residential Segregation Is the Linchpin of Racial Stratification," *City & Community* 15, no. 1 (March 2016): 4–7; Jacob S. Rugh and Douglas S. Massey, "Racial Segregation and the American Foreclosure Crisis," *American Sociological Review* 75, no. 5 (2010): 629–651, doi: 10.2307/2117754.

43. Logan, "How Race Counts."

44. Logan, "How Race Counts." Also see López and Gonzalez-Barrera, "Afro-Latino: A Deeply Rooted Identity."

45. This can also include pre-1959 Cuban communities, as well as post-revolution migrations who are of mixed-race backgrounds. For background literature, see Alan A. Aja, *Miami's Forgotten Cubans: Race, Racialization and the Local Afro-Cuban Experience* (London, United Kingdom: Palgrave Macmillan, 2016); Nancy Mirabal, "Melba Alvarado, El Club Cubano Inter-Americano, and the Creation of Afro-Cubanidades in New York City," in Miriam Jiménez Román and Juan Flores, eds. *The Afro-Latin@ Reader* (Durham: Duke University Press, 2010); Yolanda Prieto, *The Cubans of Union City: Immigrants and Exiles in a New Jersey Community* (Philadelphia: Temple University Press, 2009); Lisandro Pérez, "Racialization Among Cubans and Cuban Americans," in *How the United States Racializes Latinos: White Hegemony and Its Consequences*, ed. José A. Cobas, Jorge Duany, and Joe R. Feagin (Boulder: Paradigm, 2009); Susan Greenbaum, *More than Black: Afro-Cubans in Tampa* (Gainesville: University of Florida Press, 2002).

46. Tafoya's study found that those (Latinos) who marked "some other race," with presumably many in the distribution who are phenotypically Black (see discussion below), are also more likely to live in cities and other metro areas with

larger Black/African American communities. See Sonya M. Tafoya, "Shades of Belonging: Latinos and Racial Identity" (Washington, DC: Pew Hispanic Center, Pew Research Center, 2004), https://www.pewresearch.org/hispanic/2004/12/06/shades -of-belonging/.

47. In a more recent report examining Afro-Latinx identities, López and Gonzalez-Barrera found that while Carribean-origin Latinxs are most likely among Latinx groups to identify as Afro-Latino (34 percent) as compared to those from elsewhere (22 percent), they are also more likely to be concentrated on the East Coast and the South of the United States relative to other Latinxs (65 percent to 48 percent respectively). See Gustavo López and Ana Gonzalez-Barrera, "Afro-Latino: A Deeply Rooted Identity among U.S. Hispanics," *Pew Research Center's Hispanic Trends Project* (blog), 2016, https://www.pewresearch.org/hispanic/2016/03/01/afro-latino -a-deeply-rooted-identity-among-u-s-hispanics/.

48. By segregation, we refer to the measurable degree in which particular groups, by their subaltern status, are systemically separated from one another at a spatial level. See Douglas S. Massey and Nancy A. Denton, "The Dimensions of Residential Segregation," *Social Forces* 67, no. 2 (December 1, 1988): 281–315, doi: 10.2307/2579183; Douglas S. Massey and Nancy A. Denton, *American Apartheid: Segregation and the Making of the Underclass* (Cambridge, MA: Harvard University Press, 1993). For more on racial wealth gap, see chapter 2.

49. In other words, residential distancing from Black groups, Afro-Latinx, and African American alike was the pattern evident among white/non-Black Latinxs. "Black Hispanics," Denton and Massey noted, were the most segregated of all groups. See Douglas S. Massey and Nancy A. Denton, "Hypersegregation in U.S. Metropolitan Areas: Black and Hispanic Segregation along Five Dimensions," *Demography* 26, no. 3 (1989): 373–91, doi: 10.2307/2061599; Douglas S. Massey and Nancy A. Denton, *American Apartheid: Segregation and the Making of the Underclass* (Cambridge, MA: Harvard University Press, 1993).

50. Denton and Massey also found that Puerto Ricans who self-identified as "Black" were more likely to emulate patterns of segregation for U.S. Blacks. Those (Puerto Ricans) who identified as white were found to experience low to moderate levels of housing segregation. See Douglas S. Massey and Nancy A. Denton, "Hypersegregation in U.S. Metropolitan Areas: Black and Hispanic Segregation along Five Dimensions," *Demography* 26, no. 3 (1989): 373–91, doi: 10.2307/2061599.

51. Logan, "How Race Counts."

52. For more on this, with findings that provide critique of the literature that views Afro-Latinxs as a "bridge" between African Americans and Latinxs for potential political coalition building, see Atiya Kai Stokes Brown, "America's Shifting Color Line? Reexamining Determinants of Latino Racial Self-Identification," *Social Science Quarterly* 93, no. 2 (2012): 309–32, https://onlinelibrary.wiley.com/doi /full/10.1111/j.1540-6237.2012.00852.x .

53. Darity Jr., Dietrich, and Hamilton, "Bleach in the Rainbow."

54. In the same way we use "Latinx" and "Latino/a" interchangeably so as to include multiple identities, we also use "Hispanic" at times when citing the census and other data. We recognize that while it is common in the economics literature, scholars

have noted that the term itself is highly problematic, stressing not only a perceived linguistic attachment of the Spanish language as central to Latinx identity (despite linguistic variation among self-identified Latinxs), but also omitting Brazilians while upholding Iberian ancestry. For more on the term's origins, see Cristina Mora, *Making Hispanics: How Activists, Bureaucrats, and Media Constructed a New American* (Chicago: University of Chicago Press, 2014).

55. U.S. Census Bureau 2017 American Community Survey Questionnaire can be accessed at: https://www2.census.gov/programssurveys/acs/methodology/question naires/2017/quest17.pdf.

56. See Pew Research Center, "What Census Calls Us: A Historical Timeline," Pew Research Center (Social & Demographic Trends), 2015, https://www.pewsocialtrends .org/wp-content/uploads/sites/3/2015/06/ST_15.06.11_MultiRacial-Timeline.pdf.

57. See PBS, "Race Timeline: Has Race Always Been the Same?," PBS, http:// www.pbs.org/race/003_RaceTimeline/003_01-timeline.htm.

58. For background, see for instance, D'Vera Cohn, "Race and the Census: The 'Negro' Controversy," *Pew Research Center's Social & Demographic Trends Project* (blog), January 21, 2010, https://www.pewsocialtrends.org/2010/01/21/race-and-the -census-the-negro-controversy/. Also, some have argued that race in Puerto Rico, despite being an American colony, operates more similarly to Latin American models when considering racial classification (Edward Telles and Stanley Bailey, "Understanding Latin American Beliefs about Racial Inequality," *American Journal of Sociology* 118, no. 6 (2013): 1559–95, doi: 10.1086/670268). In post-migration contexts, attempts by the state to classify them (along with Mexicans) as "white" (such as census takers post-1960) went as far as their observed phenotype—they would be classifed as such "unless they were definitely 'Negro,' 'Indian,' or some other race."

59. In another example, survey research by the Pew Research Center found that one-quarter of Latino adults self-identified as Afro-Latino. Yet, when they were asked directly to specify their race, more preferred "white" or "Hispanic" (over 60 percent in aggregate) while 18 percent reported as "Black." Gustavo López and Ana Gonzalez-Barrera, "Afro-Latino: A Deeply Rooted Identity among U.S. Hispanics," *Pew Research Center's Hispanic Trends Project* (blog), 2016, https://www.pewresearch .org/fact-tank/2016/03/01/afro-latino-a-deeply-rooted-identity-among-u-s-hispanics/.

60. In contrast to the very low percentage of Latinxs who classify themselves as Black in U.S. Census Bureau data, findings from the Pew Research Center's 2014 National Survey of Latinos (n=1,520) indicate that when given the option of "Afro Latino/Afro Caribbean" as a racial identity, 24 percent of Latinxs indicated as such. The disparate findings of Census Bureau data versus the National Survey of Latinos underscores the complexity of racial identification in the Latinx community (discussed more so in *Latinxs and Identity* section), in that more specific terms may be interpreted as more meaningful (especially for foreign-born respondents who may not see themselves as "African American/Black"). The 2015 Pew Report is available here: Kim Parker et al., "Chapter 7: The Many Dimensions of Hispanic Racial Identity," in *Hispanic Racial Identity: Multidimensional Issue for Latinos*, by Pew Research Center (Washington, DC: Pew Research Center, 2015), https://www

.pewsocialtrends.org/2015/06/11/chapter-7-the-many-dimensions-of-hispanic-racial-identity/.

61. Darity Jr., Dietrich, and Hamilton, "Bleach in the Rainbow."

62. As we discuss in more detail throughout the book, Darity Jr. et al. (2003) also challenged the notion that "culture" is explanatory in wage disparities among Latinxs. William Darity Jr., Darrick Hamilton, and Jason Dietrich, "Passing on Blackness: Latinos, Race, and Earnings in the USA," *Applied Economics Letters* 9, no. 13 (2002): 847–53, doi: 10.1080/13504850210149133. And while we refer to "passing" here in context of Afro-descendants (and other racialized, subaltern groups) passing so as to access economic opportunities reserved for whites (non-Latinxs), or Black to white passing, there is also an important value in understanding the opposite, or appropriating Blackness. See for example: Kristen E. Broady, Curtis L. Todd, and William A. Darity Jr., "Passing and the Costs and Benefits of Appropriating Blackness," *Review of Black Political Economy* 45, no. 2 (June 1, 2018): 104–22, https://doi.org/10.1177/0034644618789182.

63. For background see Tanya Golash-Boza and William Darity Jr., "Latino Racial Choices: The Effects of Skin Colour and Discrimination on Latinos' and Latinas' Racial Self-Identifications," *Ethnic and Racial Studies* 31, no. 5 (July 1, 2008): 899–934, doi: 10.1080/01419870701568858; Edward Telles, "Latinos, Race, and the U.S. Census," *ANNALS of the American Academy of Political and Social Science* 677, no. 1 (May 1, 2018): 153–64, https://journals.sagepub.com/doi/abs/10.1177/0002716218766463?journalCode=anna; Nicholas Vargas and Kevin Stainback, "Documenting Contested Racial Identities Among Self-Identified Latina/os, Asians, Blacks, and Whites," *American Behavioral Scientist* 60, no. 4 (April 1, 2016): 442–64, https://doi.org/10.1177/0002764215613396.

64. See for example Allen et al., who argue that when feasible, combined race and ethnicity questions (and open-ended race and ethnicity questions) will help produce more robust data in meeting the community's health needs. Vincent C. Allen et al., "Issues in the Assessment of 'Race' among Latinos: Implications for Research and Policy," *Hispanic Journal of Behavioral Sciences* 33, no. 4 (November 2011): 411–24, https://www.ncbi.nlm.nih.gov/pmc/articles/PMC3519364/; Nancy López (2018) provides rebuttal and implications for this approach for the Afro-Latinx community, accessed here: Nancy López, "Why the 2020 Census Should Keep Longstanding Separate Questions about Hispanic Origin and Race," Scholars Strategy Network, December 3, 2018, https://medium.com/scholars-strategy-network/why-the-2020-census-should-keep-longstanding-separate-questions-about-hispanic-origin-and-race-7969ab1e56d8.

65. William A. Darity Jr., "The Latino Flight to Whiteness," *The American Prospect*, 2016, http://prospect.org/article/latino-flight-whiteness.

66. Miriam Jiménez Román, "Check Both! Afro-Latin@s and the Census," NACLA, November 18, 2010, https://nacla.org/article/check-both-afro-latins-and-census.

67. See Danielle Clealand, *The Power of Race in Cuba: Racial Ideology and Black Consciousness during the Revolution* (Oxford: Oxford University Press, 2017); Peter Wade, *Race and Ethnicity in Latin America* (London: Pluto Press, 1997); Norman E. Whitten and Arlene Torres, *Blackness in Latin America and the Caribbean: Eastern*

South America and the Caribbean (Bloomington: Indiana University Press, 1998); Peter Wade, *Race and Ethnicity in Latin America* (Pluto Press, 2010).

68. Eduardo Bonilla-Silva, "From bi-racial to tri-racial: Towards a new system of racial stratification in the USA," *Ethnic and Racial Studies* 27, no. 6 (2004): 931–50, doi: 10.1080/0141987042000268530; Eduardo Bonilla-Silva, "We are all Americans! The Latin Americanization of racial stratification in the USA," *Race and Society* 5 (2002): 3–16, https://doi.org/10.1016/j.racsoc.2003.12.008.

69. Patrick L. Mason, "Annual Income, Hourly Wages, and Identity Among Mexican-Americans and Other Latinos," *Industrial Relations: A Journal of Economy and Society* 43, no. 4 (2004): 817–34, https://ssrn.com/abstract=591471.

70. Darity Jr., Dietrich, and Hamilton, "Bleach in the Rainbow"; Darity Jr., Hamilton, and Dietrich, "Passing on Blackness."

71. Important to note research that underscores when Latinxs are asked to report their own skin shade, they do so at rates similar to how they self-report their "race." For background, see Alexis Rosenblum et al., "Looking through the Shades: The Effect of Skin Color on Earnings by Region of Birth and Race for Immigrants to the United States," *Sociology of Race and Ethnicity* 2, no. 1 (January 1, 2016): 87–105, https://journals.sagepub.com/doi/abs/10.1177/2332649215600718. Note: they find not only that darker-skinned immigrants are more prone to experience labor market penalties (measured by wages), but also when they disaggregate by region of origin, it is Latin American immigrants who skew the findings. Also see Darity Jr., Dietrich, and Hamilton, "Bleach in the Rainbow."

72. López and colleagues' research serves as a key accompaniment to ours, in that they found when people report their "street race-gender" along racialized lines, odds increase of reporting disparate economic and health outcomes, especially for women. Nancy López, Edward Vargas, Melina Juárez, Lisa Cacari-Stone, and Sonia Bettez, "What's Your 'Street Race'? Leveraging Multidimensional Measures of Race and Intersectionality for Examining Physical and Mental Health Status among Latinxs," *Sociology of Race and Ethnicity*, 2017, https://doi.org/10.1177/2332649217708798. See chapter on "Intersectionality" and Afro-Latinas.

73. The role of neighborhood proximity also played a role here. As Holder notes: "Personally, when I was growing up in Bed-Stuy, the main Latinx group in close proximity to Blacks with southern roots were Puerto Ricans living in Bushwick, Brownsville, and Bed-Stuy. Culturally, therefore, my earliest experiences were influenced by the Black south and the Caribbean, especially Puerto Rico and Jamaica. The cultures became so interwoven you could hardly differentiate them, except for the Spanish language, and even there many Puerto Ricans born in NYC weren't always fluent."

74. Nancy Mirabal, "Melba Alvarado, El Club Cubano Inter-Americano, and the Creation of Afro Cubanidades in New York City," in Miriam Jiménez Román and Juan Flores, eds. *The Afro-Latin@ Reader* (Duke University Press, 2010); Antonio López, *Unbecoming Blackness: The Diaspora Cultures of Afro-Cuban America* (NYU Press, 2012); Susan Greenbaum *More than Black; Afro-Cubans in Tampa* (University of Florida Press, 2002); Frank Andre Guridy, *Forging Diaspora: Afro-*

Cubans and African Americans in a World of Empire and Jim Crow (Chapel Hill: University of North Carolina Press, 2010).

75. Not surprisingly, the literature has persistently ignored the role of anti-Blackness in the racialized migrations of post-1959 Cubans, save for a few books and articles that have sought to correct for this erasure. See for example Monika Gosin, *The Racial Politics of Division: Interethnic Struggles for Legitimacy in Multicultural Miami* (Ithaca: Cornell University Press, 2019); Alan A. Aja, *Miami's Forgotten Cubans: Race, Racialization and the Local Afro-Cuban Experience* (London, United Kingdom: Palgrave Macmillan, 2016); Michelle A. Hay, *"I've Been Black in Two Countries": Black Cuban Views on Race in the US*, New Americans (El Paso: LFB Scholarly Pub, 2009); Heriberto Dixon, "The Cuban-American Counterpoint: Black Cubans in the United States," *Dialectical Anthropology* 13, no. 3 (September 1, 1988): 227–39, https://doi.org/10.1007/BF00253917; Lisandro Pérez, "Racialization Among Cubans and Cuban Americans," in *How the United States Racializes Latinos: White Hegemony and Its Consequences*, ed. José A. Cobas, Jorge Duany, and Joe R. Feagin (Boulder: Paradigm, 2009).

76. See for example Eduardo Bonilla-Silva, "We are all Americans! The Latin Americanization of racial stratification in the USA," *Race and Society* 5 (2002): 3–16, https://doi.org/10.1016/j.racsoc.2003.12.008.

77. Alan A. Aja, Stephan LeFebvre, Nancy López, Darrick Hamilton, and William Darity Jr., "Toward a Latinx/a/o Stratification Economics," *Review of Black Political Economy*, forthcoming 2021.

78. Laura Pulido and Manuel Pastor, "Where in the World Is Juan—and What Color Is He? The Geography of Latina/o Racial Identity in Southern California," *American Quarterly* 65, no. 2 (2013): 309–41, for example, studied racial identities among Latinx communities in Southern California, and considered time and space alongside other demographic variables. Related to our discussion of segregation and racialization above, they found that Latinxs who live in more segregated neighborhoods are more likely to identify as "some other race." For more on this, also see William Darity Jr., "The Latino Flight to Whiteness," *American Prospect*, February 11, 2016, https://prospect.org/api/content/7d141e89-f909-5577-a5ca-e2692770deb9/; Patrick L. Mason, "Annual Income, Hourly Wages, and Identity Among Mexican-Americans and Other Latinos," *Industrial Relations: A Journal of Economy and Society* 43, no. 4 (2004): 817–34, https://ssrn.com/abstract=591471; Alexis Rosenblum et al., "Looking through the Shades: The Effect of Skin Color on Earnings by Region of Birth and Race for Immigrants to the United States," *Sociology of Race and Ethnicity* 2, no. 1 (January 1, 2016): 87–105, https://journals.sagepub.com/doi/abs/10.1177/2332649215600718, among others.

79. For detailed reviews of the literature, see Clara E. Rodríguez, Michael H. Miyawaki, and Grigoris Argeros, "Latino Racial Reporting in the US: To Be or Not to Be," *Sociology Compass* 7, no. 5 (2013): 390–403, https://doi.org/10.1111/soc4.12032; also see Tanya Golash-Boza and William Darity Jr., "Latino Racial Choices: The Effects of Skin Colour and Discrimination on Latinos' and Latinas' Racial Self-Identifications," *Ethnic and Racial Studies* 31, no. 5 (July 1, 2008): 899–934, doi:10.1080/01419870701568858; Atiya Kai Stokes-Brown, "America's Shift-

ing Color Line? Reexamining Determinants of Latino Racial Self-Identification," *Social Science Quarterly* 93, no. 2 (2012): 309–32, https://onlinelibrary.wiley.com /doi/full/10.1111/j.1540-6237.2012.00852.x; Nicholas Vargas and Kevin Stainback, "Documenting Contested Racial Identities Among Self-Identified Latina/os, Asians, Blacks, and Whites," *American Behavioral Scientist* 60, no. 4 (April 1, 2016): 442–64, https://doi.org/10.1177/0002764215613396; Linda M. Burton et al., "Critical Race Theories, Colorism, and the Decade's Research on Families of Color," *Journal of Marriage and Family* 72, no. 3 (2010): 440–59, doi:10.1111/j.1741 -3737.2010.00712.x; José A. Cobas, Jorge Duany, and Joe R. Feagin, *How the United States Racializes Latinos: White Hegemony and Its Consequences* (London: Routledge, 2009); Douglas S. Massey, "The Racialization of Latinos in the United States," in *The Oxford Handbook of Ethnicity, Crime, and Immigration*, by Sandra Bucerius and Michael Tonry (Oxford, UK: Oxford University Press, 2014).

80. Zhenchao Qian and José A. Cobas, "Latinos' Mate Selection: National Origin, Racial, and Nativity Differences," *Social Science Research* 33, no. 2 (June 1, 2004): 225–47; also see Logan, "How Race Counts."

81. Zhenchao Qian, Daniel T. Lichter, and Dmitry Tumin, "Divergent Pathways to Assimilation? Local Marriage Markets and Intermarriage Among U.S. Hispanics," *Journal of Marriage and Family* 80, no. 1 (2018): 271–88, https://onlinelibrary.wiley .com/doi/full/10.1111/jomf.12423.

82. Zhenchao Qian, Daniel T. Lichter, and Dmitry Tumin, "Divergent Pathways to Assimilation? Local Marriage Markets and Intermarriage Among U.S. Hispanics," *Journal of Marriage and Family* 80, no. 1 (2018): 271–88, https://onlinelibrary.wiley .com/doi/full/10.1111/jomf.12423.

83. There are numerous studies in the Black/Latinx relations literature which focus on the economic overlaps between Puerto Ricans and African Americans, especially in a New York/Northeastern U.S. context. See for example Andrés Torres, *Between Melting Pot and Mosaic: African Americans and Puerto Ricans in the New York Political Economy* (Philadelphia, PA: Temple University Press, 1995). For analyses on the political context of competition for scarce resources, see John Betancur, "Framing the Discussion of African American–Latino Relations: A Review and Analysis," in *Neither Enemies nor Friends*, eds. Susanne Oboler and Anani Dzidzienyo (2005): 159–72.

84. Sharon M. Lee and Sonya M. Tafoya, "Rethinking US Census Racial and Ethnic Categories for the 21st Century," *Journal of Economic and Social Measurement* 31, no. 3–4 (January 1, 2006): 233–52, doi: 10.3233/JEM-2006-0279; Sonya M. Tafoya, "Shades of Belonging: Latinos and Racial Identity" (Washington, DC: Pew Hispanic Center, Pew Research Center, 2004), https://www.pewresearch.org /hispanic/2004/12/06/shades-of-belonging/.

85. Susan Greenbaum, "Afro-Cubans in Tampa," in Jiménez Román and Flores, eds., *The Afro-Latin@ Reader* (Duke University Press, 2010), 51.

86. Tanya Golash-Boza and William Darity Jr., "Latino Racial Choices: The Effects of Skin Colour and Discrimination on Latinos' and Latinas' Racial Self-Identifications," *Ethnic and Racial Studies* 31, no. 5 (July 1, 2008): 899–934, doi: 10.1080/01419870701568858; also see Atiya Kai Stokes-Brown, "America's Shift-

ing Color Line? Reexamining Determinants of Latino Racial Self-Identification," *Social Science Quarterly* 93, no. 2 (2012): 309–32, https://onlinelibrary.wiley.com /doi/full/10.1111/j.15406237.2012.00852.x.

87. For background literature, see Mary C. Waters, Philip Kasinitz, and Asad L. Asad, "Immigrants and African Americans," *Annual Review of Sociology* 40, no. 1 (2014): 369–90; also see Philip Kasinitz, *Caribbean New York: Black Immigrants and the Politics of Race* (Ithaca, NY: Cornell University Press, 1992); for excellent empirical rebuttal on the role of "culture" and assumed "lower quality" labor market skills, see William Darity Jr., "Revisiting the Debate on Race and Culture: The New (Incorrect) Harvard/Washington Consensus," *Du Bois Review: Social Science Research on Race* 8, no. 2 (2011): 467–76, doi: 10.1017/S1742058X11000439; Patrick L. Mason, "Race, Culture, and Skill: Interracial Wage Differences among African Americans, Latinos, and Whites," *Review of Black Political Economy* 25, no. 3 (1997): 5–39, https://doi.org/10.1007/s12114-997-1001-5.

88. Our findings, given that a signficant portion have already intermarried into the U.S. Black community, coincides with some social science literature. Michelle A. Hay, *"I've Been Black in Two Countries": Black Cuban Views on Race in the US*, New Americans (El Paso: LFB Scholarly Pub, 2009), and Alan A. Aja, *Miami's Forgotten Cubans: Race, Racialization and the Local Afro-Cuban Experience* (London, United Kingdom: Palgrave Macmillan, 2016), independently found that among Black Cubans, distancing by white Cubans through outright discrimination on one hand, and simultaneously finding acceptance among native Black/African American communities through their institutions and traditions, was key to their economic survival and future identity formation.

89. Authors' analysis of ACS data for 2011–2015 from IPUMS.

90. U.S. Census Bureau American Community Survey 5-Year Estimates, 2011–2015.

91. Justin Wolfers, David Leonhardt, and Kevin Quealy, "1.5 Million Missing Black Men," *New York Times*, The Upshot, April 21, 2015, https://www.nytimes .com/interactive/2015/04/20/upshot/missing-black-men.html.

92. U.S. Census Bureau American Community Survey 5-Year Estimates, 2011–2015.

93. Antonio Flores, "How the U.S. Hispanic Population Is Changing," *Pew Research Center* (blog), September 18, 2017, http://www.pewresearch.org/fact-tank /2017/09/18/how-the-u-s-hispanic-population-is-changing/.

94. We also ran the mean for family size but were careful with analysis considering the role of outliers. Our findings nevertheless show that among the Latinx community, Afro-Latinos demonstrate a smaller family size (compared to White Latinxs and the Latinx community on average).

95. At the timing of final edits, we also ran the marriage figures using more recently available data (2017 ACS data) and found the same pattern with the "Married, Spouse Present" variable. Black Latinx individuals were least likely to be married (measured by the mean) among all compared groups (21 percent), followed closely by non-Latinx Blacks (23 percent) and Native Americans (26 percent). White Latinx individuals demonstrated a middle position in the figures at 33 percent, compared to

whites (non-Latinx) at 46 percent and Asians at 47 percent. This measure is also important given the variable economic effect of "spouse present" on family or household income (see chapter 2).

96. Camille L. Ryan and Kurt Bauman, "Educational Attainment in the United States: 2015" (Washington, DC: U.S. Census Bureau, March 2016), https://www.census.gov/content/dam/Census/library/publications/2016/demo/p20-578.pdf.

97. Carmen DeNavas-Walt and Bernadette D. Proctor, "Income and Poverty in the United States: 2014," Current Population Reports (Washington, DC: U.S. Census Bureau, September 2015), https://www.census.gov/content/dam/Census/library/publications/2015/demo/p60-252.pdf.

98. Urban Institute, "Nine Charts about Wealth Inequality in America," https://apps.urban.org/features/wealth-inequality-charts/ Updated June 2017.

99. U.S. Census Bureau Table "Poverty Status in the Past 12 Months: 2014 American Community Survey 1-Year Estimates," https://data.census.gov/cedsci/table?q=B17&d=ACS%201-Year%20Estimates%20Detailed%20Tables&tid=ACSDT1Y2019.B17020.

100. We must note that we conduct original quantitative analysis in many parts of the book when more common data sets and measures do not produce such data for Afro-Latinxs. In chapter 3 for instance, we produce current labor force indicators for Afro-Latinxs since the Bureau of Labor Statistics, the U.S. agency responsible for providing national labor force data, does not produce such data.

101. Kimberlé Crenshaw, "Mapping the Margins: Intersectionality, Identity Politics, and Violence Against Women of Color," *Stanford Law Review* 43, no. 6 (July 1991): 1241–1300, https://doi.org/10.2307/1229039.

102. Nick Peterson et al., "Unequal Treatment: Racial and Ethnic Disparities in Miami-Dade Criminal Justice" (ACLU of Florida, 2018), https://www.aclufl.org/en/publications/unequal-treatment-racial-and-ethnic-disparities-miami-dade-criminal-justice.

Chapter Two

Income, Poverty, and Wealth among Afro-Latinxs

Over the last few years, a number of technical reports and journal articles have emerged documenting the current and forecasted wealth position of African Americans and Latinxs in comparison to other groups, especially white non-Latinxs.[1] Wealth, or the aggregate value of an individual or family's assets minus their debts or liabilities, is arguably a more robust measure of intergroup inequality than income and other socioeconomic indicators.[2] Eliciting sometimes alarming media headlines that Latinxs and African Americans "will be broke soon" or are on the "road to zero wealth," the research nevertheless underscores the extent of rising *racialized* wealth inequality in the United States, especially since the Great Recession.[3] One recent report by researchers Rakesh Kochhar and Anthony Ciluffo of the Pew Research Center showed that while there was a slight improvement in the wealth position for American households since late 2007 (start of the Great Recession), this was the case primarily for white (non-Latinx) households, but not for Black and Latinx households (measured as separate groups).[4] In 2016, the median wealth of non-Latinx white households was found to be $171,000, an astonishing ten times greater than that found for Black households ($17,100), and eight times greater than that of Latinx households ($20,600).[5] And, here is the clincher: the wealth gap in 2017 was found to be *greater* between white and Black households than it was in 2007, and the same pattern held true for the wealth gap between non-Latinx white and Latinx households over the same time period.[6] In other words, the typical white (non-Latinx) family recovered after the Great Recession, but this was not the same reality for Black and Latinxs families.

That the wealth position improved for non-Latinx whites after a major economic crisis yet worsened for Blacks and remained unchanged for Latinxs isn't an empirical surprise. Given a long history of racialized public policy based on outright confiscation, systemic exclusion, and/or predatory inclusion, wealth has been unevenly distributed by race and ethnicity for centuries in the U.S., and non-Latinx whites simply have more wealth to rely on, even in the context of macro-level economic calamity and micro-level volatility. In fact, even when considering the role of education as a potentially mitigating factor for disparities in wealth distribution by race and ethnicity, Darrick Hamilton, William Darity Jr., Anne Price, Vishnu Sridharan, and Rebecca Tippett found that the typical non-Latinx white household where the head does *not* have a college degree had exponentially more wealth than the typical Black household where the head does.[7]

These documented economic disparities raise unanswered questions for Afro-Latinxs, given that, too often, African Americans and Latinxs are measured and compared independently, without accounting for intersecting identities and experiences. Even as economic realities, measured by indicators such as poverty status and income, may be, in some geographic and socio-political contexts, comparable between both groups, Latinxs overall have been found to perform economically better than African Americans (though both groups compare poorly to Asians as well as non-Latinx whites). This poses the usual inter/intra-group questions: Where do U.S. Afro-Latinxs fit within the typical Black-Latinx economic frame? Do they experience levels of wealth, income, and poverty analogous to the Latinx community as a whole, or are they closer to African Americans and other racialized groups in a larger "Black collective" frame? Or, do Afro-Latinxs fit in their own independent space?[8] What are the related or unrelated factors that determine the U.S. Afro-Latinx economic position?

In the following pages, we attempt to answer these questions, outlining the current Afro-Latinx economic position with regard to income, wealth, and poverty, juxtaposing this against similar data for non-Latinx whites, African Americans, and Latinxs overall, and, in some contexts, Asians. We include original quantitative analysis using the American Community Survey (ACS) and other data, including localized findings from the recent *Color of Wealth* publication series, and do so applying a critical Black/Latinx/Afro-Latinx wealth frame.[9] This theoretical frame, an extension and application of the emerging subfield of "stratification economics," helps us explain how individuals experience material stratification based on the relative status of a larger subaltern group to which they belong.[10] In other words, Afro-Latinxs, belonging both to the larger Black and Latinx communities (as well as varying degrees of competing and overlapping identities within those groups) experience economic penalties related to this group's position, based on both race and ethnicity, in the larger social hierarchy. Pointedly, stratification economics also holds as a priori that economic disparities are functions of intentional socioeconomic and political barriers, not to the presence of self-defeating behaviors on the part of subaltern groups, including Afro-Latinxs.[11] Thus, tropes that suggest Black and Latinx groups simply don't work hard enough, need more education, must "pull themselves up by their bootstraps," or, more specifically, that intergroup wealth inequality is a function of a lack of financial literacy or self-sabotaging values, are countered by our findings.[12] In this chapter, the U.S. Afro-Latinx community's economic position, as measured by income, poverty status and wealth, "Blackness," or rather "anti-Blackness," matters. We find further evidence that coincides with other interdisciplinary studies that, in spite of higher relative levels of educational attainment, one's race, including one's skin shade given colorism, is determinant in one's economic position, and this is especially true among Afro-Latinxs regardless of Hispanic/Latinx ancestral origin.

SETTING THE HISTORICAL CONTEXT

In the previous chapter, we provided a general demographic profile of the U.S. Afro-Latinx community. We find, for instance, that a sizable percentage identify their primary ancestry as African American, while the rest of the group identifies alongside their Caribbean or Latin American countries of direct or familial origin. We also found that a larger percentage of Afro-Latinxs are born in the United States as compared to the Latinx community overall, and that the former group is more educated, on average, than the latter group. But whether Afro-Latinxs have been racialized as Black in the U.S. as part of long-past as well as more recent diasporic migrations, a critical "Black/Afro-Latinx" stratification theoretical lens allows us to better understand Afro-Latinxs' current economic position. Per economists Darrick Hamilton and William Darity Jr., we "look beyond the individual factors and investigate structural and context factors that preserve the relative status of dominant groups" by examining the role of wealth stripping and asset prevention that have long been institutionalized in America.[13] Let's use the racialized history of home ownership as an example.

Home ownership is a central wealth-generating feature of the American economy. As a private asset, it is one of the most commonly studied intergenerational forms of wealth and indicators of economic stratification.[14] The typical American household, for instance, regardless of racial or ethnic background, holds most of its wealth in home equity. It is also an asset that normally appreciates over time, though this is less likely to be true for communities of color, especially African Americans. It isn't, however, the primary factor in the "racial wealth gap," nor does it fully explain the gap; between non-Latinx whites and Blacks who own homes in the U.S., non-Latinx whites still hold substantially more wealth in other assets which can be relied upon in the presence of sudden financial calamity.[15]

During the last housing crisis in the U.S., a narrative emerged asserting "financially irresponsible" behavior on the part of subaltern groups—Blacks and racialized Latinxs—as a primary cause. This isn't a surprise—economists and other scholars have delved into behavioralist, "personal responsibility" frames to place the burden of structural inequality on subaltern groups themselves.[16] On home ownership specifically, ignored was that *prior* to the housing crisis, banks and lenders were engaging in predatory practices, charging higher interest rates to people of color compared to non-Latinx whites.[17] This is an example of what scholars call "predatory inclusion" in credit markets, where the exploitative behaviors of lenders not only limit the long-term benefit of holding an asset, but also, under the guise of "access" and "inclusion," longtime racial inequalities are maintained.[18]

These racialized practices are not new, as the history of home ownership, and asset accumulation in general is one of confiscation, outright exclusion, and disparate outcomes by race and ethnicity. Sociologist Joe Feagin's classic analysis on systemic racism over four centuries examined the role of home ownership rooted in the 1862 Homestead Act, highlighting the range of covert and violent exclusionary tactics that prohibited Black ownership.[19] Economist William Darity Jr. noted that, from 1880 to 1910, if land owned by the formerly enslaved wasn't violently confiscated and given to whites, any subsequent possession by Blacks was likely to be stripped, and, hence, crucial intergenerational asset transfers lost. During Jim Crow, numerous exclusionary tactics emerged as Blacks and Latinx groups (e.g., Puerto Ricans and Mexicans) with long histories in the U.S. asserted themselves economically. George Lipsitz's crucial argument that the "possessive investment in whiteness" yields propertied disparities delves into the early years of the Federal Housing Authority's (FHA) openly racist practices through its own "appraisers' manuals," ultimately chaneling "almost all of the loan money toward whites and away from communities of color."[20] During the post–World War II era, asset development was further geared toward creating a middle class through legislation like the "G.I. Bill"—but again, it was non-Latinx white veterans and their families who overwhelmingly benefited while Blacks, most Latinxs, and other racialized groups were subject to disparate outcomes based on race and ethnicity.[21] Political scientist Ira Katznelson's prolific work showed how home mortgage assistance promised by the bill did not yield "equal opportunities," in that local officials in charge of dispersing federal subsidies practiced race-based discrimination, especially local banks.[22] This decentralized arrangement created the likelihood that Black veteran families ending up renting, while non-Latinx whites became homeowners. Katznelson unapologetically referred to this time and its practices as "when affirmative action was white."[23]

Other policies, including redlining, where lenders disallow qualified home-buyers (predominantly Black, Latinx, and low-income) to purchase homes in certain neighborhoods, along with restrictive covenants (prohibitive land use/acquisition contracts), independently and in the aggregate contributed to racialized outcomes. Sociologist Keeanga-Yamahtta Taylor provides a succinct summary of this history boldly and frankly:

> From racial zoning to restricted covenants to LICs to FHA-backed mortgages to the subprime mortgage loan, the U.S. housing industry has sought to exploit and financially benefit from the public perceptions of racial difference. This has meant that even when no discernable discrimination is detected, the fact that Black communities and neighborhoods are perceived as inferior means that African Americans must rely on an inherently devalued "asset" for maintenance of their quality of life. This has created a permanent disadvantage.[24]

Yet, as public policy played a central role in racialized wealth distribution, arguments remain that placed the burden of material poverty, educational inequity, and asset inequality on racialized groups themselves. As the argument goes, if "they" (Blacks, Latinxs, and low-income individuals) simply acquired more education or better-paying occupations, were more frugal with savings, gained financial literacy, emulated supposedly successful "minority" groups, implored the right family values and structures, got off welfare programs, and a host of behavioralist expectations, economic disparities would simply disappear.[25] In subsequent pages of this book, our portrait presents evidence that counters these narratives, and we begin with the central role education is expected to play in income generation. We find that Afro-Latinxs in the U.S. possess *more* education than their white Latinx and other peers, yet experience disparate economic outcomes. Taken together with evidence which suggests Afro-Latinxs are more likely to possess African phenotypical attributes, and hence are subject to labor market and asset-based anti-Black discrimination, the aggregation of evidence places them well within the frame of the experience of African Americans, in that education alone does not suffice as an efficient instrument of economic mobility, nor does it serve as an anti-discriminatory shield.[26]

INCOME, EDUCATION, AND AFRO-LATINXS

In early 2018, an Economic Policy Institute (EPI) report by Janelle Jones, John Schmitt, and Valerie Wilson reflected on the 50-year anniversary of the historic *Kerner Commission Report.*[27] The initial Kerner report, written in the context of the civil rights movement so as to understand the causes of uprisings in urban Black communities, examined a vast array of economic and social measures confronting this group.[28] The 1968 report, we should emphasize, has received a lot of critique in the interdisciplinary literature, in that though the report acknowledged the oppressive role of white racism, it nevertheless asserted that the burden of economic justice rests on Black communities themselves.[29] Keisha Bentley-Edwards et al.'s recent critique is an example, stating:

> Rather than seeing racial uprisings by black people as a normal response to incessant oppression and degradation, racial discontent and uprisings are seen through the lenses of black deficiency.[30]

Fifty years since the report's publication, Jones et al. found that, among key inequities the Kerner report measured, income inequality between Blacks and non-Latinx whites remained constant and persistent. Adjusting for inflation, the hourly wage between 1968 and 2016 grew about 0.6 percent per year (30.5 percent over the nearly 50-year period) for African Americans overall, a disappointing outcome considering the impressive educational attainment documented among African Americans over that time (see discussion below).[31] Despite some absolute improvement in wages for all groups, Black workers still make 82.5 cents on the dollar earned by non-Latinx white workers. Figures for inflation-adjusted household income were even more telling—despite a 42.8 percent increase in household income overall since 1968, the racial disparity remains stark—the typical Black household earned only 61.6 percent of annual income earned by the typical non-Latinx white household.[32]

We purposely begin with the African American community so as to set the empirical context—as we previously noted, some Afro-Latinxs are found to self-identify in ways incongruent to their phenotype (see chapter 1), in that they may be perceived, hence discriminatorily treated in all economic spheres, as Black regardless of geographic origin/ancestry. In other words, amid this disjuncture between one's self-identity and one's actual racialized treatment, nuanced research on colorism underscores the reality of wage and other forms of discrimination against people with darker skin tones, which, both intentionally and by default, has included Afro-Latinxs in the methodology.[33] Given this coloristic backdrop, what does the latest research tell us about how Afro-Latinxs compare to their African American counterparts when measuring income, and to what extent does educational attainment play a role? Few studies have explored this question.

One such well-cited study by John Logan, "How Race Counts for Hispanic Americans," in Miriam Jiménez Róman and Juan Flores, eds., *The Afro-*

Latin@ Reader, provides us an introductory window into these questions.[34] Applying a micro-analysis of the 1980, 1990, and 2000 U.S. censuses, the author measured a series of socioeconomic indicators of Latinxs by self-reported race, finding that median household income for Afro-Latinxs (defined as "Hispanic Blacks" in his study) was close to only one group— African Americans ("non-Hispanic Blacks").[35] On an intra-group level, while Afro-Latinxs in the sample have an "advantage in education" (measured by mean years of schooling) compared to white and "other" Latinxs, their economic position, as measured by median household income (as well as poverty rate and unemployment), was not within the range that would be predicted given their educational attainment or "human capital."[36] This is an important finding we explore in subsequent pages and throughout the book—despite relatively higher levels of educational attainment, a host of economic indicators for Afro-Latinxs fall behind expected levels. As we discuss below, this is even more profound in the context of debt accumulation in a "new economy," characterized by low wages, precarious employment, and the role higher education plays through student loan financing for Blacks (and Latinxs).[37]

In our analysis of educational attainment data, we detected a similar dynamic for Afro-Latinxs as that found for Blacks in the U.S. For larger context, let's consider that in 2015, 29 percent of everyone 25 years of age and over in the U.S. completed some college or an associate's degree, while 28 percent possessed only a high school diploma or its equivalent.[38] About 30 percent of the U.S. population 25 years and older completed college, while roughly 13 percent did not complete high school. Deconstructing educational attainment by race and ethnicity, the median educational attainment level for non-Latinx whites in 2015 was at least one but less than two years of college, while for African Americans it was less than one year of college, and for Latinxs, regardless of citizenship status, it was high school completion.[39]

Table 1.2 in chapter 1 provides nuance to the data, centering the Afro-Latinx community by measuring their median level of educational attainment relative to other groups. While African Americans tend to have higher educational attainment levels than Latinxs overall, in examining Afro-Latinxs specifically, the latter group also has higher educational attainment levels than Latinxs overall; the median educational attainment level of Afro-Latinxs, regardless of citizenship status, is less than one year of college.[40] Comparing select demographic groups, which includes non-Latinx whites, African Americans, Asians, Native Americans, Latinxs, Afro-Latinxs, and white Latinxs, it is evident that the most educated group remains Asians followed by non-Latinx whites. Yet, of note is that Afro-Latinxs are the third most educated group, and they also report more educational attainment than their white Latinx peers.

But as we noted above, despite an expected positive economic relationship between educational level and income, we find, similar to other researchers' findings from several years ago, that education is still not paying off for Afro-Latinxs when measured by income and other indicators.[41] Table 2.1 provides two measures of median income—household and personal. At the household level, Afro-Latinxs report a median income of $55,000, significantly less than their white Latinx counterparts reporting at $60,900, despite the fact the former possesses a higher overall educational attainment level. When we consider the same measure using the mean, Afro-Latinx household income trends closer to that of the groups in the lower part of the distribution, which includes African Americans and Native Americans.

Table 2.1.   Household and Personal Income among Latinxs and Comparable Demographic Groups

	Household Income (Thousands)		Personal Income (Thousands)	
	Median	Mean	Median	Mean
Latinxs				
All Latinx	60.00	78.11	17.00	26.80
White Latinx	60.90	80.11	17.50	28.22
Afro-Latinx	55.00	74.51	14.40	25.05
Non-Latinx				
White	78.70	105.04	28.00	45.44
Black/African American	49.90	67.03	16.00	27.02
Asian	100.00	129.99	23.30	46.47
Native Americans	46.60	62.68	13.50	24.17

Note: Mean values between one group and white non-Latinx are all significant at the 0.001 level.

Source: Author Analysis of American Community Survey, 2017 via Steven Ruggles, Sarah Flood, Ronald Goeken, Josiah Grover, Erin Meyer, Jose Pacas, and Matthew Sobek. IPUMS USA: Version 9.0 [dataset]. Minneapolis, MN: IPUMS, 2019. https://doi.org/10.18128/D010.V9.0.

Table 2.1 also reports mean and median personal income for Latinx and non-Latinx groups, and the above patterns continue to hold for Afro-Latinx respondents. When considering the mean, Afro-Latinxs are at the lower end of the income distribution within the Latinx community, with the former group situated in the middle between African American and Native American households.[42] The median figure, which is used to control for outliers, provides a similar picture. Afro-Latinxs have the lowest personal income among Latinx groups, comparable to African Americans ("Non-Latinx Black" in the table) and Native/tribal communities.

Taken together, there are several findings here worthy of further discussion. According to our figures, and consistent with the literature, Afro-Latinxs hold an advantage in educational attainment over white Latinx respondents, yet experience lower returns in income. At the same time, it appears that white Latinxs are not that much more well off with respect to income when compared to other non-Latinx groups, especially whites and Asians.[43] But this finding can be deceiving, considering the undercount of Afro-Latinxs already present in the data, and the inflation of white Latinx respondents (see chapter 1). Analogously, also "undercounted" is the role of skin shade/ racial discrimination faced by the U.S. Afro-Latinx community with regard to wages, of importance given Afro-Latinxs' higher overall educational attain- ment among Latinx subgroups. The next section explores a similar dynamic involving poverty rates.

POVERTY AND AFRO-LATINXS

In this section we use U.S. census data and its measurement of poverty, based on a calculated income threshold designed to determine whether a family lives in poverty.[44] We are aware of the literature that questions and seeks to improve this measure; the Census Bureau's poverty estimates don't take into account numerous interacting demographic and socioeconomic factors that are occur- ring at present and over time.[45] For example, the typical Afro-Latinx family who falls under the Census-estimated poverty threshold in New York City, as compared to such a family living in Miami, can be materially poor, but factors like a higher cost of living in one locality or the other, tighter relative labor market conditions in one locality or the other, mass divestment in local and state public goods, and other structural forces may impose a different set of challenges for Afro-Latinx families in different regions of the country.

To set the overall context, about 15 percent of the U.S. population lives at or below the U.S. Census Bureau's poverty threshold, but this rate shows great variation by age, gender, race, ethnicity, educational attainment, and employment status.[46] Children tend to be poorer than adults, women tend to be poorer than men, Native Americans tend to have the highest poverty rate of all major racial and ethnic demographic groups (followed closely by African Americans and then Latinxs) while non-Latinx whites tend to have the lowest. This variation is also found within the Latinx community across ancestry groups: Dominicans, Mexicans, Puerto Ricans, and other Central American groups tend to be poorer than other Latinx groups (such as South Americans measured as a whole), but this can also be tricky given divergent histories and (im)migration contexts. Intra-group poverty can vary by nativ- ity, wave and timing of (im)migration, locality, and other variables.[47] And, contrary to conventional narrative, Cubans in the U.S. are not much poorer than their Caribbean or other Latinx cohorts, and previous literature shows that this varies by self-reported race or skin shade.[48] But what about Afro-Latinxs in the U.S. as a whole? How do they compare to African Americans and/or Latinxs more broadly?

According to American Community Survey (ACS) data for the period 2011–2015, poverty estimates show inequities for the U.S. Afro-Latinx community (see figure 2.1). Our graph depicts poverty rates for typical demographic groups in the U.S., but it also includes supplemental data that examine Latinxs by self-reported race, and Afro-Latinxs are found to have the highest poverty rate, comparable only to African Americans and Native Americans. While non-Latinx whites and Asians had the lowest poverty rates, with 14 percent and 13 percent, respectively, the Afro-Latinx community had the highest rate at 35 percent, slightly higher than the African American and Native American communities (each at 34 percent).[49]

In addition, among Latinxs as a collectivity, an intra-group picture that stresses the role of race operating within the group emerges. Latinxs who identify as white have a lower poverty rate (25 percent) than their Afro-Latinx peers (35 percent). This is even more telling given the discussion in chapter 1 on the methodological limitations of applying self-reported race data, notably the issue of "passing on Blackness" among Latinxs that William Darity Jr., Jason Dietrich, and Darrick Hamilton underscored in their study, among others.[50] In other words, since it is likely that some Afro-Latinxs have self-identified as "white" or "some other race," coupled with existing evidence that "white/white-passing" Latinxs experience lower levels of

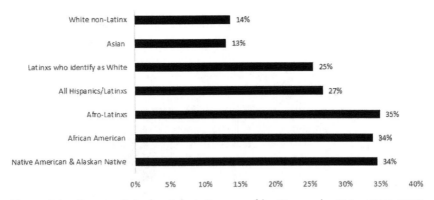

Figure 2.1. Poverty Rate by Select Demographic Groups in U.S., 2011–2015. *Data Source*: Author analysis of 2011–2015 American Community Survey 5-year data obtained from Steven Ruggles, Katie Genadek, Ronald Goeken, Josiah Grover, and Matthew Sobek. Integrated Public Use Microdata Series, Version 6.0 [dataset]. Minneapolis, University of Minnesota, 2015. http://doi.org/1018128/D010.V6.0. *NOTE the categories "white non-Latinx" and "Asian" are restricted to U.S. citizens.

economically-based discrimination than their Afro-Latinx peers (see chapter 6 for more discussion on discrimination), a larger poverty gap likely exists between Black and white Latinxs than is evident in the data.

In exploring the reasons for disparate intergroup poverty rates, in that African Americans have historically had a higher poverty rate than Latinxs, the evidence that Afro-Latinxs are among the most impoverished demographic groups in the U.S. provides nuance to the literature on poverty. Based on an overlapping set of economic experiences, sociologist Eduardo Bonilla-Silva has argued that a "tri-racial order" is emerging in the U.S. (similar to race models in Latin America), one in which particular Latinx groups occupy different social positions grounded in their racialization. While assimilated white Latinxs occupy upper echelons of this hierarchical arrangement, and light-skinned Latinxs join some Asian groups in an intermediary position, Bonilla-Silva posits that Afro-Latinxs have joined Afro-Caribbean, African American, and other racialized communities in a "collective Black" formation.[51]

To reconnect this to a stratification economics frame, we challenge the position that unequal economic outcomes of Blacks and Latinxs are by-products of self-defeating behaviors that affect their "productivity." High levels of poverty, within these frames, are conventionally thought of as due, in part or in whole, to a "culture of poverty" (i.e., recycled self-defeating behaviors passed down through generations among groups), to a lack of desirable labor market characteristics (such as "soft skills"), and other deficiency-based narratives. This is accompanied by the frame that if the state reduces public spending on social programs (which are viewed to cause dependency and disincentivize working), and that, as noted previously, if subaltern groups simply adjust their behavior, work harder, play by the rules, acquire more education, possess the "right" family values, save more, or emulate so-called "successful" minorities, their economic positions will improve.[52] The reality is that when we use a wealth analysis, not just one that is income or poverty-based, we can more vividly see that "culture" or dysfunctional behaviors are not sufficient predictors of economic immobility for Afro-Latinxs and U.S. Black communities broadly speaking, and that instead such disparities are grounded in historical to present, overt to covert, direct to indirect structural discriminatory forces based on anti-Blackness.[53]

WEALTH DISPARITIES—HOME OWNERSHIP AND AFRO-LATINXS

At present, there is considerable empirical evidence that Blacks, Latinxs, and Native Americans, studied as distinct groups, are less likely to own homes than Asians and non-Latinx whites. There is also evidence that across the Latinx community in the U.S., groups like South Americans, Cubans, and other select groups have higher rates of home ownership as compared to other Latinxs. For example, in the Pew Research Center 2017 report "Hispanic-Origin Profiles" (which uses 2015 ACS data) by Luis Noe-Bustamente, Danielle Alberti, and Adriana Rodriguez-Gitler, patterns of home ownership emerged that reflect histories of racialization and intra-group hierarchies in the U.S.[54] According to the report, Argentinians (58 percent), Cubans (52 percent), Mexicans (48 percent), and Colombians (47 percent) were the most likely Latinxs to be homeowners. Noteworthy is that at the bottom of the rankings were groups with larger shares of Afro-Latinxs, with Puerto Ricans (36 percent) and Dominicans (24 percent) ranking last; the data in this report suggest that those Latinx groups with more self-declared "whites" indicated higher levels of home ownership. However telling, we must note that hidden in these figures are numerous interacting factors amid the entangled roles of race, gender, education, and class: wave of immigration (if applicable); locality; nativity; and other demographic factors.[55]

With these limitations in mind, table 2.2 illustrates two important measures of wealth—percentage of home ownership and mean/median home value, with attention paid to the U.S. Afro-Latinx experience. We must first note that ACS data is limited in capturing measures of wealth. In addition, while home ownership and home value are two of the few asset-specific measures from the ACS, they do not represent the entirety of what is defined as "wealth" (see discussion above). We must also re-emphasize that while home ownership is an important aspiration of Black and Latinx families for its intergenerational transfer value, and the most commonly owned asset among subaltern groups, homeownership rates among these groups pale in comparison to levels for whites.[56] Homeownership is also not the primary factor in the racial wealth gap, nor do we believe that equalizing home ownership levels among groups will fully bridge the racial wealth gap.[57] Nevertheless, our findings are insightful.

The first column in table 2.2 shows that the typical Afro-Latinx household in the U.S. is the least likely among groups to own a home (measured at the mean). At 41 percent, Afro-Latinxs not only fall considerably below the Latinx average but also pale in comparison to the level of home ownership for white Latinxs. This is even truer when Afro-Latinxs are compared to other non-Latinx groups; Afro-Latinxs, along with African Americans, have the lowest homeownership rates compared to whites, Asians, and Native Americans.

The second column in the table, which outlines median and mean home values, is also telling. Compared to other Latinx respondents, Afro-Latinxs'

Table 2.2.   Homeownership Percentage and Home Value by Demographic Groups

Groups	Homeownership (%) Mean	Home Value (thousands) Mean	Median
Non-Latinx			
Whites	79%	321.43	215.00
African Americans/Blacks	51%	217.45	150.00
Asians	69%	564.63	440.00
Native Americans	66%	176.53	100.00
Latinx			
All Latinx	56%	287.96	200.00
White Latinx	59%	282.09	200.00
Afro-Latinx	41%	297.99	230.00

Note: Mean values between one group and white non-Latinx are all significant at the 0.001 level.
Source: Author Analysis of American Community Survey, 2017 via Steven Ruggles, Sarah Flood, Ronald Goeken, Josiah Grover, Erin Meyer, Jose Pacas, and Matthew Sobek. IPUMS USA: Version 9.0 [dataset]. Minneapolis, MN: IPUMS, 2019. https://doi.org/10.18128/D010.V9.0.

home values are higher. In addition, compared to other non-Latinx groups, Afro-Latinxs also hold a better position in terms of home value. So why is there a discrepancy for Afro-Latinxs between their rate of home ownership (which is the lowest, followed by African Americans) and their home values (which places them in a middle position in the estimates)? Does this suggest that when Afro-Latinxs do become homeowners, they are more likely to live in neighborhoods with higher home values, freer from the reality of racial disparities perpetuated by redlining, racialized appraisals, and steering?[58]

A closer look at our figures suggests none of this is, or would be, the case—instead, Afro-Latinxs, by matter of skin shade to shared racialized experience, are more likely to receive the same kind of housing-based penalties as other Blacks in the U.S. We believe this to be the case for the reasons of evasion or "passing on" Blackness we highlighted in chapter 1 of this book, evident in the uneven distribution of those who self-identify as white compared to those who "choose Blackness" in national demographic data.[59] Estimates for white Latinxs should reflect the advantages to "whiteness," while estimates of the size of the Afro-Latinx community in the U.S. are likely lowball figures, which would contribute to an underestimation of discriminatory behavior in market activities. The next section, which shows the need for more localized studies to measure wealth by various asset types across Latinxs by ancestry group and race, is both instructive and demonstrative.

CASE STUDIES IN WEALTH DISPARITIES—
WHERE DO AFRO-LATINXS FIT?

In a recent series of collaborative studies (The Colors of Wealth in the United States) spearheaded by economists Darrick Hamilton and William Darity Jr. and produced out of the Cook Center on Social Equity at Duke University, Kirwan Center for the Study of Race and Ethnicity at Ohio State University, The New School, Insight Center for Community Economic Development, UCLA, the Federal Reserve, and other institutions, researchers sought to measure the various contours of the "racial wealth gap" in select U.S. metropolitan areas. The studies examine a host of demographic variables across a few cities and disaggregates both Asian and Latinx groups by ancestry in Los Angeles and Washington, DC, respectively, for inter- to intra-group comparisons. For Boston and Miami, the studies provide a wealth-based examination for Latinx ancestry groups that have large percentages of Afro-Latinx members, such as Dominicans and Puerto Ricans (see figure 1.1 in chapter 1).[60]

Before we continue, let's revisit the definitions of wealth. In short, wealth can be classified as public assets, such as assets co-owned publicly through a trust or cooperative, or as private assets. The latter, the focus of our analysis, can be calculated in different ways, but arguably the most common measure is to determine an individual or household's net worth, which is the numerical difference between assets and debts/liabilities. Debt can include student and car loans, a mortgage, credit cards, and outstanding medical costs. Assets can include checking and savings accounts, bonds, stocks, retirement funds, and home, vehicle, or business equity. Assets classified as "liquid assets" can be readily converted to cash, can serve as rainy day funds in case of a financial emergency, unexpected job loss, or a larger structural effect, such as an economic recession.[61]

As we previously noted, during the Great Recession non-white communities, especially African Americans, were among groups (including Latinxs) hit the hardest, especially with regard to home equity.[62] This is in the context of wealth being hoarded by a small number of people domestically and worldwide, with this wealth-holding vastly inequitable when race, gender, ethnicity, and other variables contributing to subaltern status are taken into account.[63] In fact, groundbreaking research on assets that compares the kinds of debt that can produce market returns to the kinds that can be debilitating in the long term has shown disparate outcomes along Black-white frames.[64] As we explore below, there are similar patterns among Latinx groups with large shares of Afro-Latinx members.[65]

Wealth is crucial not only for a household's economic well-being, but also for one's health outcomes.[66] But, literature on the wealth position of Afro-

Latinxs in the U.S. is virtually non-existent, in that their "wealth stories" are likely to be hidden in group-based studies that separate Hispanics/Latinos and Blacks/African Americans, ignoring intersecting identities, histories, and discriminatory experiences. At present, one way to consider Afro-Latinx wealth positioning is to produce an analysis that involves a circuitous route which infers Afro-Latinx presence in a larger group with similar subaltern sociohistorical experiences. In our case, this can be done by examining the wealth position of Latinx ancestry groups with large shares of self-identified Afro-Latinxs, such as Dominicans, Puerto Ricans, and Panamanians (see chapter 1), then compare these groups to other demographic groups.

In some cases, sample size limitations force researchers to collapse ancestry-based groups into larger catchall demographic categories, such as placing Central and South Americans into one large category. The recent Colors of Wealth series, which examines groups in five different U.S. cities via the National Asset Scorecard for Communities of Color (NASCC) survey, so as to consider localized effects of the recent housing crisis, is arguably a study we can use for these reasons.

Table 2.3 outlines the comparative position of Black and Latinx net household worth in four U.S. cities: Boston, Miami, Los Angeles, and Washington, DC.[67] In Boston, for instance, which is home to large Dominican and Puerto Rican populations, a tremendous gap was found between non-Latinx white and non-white (e.g., African American and Latinx, including Afro-Caribbean) households when measuring net worth.[68] Non-Latinx white households had a median net worth of $247,500 compared to Dominican and African American households with a net worth close to zero (and Puerto Ricans, the group

Table 2.3. Median Household Net Worth by Select U.S. Localities—Colors of Wealth Reports (Combined), 2013–2016 NASCC Data

	Los Angeles	*Boston*	*Miami*	*Washington, DC*
African Americans	$4,000*	$8.00	$3,700	$3,500***
Mexicans	$3,500**	NA	NA	NA
Puerto Ricans	NA	$3,020	NA	NA
Dominicans	NA	$0	NA	NA
Cubans	NA	NA	$22,000	NA
All Latinx	NA	NA	NA	$13,000***
Whites (Non-Latinx)	$355,000	$247,500	$107,000	$284,000
Other Latinxs	NA	NA	$1,200	NA

Source: NASCC Sample—Colors of Wealth Reports (Boston, Miami, Los Angeles, Washington DC)— Permission (and special thanks!) to create table courtesy of Colors of Wealth Report sponsoring institution Prinicipal Investigators: William Darity Jr. at Duke University (Cook Center for Social Equity) and Darrick Hamilton at Ohio State University (Kirwan Center for Study of Race and Ethnicity). *, **, *** represent statistical significance.

that reports the largest number of Afro-Latinxs in the U.S., doing not much better at just over $3,000 of net worth). In Los Angeles, where there is a considerable Mexican-origin population (some of whose ancestors owned property and other assets prior to U.S. colonial expansion westward), the gaps were astonishing—Blacks and Mexicans possessed $4,000 and $3,500 median net worth, respectively, compared to non-Latinx whites at $355,000 median net worth.[69] Washington, DC, yielded a different localized scenario, where Latinxs (measured as one group) fared comparably better than African Americans in terms of net worth ($13,000 to $3,500, respectively), yet neither could compete with non-Latinx whites ($284,000 of net worth). In each of the cities above, other measures of asset formation—from home ownership to liquid assets—in most instances yielded intersecting findings across Black and select Latinx groups (such as Puerto Ricans and Dominicans), while in other cities a gradient pattern emerged, with some Latinx groups taking a modest yet more favorable position compared to African Americans.[70]

In the Miami study, where the intersections of race and Latinx ancestry were analyzed in more detail, the median net worth of two local groups often compared (and with sometimes acrimonious histories), African Americans (called "U.S. Blacks" in the study) and Cubans, stood at $3,700 and $22,000, respectively. "Other" Latinxs (rest of the sample grouped together) had a median net worth of $1,200, while the comparable figure for non-Latinx whites stood at $107,000.[71] To some extent, the wide range of net worth across groups could be considered surprising given the pervasive "successful minorities" trope often applied to promote a narrative that Blacks and racialized Latinxs should simply work harder.[72] In Miami, this obfuscates the actual lived experience of more recent Cuban arrivals, especially Afro-Cubans. Their "wealth stories" are often supplanted by the relatively more favorable experience of earlier post-revolution Cuban arrivals, largely white Latinxs who received federal assistance specifically designed for asset development, whether through the Cuban Refugee Program, the Small Business Administration, or other state-level programs.[73] Local African Americans, as defined by their ancestral relationship to U.S. slave descendants and Caribbean slave descendants (specifically Bahamians), did not receive the same level of asset-development assistance; as the group upon whose backs the city of Miami was initially built, government and private actors colluded throughout the twentieth century to strip them of their wealth (and prevent further accumulation), especially home ownership.[74]

The results were captured not only in the study's analysis of net worth and other asset measures, but the study also yielded another important finding with implications for Afro-Latinxs. When examining local Latinx groups by ancestry and race, it was clear that an overall preference toward a white identity prevails, despite the presence of longtime Latinx groups with racialized histories, with few local Latinxs asserting a Black identity (see discussion in chapter 1). Also found was that in particular Latinx ancestry groups, including Cubans and Colombians, Afro-Latinxs "out-educated" white Latinxs in those groups, but possessed lower median household incomes and rates of homeownership. This is consistent with our larger findings highlighted in this and other chapters in this text. Taken together with figures for local Afro-Caribbean groups, it's clear that one's race was a greater predictor of local economic experience than one's ancestry. Regardless of one's ancestral origins, on most socioeconomic and asset-centered measures, Blacks of all ancestry groups (Latinx, U.S. slave descendants, and Afro-Caribbeans) shared similar economic profiles, with U.S. Blacks holding the least favorable position.

In summation, this chapter measured indicators of socioeconomic well-being (poverty, income, and wealth) for U.S. Afro-Latinxs, finding that, as a collectivity, this demographic group appears quite similar in profile to the African American community. We must emphasize that, despite narratives which suggest educational attainment is key in all facets of economic well-being, Afro-Latinxs do demonstrate impressive levels of educational attainment yet do not experience expected material returns. Our findings are also consistent with evidence, based on wealth measures in localized contexts, that Latinx communities with a larger distribution of Afro-Latinx members also possess economic realities quite similar to the African American community. In essence, through these economic indicators we study, Blackness, or "anti-Blackness," matters.

In the next chapters, we continue to hold these findings as instructive and correlated. The next chapter examines the labor market status of Afro-Latinxs, providing occupational and employment-based analyses of the U.S. Afro-Latinx community. This chapter is followed by an exposition on the Afro-Latina experience.

NOTES

1. Much of the "wealth gap" research is situated in the Black/white dichotomy, referring largely to African Americans/Blacks as descendants of U.S. slavery experience and whites (non-Latinx). More nuanced studies, including the Colors of Wealth series (described in the latter part of the chapter) include and measure Native American, Asian, and Latinx groups as collectivities and disaggregated by nationality/ancestral origins. For more on the many facets of the racial wealth gap considering race and ethnicity, see Maury Gittleman and Edward N. Wolff, "Racial and Ethnic Differences in Wealth," in Marlene Kim (ed.), *Race and Economic Opportunity in the Twenty-First Century, Chapter 2* (London: Routledge, 2007), 29. Also see for background

William Darity Jr., Darrick Hamilton, Mark Paul, Anne Price, Alan Aja, Antonio Moore, Caterina Chiopris, "What We Get Wrong about Closing the Wealth Gap," DuBois Cook Center on Social Equity, Insight Center for Community Economic Development, 2018, https://socialequity.duke.edu/portfolio-item/what-we-get-wrong -about-closing-the-racial-wealth-gap/; Darrick Hamilton, William A. Darity Jr., Anne Price, V. Sridharan, and Rebecca Tippett, "Umbrellas Don't Make It Rain: Why Studying and Working Hard Isn't Enough for Black Americans," Samuel DuBois Cook Center on Social Equity at Duke University, the New School, and Insight Center for Community Economic Development, 2015, http://www.insightcced.org /uploads/CRWG/Umbrellas-Dont-Make-It-Rain8.pdf; Yunju Nam, Darrick Hamilton, William A. Darity Jr., and Anne E. Price, "Bootstraps Are for Black Kids: Race, Wealth, and the Impact of Intergenerational Transfers on Adult Outcomes," Insight Center for Community Economic Development, September 2015; http://www.insight cced.org/wp-content/uploads/2015/07/Bootstraps-are-for-Black-Kids-Sept.pdf; Thomas Shapiro, Tatjana Meschede, and Sam Osoro, *The Roots of the Widening Racial Wealth Gap: Explaining the Black-White Economic Divide*, Institute for Assets & Social Policy, 2013, https://heller.brandeis.edu/iasp/.

2. In their classic publication *Black Wealth/White Wealth*, Melvin Oliver and Thomas Shapiro (2006, 2003) make the case that income differences across groups obfuscate profound intergroup wealth disparities overall (Blacks were found to hold one-tenth in family wealth as to what whites hold)—and these disparities also varied by different types of wealth, including those that have longer-term positive effects on one's material livelihood. Melvin Oliver and Thomas Shapiro, *Black Wealth/White Wealth: A New Perspective on Racial Inequality* (2nd Ed.) (New York: Routledge, 2006; 2003). Also see Louise Seamster, "Black Debt, White Debt," *Contexts* 18, no. 1 (2019): 30–35, https://doi.org/10.1177/1536504219830674.

3. See for example Josh Hoxie, "Blacks and Latinos will be broke in a few decades," *Fortune*, September 19, 2017, http://fortune.com/2017/09/19/racial-inequality -wealth-gap-america/; Dedrick Asante-Muhamad and Chuck Collins, "Inequality Crisis: Blacks and Latinos on the Road to Zero Wealth," *USA Today*, September 17, 2017. For a larger examination of wealth inequality in the United States and Europe, especially a strong critique of the increasing concentration of wealth's deleterious effects on political economies and current role in economic instability, see Thomas Piketty, *Capital in the 21st Century* (Cambridge: Harvard University Press, 2013).

4. Rakesh Kochhar and Anthony Cilluffo, "How wealth inequality has changed in the U.S. since the Great Recession, by race, ethnicity and income," *Pew Research Center*, 2017, https://www.pewresearch.org/fact-tank/2017/11/01/how-wealth-inequality-has -changed-in-the-u-s-since the-great-recession-by-race-ethnicity-and-income/.

5. Kochhar and Cilluffo, "How wealth inequality."

6. Kochhar and Cilluffo, "How wealth inequality."

7. As we similarly challenge in this chapter with regard to the relationship between education and Afro-Latinx economic mobility, Darrick Hamilton and colleagues underscored the point that simply because wealthier households tend to have more educational attainment, there is not a causal relationship here. When considering a race and wealth empirical lens, that white households still have more wealth absent

that education speaks volumes about anti-Black racism. See Darrick Hamilton et al., 2015, "Umbrellas Don't Make It Rain," The New School, Duke Center for Social Equity, and Insight Center for Economic and Community Development, http://www .insightcced.org/uploads/CRWG/Umbrellas-Dont-Make-It-Rain8.pdf. Highlighted in the subsequent chapter more thoroughly, Janelle Jones and John Schmitt found that after the Great Recession, Blacks with college degrees were more likely to be unemployed. See Janelle Jones and John Schmitt, "A College Degree is No Guarantee," Center for Economic and Policy Research, 2014, http://cepr.net/documents/black -coll-grads-2014-05.pdf.

8. In his original essay, Eduardo Bonilla-Silva challenged the notion of a typical bi-racial alignment of racial stratification and argued a "reshuffling" was occurring based on a tri-racial formation similar to Latin American and Caribbean societies. This includes "whites" (which includes assimilated white Latinxs and other privileged immigrant groups), "honorary whites" (includes most Asian American groups and light-skinned Latinxs), and a "collective Black" formation (comprised of African Americans/Blacks, particular racialized Asians, Native/tribal communities, Afro-Caribbean/African groups, and "dark-skinned Latinos"). See Eduardo Bonilla-Silva, "We are all Americans! The Latin Americanization of racial stratification in the USA," *Race and Society* 5 (2002): 3–16, https://doi.org/10.1080/014198704200026 8530.

9. The Color of Wealth reports, which examined wealth inequality across racial and ethnic groups in five select localities (Los Angeles, Boston, Tulsa, Miami, and Washington, DC) were based off analyses of the National Asset Scorecard for Communities of Color (NASCC). The survey was developed to supplement existing national data sets on household wealth with more robust information on asset accumulation by locality and national origins. For more on the survey's origins, see the first study of the series—Melany De La Cruz-Viesca, Zhenxiang Chen, Paul M. Ong, Darrick Hamilton, and William A. Darity Jr., "The Color of Wealth in Los Angeles," Cook Center for Social Equity, Duke University, The New School, University of California, Los Angeles, Asian American Studies Center, and the Insight Center for Community Economic Development, Federal Reserve Bank of San Francisco, 2015, http://www.aasc.ucla.edu/besol/Color_of_Wealth_Report.pdf. Also see background information available via Cook Center at Duke University: https://socialequity.duke .edu/news/national-asset-scorecard-communities-color-and-city-findings.

10. Stratification Economics (SE) strengthens the economics canon by drawing from sociology, social pscyhology, and other disciplines to help explain the material rewards and penalities associated with group positionality in the U.S. In William Darity Jr.'s key explanatory paper, he identifed a set of central tenets a stratification economists brings with them to analyses and to which we apply in this chapter. They are that intergenerational transmissions (wealth inequality) play a predictive role on material realities, dominant groups are motivated and engage in efforts (discrimination) to retain their material privilege, human capital (e.g., education, skills) does not serve as a sufficient shield of discrimination, and that self-defeating behaviors (e.g., culture of poverty) are not explanatory in observed or empiricized intergroup disparities. William Darity Jr., "Stratification Economics: The Role of Intergroup

Inequality," *Journal of Economics and Finance* 29, no. 2 (Summer 2005): 144–153, https://doi.org/10.1007/bf02761550. For a recent update on SE, see William Darity Jr., Darrick Hamilton, Patrick Mason, Gregory Price, Alberto Davila, Marie T. Mora, and Sue Stockly, "Stratification Economics: A General Theory of Intergroup Inequality," in *Hidden Rules of Race: Barriers to an Inclusive Economy*, Andrea Flynn, Dorian T. Warren, Felicia Wong, and Susan Holmberg (Cambridge University Press, 2017), 35–51. For a consideration of the Latinx community within an SE frame, see Alan A. Aja, Stephan LeFebvre, Nancy López, Darrick Hamilton, and William Darity Jr., "Toward a Latinx/a/o Stratification Economics," for *Review of Black Political Economy*, forthcoming 2022.

11. William Darity Jr., Darrick Hamilton, Mark Paul, Anne Price, Alan Aja, Antonio Moore, Caterina Chiopris, "What we get wrong about Closing the Wealth Gap," DuBois Cook Center on Social Equity, Insight Center for Community Economic Development, 2018, https://socialequity.duke.edu/portfolio-item/what-we-get-wrong-about-closing-the-racial-wealth-gap/; Darrick Hamilton, William A. Darity Jr., Anne Price, V. Sridharan, and Rebecca Tippett, "Umbrellas Don't Make It Rain: Why Studying and Working Hard Isn't Enough for Black Americans," Samuel DuBois Cook Center on Social Equity at Duke University, the New School, and Insight Center for Community Economic Development, 2015, http://www.insightcced.org/uploads/CRWG/Umbrellas-Dont-Make-It-Rain8.pdf. Also see Alan A. Aja, Daniel Bustillo, Darrick Hamilton, and William Darity Jr., "From a Tangle of Pathology to a Race-Fair America," *Dissent* 2014, https://www.dissentmagazine.org/article/from-a-tangle-of-pathology-to-a-race-fair-america.

12. Take for example William Mangino's important study which empirically counters the frame that subaltern groups do not value education. He compares the educational attainment of whites, men, and a measure dileneating the "super-rich" as compared to women, non-white groups and the 99 percent. Found was that the former (elites, whites, men) demonstrate lower rates of four-year college completion. In fact, single white men were shown to complete less college as compared to everyone else. The author argues that privileged groups, due to heightened levels of informal opportunities to advance their "human capital" (see our similar discussion on statistical discrimination in chapter 6), can therefore afford to "opt out" of schooling much earlier than less privileged groups. Mangino's study further underscores that among people of similar socioeconomic backgrounds, Asians, African Americans, and Latinxs not only achieve their college degrees at similar rates (contrary to "model minority" myths usually circulating that emphasize cultural values as determinant), but collectively do so more so than whites. See William Mangino, "The Negative Effects of Privilege on Educational Attainment: Gender, Race, Class, and the Bachelor's Degree," *Social Science Quarterly* 95, no. 3 (2014): 760–84, https://doi.org/10.1111/ssqu.12003. Also see William Mangino, "Why Do Whites and the Rich have Less Need for Education?," *American Journal of Economics and Sociology* 71, no. 3 (2012): 562–602, https://doi.org/10.1111/j.1536-7150.2012.00823.x.

13. Darrick Hamilton and William Darity Jr. (p. 71), "The Political Economy of Education, Financial Literacy, and the Racial Wealth Gap," *Federal Reserve*

Bank of St. Louis Review, First Quarter, 99, no. 1 (2017): 59–76, http://dx.doi.org /10.20955/r.2017.59-76.

14. Thomas M. Shapiro, "Race, Home Ownership and Wealth," *Journal of Law and Policy*, Washington University, 20 (2006).

15. For instance, Alexandra Killewald and Brielle Bryan demonstrated that the residual race gaps in access to and returns to homeownership, measured as the net of race differences in prior wealth and income, do contribute to the racial/ethnic wealth chasm, but that eliminating homeownership as a mechanism of wealth accumulation does not change either the "Black-white" or "Hispanic-white" wealth ratios. Thus homeownership is indeed a mechanism of unequal wealth accumulation, but relative to other asset disparities, it is not particularly more unequal, so simply addressing homeownership disparities alone as public policy would not have an equalizing effect. See Alexandra Killewald and Brielle Bryan, "Does your Home Make you wealthy?," *Russell Sage Foundation Journal of the Social Sciences* 2, no. 6 (2018): 110, doi: 10.7758/rsf.2016.2.6.06. Also see Rebecca Tippett, Avis Jones-DeWeever, Maya Rockeymoore, Darrick Hamilton, and William Darity Jr., "Beyond Broke: Why Closing the Wealth Gap is a Priority for National Economic Security," Center for Global Policy Solutions, 2014, http://globalpolicysolutions.org/report/beyond-broke/.

16. Another facet of this argument argues that if Blacks and Latinxs simply acquire more education, this will thus bridge the racial wealth gap. If this were true, consider that Tatjana Meschede and colleagues found that, for college-educated families, the racial wealth gap *tripled* between white and Black families—to a ratio of fifteen to one—between 1989 and 2013. In other words, Black families' net worth dropped by half over that time period. Meanwhile, for most whites (non-Latinx), it improved even after the Great Recession (see introductory discussion to this chapter). See Tatjana Meschede, Joanna Taylor, Alexis Mann, Thomas Shapiro, "Family Achievement? How a College Degree Accumulates Wealth for Whites and Not for Blacks," *Federal Reserve Bank of St. Louis Review* 99, no. 1 (2017): 121–37, https:// dx.doi.org/10.20955/r.2017.121-137. Also see related discussion and debunking of cultural arguments in sociological literature in Stephen Steinberg, *Race Relations: A Critique* (Stanford University Press, 2008). Also see Patrick Bayer, Fernando Ferreira, and Stephen L. Ross, "What Drives Racial and Ethnic Differences in High Cost Mortgages: The Role of High Risk Lenders," *Review of Financial Studies* 31, no. 1 (2018): 175–205, https://doi.org/10.1093/rfs/hhx035; also see Jacob S. Rugh and Douglas Massey, "Racial Segregation and the American Foreclosure Crisis," *American Sociological Review* 75, no. 5 (2010): 629–51; Maury Gittleman and Edward N. Wolff, "Racial Differences in Patterns of Wealth Accumulation," *Journal of Human Resources* 39, no. 1 (2004): 193–227, https://doi.org/10.2307/3559010.

17. Among many examples in the literature, Patrick Bayer, Fernando Ferreira, and Stephen L. Ross studied select metropolitian areas in the years prior to the mortgage-debt crisis (2004–2007) to find that Black and Latinx home buyers were 105 and 78 percent respectively more likely to hold high-cost mortgages as compared to non-Latinx whites. The authors suggest this is attributable to a combination of sorting by lenders and inequitable treatment of equally qualified lenders.

18. For an excellent example of "predatory inclusion" in asset markets, specifically with regard to educational debt, see Louise Seamster and Raphael Charron-Chénier's analysis of the 2001 to 2013 Survey of Consumer Finances. They found that, compared to other forms of debt, the white-Black educational debt gap increased during the previous decade, and did so directly as a result of exploitative practices by lenders. They also underscore that these racialized educational debt gaps are not a product of differences in educational attainment among groups, as per conventional wisdom. Louise Seamster and Raphael Charron-Chénier, "Predatory Inclusion and Educational Debt: Rethinking the Racial Wealth Gap," *Social Currents* 4, no. 3 (2017): 199–207, January 3, https://doi.org/10.1177/2329496516686620. For a critique of debt as a mechanism of social control, also see Hannah Appel, SA Whitley, and Caitlin Kline, "The Power of Debt: Identity and Collective Action in the Age of Finance," Institute on Inequality and Democracy, 2019, https://challengeinequality.luskin.ucla.edu/2019/04/12/the-power-of-debt/.

19. Joe R. Feagin, *Systemic Racism: A Theory of Oppression* (Routledge Press, 2006).

20. George Lipsitz, *The Possessive Investment in Whiteness* (Temple University Press, 2011), 5.

21. Lipsitz, *The Possessive Investment*; also see Richard Rothstein, *The Color of Law: A Forgotten History of How Our Government Segregated America* (New York: Liveright, 2017); Ira Katznelson, *When Affirmative Action Was White* (New York: W.W. Norton, 2005); Oliver and Shapiro, *Black Wealth/White Wealth*.

22. We need to emphasize here that as whites were the ulitmate beneficiary, the G.I. Bill's outcomes varied by race and ethnic group, underscoring differential patterns of group racialization in the United States. Puerto Rican veterans on the island, especially, overwhelmingly benefited from the bill as the island's government sought to center their success as it attempted to modernize the economy (see for example Operation Bootstrap). Making use of promised provisions regarding education, housing, employment training, and other benefits, the G.I. Bill was crucial in propelling Puerto Rican veteran families into the middle class (see Harry Franqui-Rivera 2018). This experience, we must note, was not the same for Puerto Rican (and Mexican American veteran) families on the "mainland," in that in the absence of an active government protecting their rights to the bill's provisions (as in the case for island-side Puerto Ricans), they were far more likely to experience a middle position with regard to "inclusion" as compared to their African American co-veteran families. See Harry Franqui-Rivera, *Soldiers of the Nation: Military Service and Modern Puerto Rico, 1868–1952* (University of Nebraska Press, 2018). This also speaks to the larger discriminatory issues of a decentralized G.I. Bill administration Ira Katznelson and others have documented, whereas for Puerto Ricans and other veteran Latinxs who were phenotypically Black on the "mainland" their experience was likely to be that of African Americans. However, we must note that at the time of publication, we are not able to locate a race-based analysis of home ownership in Puerto Rico. We suspect, given the historical to present evidence, that Afro-Puerto Ricans were not treated the same way as their white or lighter-skinned peers.

23. On Mexican Americans, see Steven Rosales's important critique of the bill's varying policy-level effects, especially on Mexican American socioeconomic mobility. Steven Rosales, "Fighting the Peace at Home: Mexican American Veterans and the 1944 GI Bill of Rights," *Pacific Historical Review* 80, no. 4 (2011): 597–627, https://doi.org/10.1525/phr.2011.80.4.597.

24. Keeanga-Yamahtta Taylor, "Against Black Homeownership," *Boston Review* (November 19, 2019): 1, http://bostonreview.net/race/keeanga-yamahtta-taylor -against-black-homeownership. Also see Keeanga-Yamahtta Taylor, *Race for Profit: How Banks and the Real Estate Industry Undermined Home Ownership* (University of North Carolina Press, 2019).

25. The role of "savings" is directly implied here, which is often part of the personal responsibility narrative applied to racialized groups—that they need better financial literacy or portfolio management skills. See Darity Jr. et al., "What we get wrong." We must note that there is no evidence that Blacks have lower savings rates as compared to white Americans after controlling for household income. Also see evidence that Blacks have a slightly higher savings rate than whites in Maury Gittleman and Edward N. Wolff, "Racial and Ethnic Differences in Wealth," in Marlene Kim (Ed.), *Race and Economic Opportunity in the Twenty-First Century, Chapter 2* (Routledge, 2007), doi: 10.4324/9780203960783. Ngina Chiteji and Darrick Hamilton contextualize this further, finding that because Blacks have more kin obligations to assist economically struggling family members, it thus reduces their capacity to save. Ngina Chiteji and Darrick Hamilton, "Family Connections and the Black-White Wealth Gap Among the Middle Class," *Review of Black Political Economy* 30, no. 1 (2002): 9–27, https://doi.org/10.1007/BF02808169. For an excellent critique of the assumption that Black banking is among the key institutional avenues to Black wealth accumulation (hence mitigating the racial wealth gap), see Mehrsa Baradaran's *The Color of Money: Black Banks and the Racial Wealth Gap* (Harvard University Press, 2017).

26. This fits in findings per the aforementioned work of Hamilton et al., "Umbrellas"; Jones and Schmitt, "A College Degree"; and Mangino, "Why do Whites."

27. Janelle Jones, John Schmitt, and Valerie Wilson, "50 Years after the Kerner Commission," Economic Policy Institute, February 26, 2018, https://www.epi.org /publication/50-years-after-the-kerner-commission/.

28. Jones, Schmitt, and Wilson, "50 Years after."

29. Keisha L. Bentley-Edwards, Malik Chaka Edwards, Cynthia Neal Spence, William A. Darity Jr., Darrick Hamilton, and Jasson Perez, "How does it feel to be a problem? The Missing Kerner Commission Report," *Russell Sage Foundation Journal of the Social Sciences* 4, no. 6 (September 2018): 20–40, doi: https:// doi.org/10.7758/RSF.2018.4.6.02. For critique and rebuttal on similar "Black deficiency" tropes, see Alan Aja, Daniel Bustillo, William Darity Jr., and Darrick Hamilton, "From a Tangle of Pathology to a Race-Fair America," *Dissent Magazine*, Summer 2014: 38–42, https://www.dissentmagazine.org/article/from-a-tangle-of -pathology-to-a-race-fair-america. Also see Stephen Steinberg's *Turning Back: The Retreat from Racial Justice in American Thought and Policy* (Beacon Press, 1995, 2001).

30. Bentley-Edwards et al., 2018.

31. Jones, Schmitt, and Wilson, "50 Years after." We must denote that while all wages are considered income, not all income sources come directly from wages. Wages are typically measured for individual workers but household income measures take into account income sources from everyone in the household—this can include reported "income" from alimony, disability benefits, capital gains/investments, and other sources.

32. Jones, Schmitt, and Wilson, "50 Years after."

33. See discussion and references in chapter 1, including aforementioned works of Darity Jr. et al., "Bleach in the Rainbow"; also see Margaret Hunter, "The Persistent Problem of Colorism: Skin Tone, Status and Wages," *Sociology Compass*, 1, Issue 1 (July 2007), https://doi.org/10.1111/j.1751-9020.2007.00006.x; on Latinxs specifically (and in comparison), see Patrick Mason, "Annual income, hourly wages, and identity Among Mexican Americans and other Latinos," *Industrial Relations* 43, no. 4 (2004): 817–34, https://ssrn.com/abstract=591471; Patrick Mason, "Race, Culture, and Skill: Interracial Wage Differences Among African Americans, Latinos, and Whites," *Review of Black Political Economy* 25, no. 3 (1997): 5–39, https://doi.org/10.1007/s12114-997-1001-5.

34. John Logan, "How Race Counts for Hispanic Americans," in Miriam Jiménez Róman and Juan Flores (eds.), *The Afro-Latin@ Reader* (Duke University Press, 2010), 471–84.

35. Logan, *How Race Counts*, 472–73. Specifically, the author compared "white Hispanics" (in our book as Latinxs who identify as white), "Hispanic-Hispanics" (those who self-reported as "some other race"), and "Black Hispanics" (e.g., Afro-Latinxs in our book). The findings demonstrated that the lowest median income in 2000 was $35,000 for Black Latinxs as compared to $39,000 and $37,500 for the above groups respectively. Notably, the income figure for Black Latinxs in 2000 was closer to the median for non-Hispanic Blacks ($34,000).

36. For an earlier strong critique of human capital theory as an explanation for racial disparities (in that racial differences in human capital acquisition are viewed as explanatory for wage gaps), see William Darity Jr. who places it, as we do, in largely outright structural discriminatory frames. William A. Darity Jr., "The Human Capital Approach to Black-White Earnings Inequality: Some Unsettled Questions," *Journal of Human Resources* 17, no. 1 (1981): 72–93, https://doi.org/10.2307/145525.

37. For more literature on how higher education plays a role in perpetuating and sustaining the racial wealth gap in a Black/white debt frame, see aforementioned analysis in Louise Seamster (2019) and Charrón-Chenier and Seamster (2018). For more on the role of for-profit colleges in racial debt accumulation and its myriad effects, see Tressie McMillan Cottom, *Lower Ed: The Troubling Rise of For-Profit Colleges in the New Economy* (New York: The New Press, 2017). Also see Brandon A. Jackson and John R. Reynolds, "The Price of Opportunity: Race, Student Loan Debt, and College Achievment," *Sociological Inquiry* 83, Issue 3 (2013), https://doi.org/10.1111 soin.12012; Sara Goldrick-Rab, Robert Kelchen, and Jason Houle, "The Color of Student Debt: Implications of Federal Loan Program Reforms for Black Students and Historically Black Colleges and Universities," Discussion paper, Wisconsin HOPE

Lab, September 2, 2014, https://www.academia.edu/15492963/The_Color_of_Stu
dent_Debt_Implications_of_Federal_Loan_Program_Reforms_for_Black_Students
_and_Historically_Black_Colleges_and_Universities.

38. U.S. Census Bureau American Community Survey data for 2015.

39. Lisette M. Garcia and Alan Bayer show that educational attainment among Latinxs in the U.S. also varies by subgroup, with Latinos of Mexican descent showing lower educational attainment levels when compared to other Latinx subgroups. Lisette M. Garcia and Alan Bayer, "Variations in Latino Groups in US Post-Secondary Educational Attainment," *Research in Higher Education* 46, no. 5 (August 2005): 511–33, doi: 10.1007/s11162-005-3363-5. Note: Latinxs of Mexican descent constitute 63 percent of all Latinxs in the United States. See U.S. Census Bureau American Community Survey data for 2015.

40. Authors' analysis of American Community Survey data for 2011–2015 from IPUMS.

41. As aforementioned, see Logan in Román and Flores, eds., 2010; also see Logan 2003.

42. We find here again that white Latinxs report higher incomes than Black Latinxs. There are several studies that also show the same by ancestry group. See Logan "How Race Counts." Also see chapters 1 and 2 discussion and notes.

43. For a recent longitudinal income-mobility study that compares racial/ethnic groups at *intra-* and *inter-group* levels and stresses the persistently subaltern "income-based" position of Blacks and Latinx communities, see Randall Akee, Maggie R. Jones, and Sonya R. Porter, "Race Matters: Income Shares, Income Inequality and Income Mobility for All U.S. Races," *Demography* 56, Issue 3 (2019): 999–1021, https://link.springer.com/article/10.1007%2Fs13524-019-00773-7. The authors did not separate out Afro-Latinxs, but the study is nevertheless useful for its documentation of variation across and within groups.

44. For the latest census definition, and a brief discussion of the history of these calculated thresholds, see: https://www.census.gov/topics/income-poverty/poverty /guidance/poverty-measures.html.

45. For an succinct background review of the poverty measurement problem and the case for alternative measures, see for example: https://poverty.ucdavis.edu/policy -brief/supplemental-poverty-measure-better-measure-poverty-america.

46. U.S. Census Bureau American Community Survey data for 2015.

47. We use the term (im)migrant since Puerto Ricans are included in our measures, who are default not immigrants but migrants due to their position as U.S. citizens.

48. For the latest Hispanic origin profiles based on self-described ancestry/ethnicity, including poverty rates and other demographic and economic measures, see Antonio Flores, "How the U.S. Hispanic Population is Changing," Pew Research Center, Facttank, September 8, 2017, https://www.pewresearch.org/fact-tank/2017/09/18/how -the-u-s-hispanic-population-is-changing/. For more on Cuban socioeconomic mobility specifically or in larger Latinx comparative "race" context, see Brandon P. Martínez, "Housing Inequality: Racial Disparities in the Homeownership and Home Equity Patterns of Cuban-Americans" (2018), *Open Access Theses*, 712, https://schol arlyrepository.miami.edu/oa_theses/712; Alan Aja, *Miami's Forgotten Cubans:*

Race, Racialization and the Afro-Cuban Experience (Palgrave Macmillan, 2016); Michelle Hay, *I've Been Black in Two Countries, Black Cuban Views on Race in the U.S.* (LFB Scholarly Publishing, 2009).

49. Author analysis of American Community Survey data for 2015 from IPUMS.

50. William Darity Jr., Darrick Hamilton, and Jason Dietrich, "Passing on Blackness: Latinos, race, and earnings in the USA," *Applied Economics Letters* 9, no. 13 (2002): 847–53, doi: 10.1080/13504850210149133.

51. Eduardo Bonilla-Silva, "From bi-racial to tri-racial: Towards a new system of racial stratification in the USA," *Ethnic and Racial Studies* 27, no. 6 (2002): 931–50, doi: 10.1080/0141987042000268530.

52. As example, Hector Cordero-Guzman's working presentation at the *American Sociological Association* in 2018 is applicable here (and in chapter 3 on the labor market status of Afro-Latinxs). In his case study on Puerto Rico, he challenged the economic orthodoxy embedded in PROMESA (current debt-restructuring board), which argues that welfare programs provide a disincentive to work and therefore perpetuate poverty. His data demonstrates otherwise; with the introduction of PAN (food stamp program) in the mid 1970s, workforce participation on the island increased as spending on the program increased. The scholar situates the effects of economic depression post-2006 as primarily responsible for low levels of labor force participation since, not necessarily public programs like PAN. See Hector Cordero-Guzmán, "Characteristics of Participants in Puerto Rico's Nutritional Assistance Program (PAN) and their connections to the Labor Market," Working Paper, American Sociological Association annual conference proceedings, August 8, 2018. Also see Darrick Hamilton and Willam Darity Jr., "The Political Economy of Education, Financial Literacy, and the Racial Wealth Gap," *Federal Reserve Bank of St. Louis Review*, First Quarter, 99, no. 1 (2017): 59–76, http://dx.doi.org/10.20955/r.2017.59-76; Patrick Mason, "Race, Culture, and Skill: Interracial Wage Differences Among African Americans, Latinos, and Whites," *Review of Black Political Economy* 25, no. 3 (1997): 5–39, https://doi.org/10.1007/s12114-997-1001-5.

53. In a formative piece on SE (stratification economics), William Darity Jr. (2005: 145) explained that wealth disparities in the U.S., situated in "structured disadvantage" that persists "over generations," is "much larger than racial gaps in earnings or income." William Darity Jr., "Stratification Economics: The Role of Intergroup Inequality," *Journal of Economics and Finance* 29, no. 2 (Summer 2005): 144–53, https://doi.org/10.1007/bf02761550.

54. See downloadable Pew Research Center—Hispanic Origin profiles, 2017 (Based on *American Community Survey*, 2015, 1 percent PUMS). Measured as "household heads living in owner-occupied homes."

55. For instance, Afro-Latinxs can belong to a particular Latinx ancestry group with higher levels of home ownership as compared to others (like Cubans, for example), which often draws into the limelight the immigrant success trope, which obfuscates race-based differences within groups (hence discriminatory experiences). A helpful theory is the lateral mobility hypothesis, which posits that the socioeconomic status of an immigrant group is related to the relative position of the adult members that constitute the bulk of the original members of that group. William Dar-

ity Jr., "The New (Incorrect) Harvard/Washington Consensus on Racial Inequality," *DuBois Review* 8, no. 2 (Fall 2011): 467–76, doi: 10.1017/S1742058X11000439; William Darity Jr., Jason Dietrich, and David K. Guilkey, "Persistent Advantage or Disadvantage? Evidence in Support of the Intergenerational Drag Hypothesis," *American Journal of Economics and Sociology* 60, no. 2 (2001): 435–70, http://www .jstor.org/stable/3487929. Also see aforementioned works of Martínez 2018; Muñoz et al. 2017; De la Cruz Viezca et al. 2016 on localized studies of home ownership (and other assets) by Latinx ancestry group.

56. Brian McCabe, "Why Buy a Home? Race, Ethnicity, and Homeowner-ship Preferences in the United States," *Sociology of Race and Ethnicity*, 2018, 2332649217753648, doi: 10.1177/2332649217753648. Also see Matthew Painter and Zhenchao Qian, "Wealth Inequality Among Immigrants: Consistent Racial/ Ethnic Inequality in the United States," *Population Research and Policy Review* 35, no. 2 (2016): 147–75, doi: 10.1007/s11113-016-9385-1.

57. As underscored by William Darity Jr., Darrick Hamilton, Mark Paul, Anne Price, Alan Aja, Antonio Moore, Caterina Chiopris, "What we get wrong about Clos-ing the Wealth Gap," DuBois Cook Center on Social Equity, Insight Center for Com-munity Economic Development, 2018, https://socialequity.duke.edu/portfolio-item /what-we-get-wrong-about-closing-the-racial-wealth-gap/.

58. Andre Perry et al.'s (2018) study attempts to answer the question, "what is the cost of racial bias?" in the context of homeownership in predominantly Black neighborhoods in the United States. They compare home values in various localities, finding that owner-occupied homes in predominantly Black neighborhoods were de-valued by a mean of $48,000 per home. For an interactive map by locality and report summary, see Andre M. Perry, Jonathan Rothwell, and David Harshbarger, "The De-valuation of Assets in Black neighborhoods: The case of residential property," Brook-ings Institute, November 27, 2018, https://www.brookings.edu/research/devaluation -of-assets-in-black-neighborhoods/; Junia Howell and Elizabeth Korver-Glenn, "Neighborhoods, Race, and the Twenty-first-century Housing Appraisal Industry," *Sociology of Race and Ethnicity*, 2018, doi: 10.1177/2332649218755178; Matthew Desmond, *Evicted: Poverty and Profit in the American City* (Portland: Broadway Books, 2017). Also see Richard Rothstein, *The Color of Law: A Forgotten History of How Our Government Segregated America*, First edition (New York: Liveright Publishing Corporation, 2017).

59. Darity Jr., Hamilton, and Dietrich, "Passing on Blackness."

60. The Colors of Wealth series is the first time data on assets and debts were collected at the local level, as well as first time disaggregation of this information for "non-white" groups was considered in a detailed way.

61. For succinct definitions and examples of "types" of wealth, see Jhumpa Bhat-tacharya, Anne Price, and Fenaba Addo, *Clipped Wings: Closing the Wealth Gap for Millennial Women* (Asset Funders Network, Texas Women's Foundation, The New York Women's Foundation, 2019), https://insightcced.org/clipped-wings-closing-the -wealth-gap-for-millennial-women/; also see each of the Colors of Wealth reports.

62. Christopher Famighetti and Darrick Hamilton, "The Great Recession, edu-cation, race and home ownership," *Working Economics* blog, Economic Policy

Institute, 2019, https://www.epi.org/blog/the-great-recession-education-race-and
-homeownership/.

63. See Thomas Piketty and Emmanuel Saez, "Inequality in the Long Run," *Science* 344, 6186 (May 2014), doi: 10.1126/science.1251936.

64. For an example of how white and Black families experience disparate outcomes, especially in a health-based frame, see Jennifer Kaufman et al. examined the relationship between dementia on wealth and found an astounding 97 percent loss of wealth for Black Americans, compared to 42 percent among non-Black Americans. They suggest the loss or sale of a home (asset) to pay for a costly disease results in a kind of "wealth exhaustion" for Black Americans not experienced by non-Blacks. Jennifer E. Kaufman, William T. Gallo, and Marianne C. Fahs, "The contribution of dementia to the disparity in family wealth between black and non-black Americans," *Ageing and Society*, August, 2018, https://www.cambridge.org/core/journals/ageing-and-society/article/contribution-of-dementia-to-the-disparity-in-family-wealth-between-black-and-nonblack-americans/A401D90931B25C0CD197CEFCA20CAC87. On Black/white debt, see Louise Seamster, "Black Debt, White Debt," *Contexts* 18, no. 1 (2019): 30–35, doi: 10.1177/1536504219830674. Also see Raphael Charron-Chénier and Louise Seamster, "(Good) Debt is an Asset," *Contexts* 17, no. 1 (2018): 88–90, doi: 10.1177/1536504218767126.

65. Louise Seamster's important piece applying "good debt/bad debt" along the "Black/white" dichotomy is key for understanding Afro-Latinx wealth positioning compared to white/white-passing Latinxs. If we consider the literature on race/ethnicity and medical and student loan debt, this is important especially in the context of an absent universal, or single-payer, healthcare system in the U.S., or a universal, tuition-free higher educational system. Sandy Baum and Patricia Steele found, for instance, Blacks and Latinxs graduate from college with higher levels of student loan debt as compared to whites. See "Who Borrows Most? Bachelor's Degree Recipients with High Levels of Student Debt," Trends in Higher Education Series, 2010, www.collegeboard.com/trends. For more specific locally based analyses that compare Latinx subgroups with African Americans (non-Latinx Blacks), see the Colors of Wealth series, in specific the Boston (Muñoz et al., 2016) report, and Miami report (Aja et al., 2019). Also see Tressie McMillan-Cottom's (2016) *Lower Ed* for this literature in the context of the rise of predatory, for-profit colleges.

66. Darrick Hamilton's working paper emphasizes the crucial role of wealth on health outcomes within a putative "post-racial" frame. Darrick Hamilton, "Post-racial rhetoric, racial health disparities, and health disparity consequences of stigma, stress and racism," *Washington Center for Equitable Growth*, 2017, https://equitablegrowth.org/working-papers/racial-health-disparities/. For Afro-Latinxs specifically, there is markedly little research on health outcomes in the community. In some studies, as expected, the small sample size of self-identified Black Latinxs serves as a hindrance to fully understanding challenges face by the community. See for example Adolfo G. Cuevas, Beverly Araujo Dawson, and David R. Williams, "Race and Skin Color in Latino Health: An Analytical Review," *American Journal of Public Health* 106 (2016): 2131–36, https://doi.org/10.2105/AJPH.2016.303452. Those that were able to measure physical health outcomes evidenced intra-group racial disparities, in that

U.S. Afro-Latinxs experienced more health issues as related to white Latinx counterparts as measured by hypertension (Borrell 2008), among other health outcomes. Luisa N. Borrell and Natalie D. Crawford, "Disparities in Self-Reported Hypertension in Hispanic Subgroups, Non-Hispanic Black and Non-Hispanic White Adults: The National Health Interview Survey," *Annals of epidemiology* 18, no. 10 (2008): 803–12, doi:10.1016/j.annepidem.2008.07.008.

67. The National Asset Scorecard for Communities of Color (NASCC) survey was undertaken in five U.S. cities: Boston, Miami, Los Angeles, Tulsa, and Washington, DC. We exclude Tulsa here because there were not enough Latinx subgroup samples in this city.

68. See Ana Patricio Muñoz, Marlene Kim, Mariko Chang, Darrick Hamilton, William Darity Jr., *The Color of Wealth in Boston: Federal Reserve Bank of Boston*, 2015, https://www.bostonfed.org/publications/one-time-pubs/color-of-wealth.aspx.

69. See Melany De La Cruz-Viesca, Zhenxiang Chen, Paul M. Ong, Darrick Hamilton, and William A. Darity Jr., "The Color of Wealth in Los Angeles," Joint publication of Cook Center for Social Equity, Duke University, The New School, the University of California, Los Angeles, Asian American Studies Center, the Insight Center for Community Development, Federal Reserve Bank of San Francisco, 2015, http://www.aasc.ucla.edu/besol/Color_of_Wealth_Report.pdf. Note: For more on the U.S. colonization of Northern Mexico and the historical processes of racialization in the Mexican American community (in comparison to African Americans and Native communities) see Laura Gómez, *Manifest Destinies: The Making of the Mexican-American Race*, 2008.

70. Muñoz et al., "The Color of Wealth."

71. See Alan A. Aja, Gretchen Beesing, Daniel Bustillo, Danielle Clealand, Mark Paul, Khaing Zaw, Anne E. Price, Darrick Hamilton, and William Darity Jr., "The Color of Wealth in Miami," Kirwan Center on the Study of Race and Ethnicity (Ohio State University), Samuel DuBois Cook Center on Social Equity (Duke University), Insight Center for Community Economic Development (Oakland, California), 2018. We must note that the Miami study in particular measured the socioeconomic position of local Latinxs by race, particularly because it is one locality where Latinxs overwhelmingly identify as "white" despite intra-group phenotypical diversity (especially among Caribbean, Central American, and South American communities). In almost all socioeconomic measures (except educational attainment), self-identified white Latinxs do significantly better than those who identified as Black. Noted is that the so-perceived successful Cuban community did not yield the kind of results as expected in the literature—South American groups did better. And overall, white Latinxs occupied a middle position, as non-Latinx whites were clearly at an advantage.

72. Darity Jr. et al., "What we get wrong"; Hamilton et al., "Umbrellas Don't Make It Rain."

73. For more on divergent patterns of racialization of the Cuban community, see for instance Alan A. Aja, *Miami's Forgotten Cubans: Race, Racialization and the Local Afro-Cuban Experience* (London: Palgrave Macmillan, 2016); Monika Gosin,

The Racial Politics of Division: Interethnic Struggles for Legitimacy in Multicultural Miami (Cornell University Press: 2019). In cross-group comparison, see Ramón Grosfoguel, *Colonial Subjects: Puerto Ricans in a Global Perspective*, First edition ed. (Berkeley: University of California Press, 2003). Also see for background, Felix Masud-Piloto, *From Welcomed Exiles to Illegal Immigrants: Cuban Migration to the U.S.* (Rowman & Littlefield, 1995).

74. Sociologist Marvin Dunn chronologically documents the history of Black Miami with consideration for socioeconomic realities of the group in a post–civil rights era context (as well as their political and economic positionality in relation to post-1960s immigration to the region from the Caribbean and Latin America). Marvin Dunn, *Black Miami in the 20th Century* (Gainesville: University of Florida Press, 2016, 1997); Nathan Connolly dissects this history through a material lens, with emphasis on the role of eminent domain, property relations (land transactions), and racist "urban renewal" projects that led to current intergroup spatial and socio-economic disparities. Nathan Connolly, *A World More Concrete: Real Estate and the Remaking of Jim Crow South Florida* (University of Chicago Press, 2016).

Chapter Three

The Labor Market Status
of Afro-Latinxs

In the State of the Union address in February 2019, former President Donald Trump boasted about the historically low unemployment rates for often-compared subaltern groups. "African American, Hispanic-American and Asian-American unemployment have all reached their lowest levels ever recorded," he stated, seemingly taking credit for the statistics.[1] Just days before the speech, economist Valerie Wilson set the empirical record straight, placing the low unemployment rates in their proper historical context. Noting that the rates for Blacks had been in steady decline since 2011 (citing federal interest rates at or near zero as a likely determinant), Wilson also referenced crucial evidence often obfuscated in the larger economics and race literature: the unemployment rate for Blacks was nearly twice as high as the rate for whites, a pattern that has persisted for decades.[2]

That African Americans have been in a "perpetual state of employment crisis," as economist Darrick Hamilton wrote in *Dissent*, is crucial in understanding the experience of Afro-Latinxs in the labor market.[3] Because of the ways in which anti-Blackness operates in U.S. society, Afro-Latinxs are closely affected. Afro-Latinxs have higher levels of unemployment than Latinxs in general, and this group's degree of attachment to the labor force, as evidenced by their labor force participation rate, is lower than that for Latinxs overall. The average unemployment rate for Afro-Latinxs for the period 2011–2015 was 14.5 percent (see figure 3.1), and this group had a labor force participation rate of 61.4 percent.[4] In comparison, the overall Latinx unemployment rate from 2011 to 2015 in the U.S. was 10.4 percent, and this group's labor force participation rate was 63.7 percent; analogous statistics for African Americans for the same period were 15.2 percent and below 60 percent, respectively.[5] As this data shows, the labor market status of Afro-Latinxs in the U.S. more closely resembles that of African Americans than of Latinxs in general.

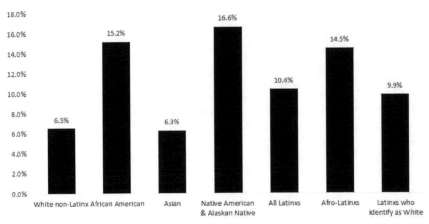

Figure 3.1. Annual Average Unemployment Rate for Select Demographic Groups in the U.S., 16+ Years of Age, 2011–2015. Data Source: Author analysis of 2011–2015 American Community Survey 5-year data obtained from Steven Ruggles, Katie Genadek, Ronald Goeken, Josiah Grover, and Matthew Sobek. Integrated Public Use Microdata Series, Version 6.0 [dataset]. Minneapolis, University of Minnesota, 2015. http://doi.org/1018128/D010.V6.0. *NOTE the categories "white non-Latinxs" and "Asians" are restricted to U.S. citizens.

In this text we've discussed the educational position of Afro-Latinxs in the U.S., noting that this group possesses a higher median educational attainment level as compared to other demographic groups, including white Latinxs (see table 1.2 in chapter 1). We also briefly underscored some of the literature that finds higher levels of educational attainment among groups like African Americans don't always result in lower unemployment rates.[6] In chapter 2, we measured this with regard to income, wealth attainment, and poverty status. Educational attainment, while important, is unfortunately insufficient in helping to equalize wealth and labor market outcomes without addressing other structural inequalities. In examining the unemployment rate for Afro-Latinxs, it's clear that higher relative educational attainment hasn't been a panacea to solve higher relative levels of unemployment for this demographic. It is important to situate these figures within longer labor market trends, in that the Black unemployment rate in the U.S. has historically been twice as high as the white unemployment rate, with the Latinx unemployment rate falling somewhere in between. Among Latinxs, race appears to matter. In other words, as we further argue in this chapter, race, or rather "Blackness," supercedes ethnicity when considering U.S. Afro-Latinx economic positioning.

This chapter outlines unemployment and labor force participation rates for Afro-Latinxs, and examines the occupational distribution of this group. We will begin with a discussion of unemployment and labor force participation estimates. This has salience given the literature on the social-psychological effects of unemployment.[7] We then continue with an examination of occupational distribution, including the Afro-Latinx presence in low-wage sectors of the American economy, and move on to look at the problematic posed by higher relative educational attainment levels of Afro-Latinxs compared to all Latinxs in the U.S., yet higher unemployment rates as well. This chapter is designed, in part, to continue our discussion in chapter 2 that a critical Latinx/ Afro-Latinx "stratification economics" theoretical view is applicable in analyzing the labor market status of Afro-Latinxs. This chapter also provides a larger relative context for the "intersectional" analysis in chapter 4, incarceration analysis in chapter 5, and empirical evidence for our policy recommendations discussed in chapter 6.

OCCUPATIONAL DISTRIBUTION OF AFRO-LATINXS

Economists, particularly labor economists, examine the occupational distribution of groups in part because it provides a sense of the average or median wage distribution across groups; group-based occupational differences therefore provide insight into wage disparities based on race, ethnicity, and gender, among other characteristics. Similar to other non-white groups as well as women (regardless of race or ethnicity), Afro-Latinxs tend to be overrepresented in low-wage occupations such as food preparation and serving, building and grounds cleaning, and personal care and service—see table 3.1. Such overrepresentation is in contradiction to this group's relatively higher educational attainment status, a recurring theme in this chapter. While Afro-Latinas, compared to non-Latinx white men and women, appear significantly overrepresented in healthcare support (including home health aides) and personal care (including hairdressers and childcare workers) occupations, Afro-Latinx men appear to be overrepresented in building and grounds cleaning occupations as well as military service (notably, African American men are also overrepresented in military service).[8]

AFRO-LATINXS AND WAGES

Afro-Latinx median wages tend to be higher than Latinx median wages in general, including that of white Latinxs—see table 3.2. This may be due, in part, to more human capital endowments in the former of increased educational attainment on the part of Afro-Latinxs compared to Latinxs overall,

Table 3.1. Occupational Distribution of White and Afro-Latinx Full-Time Workers 18+ Years Old, U.S., 2015

Major Occupational Category	All	White Non-Latinx Men	White Non-Latinx Women	All Afro-Latinxs (Men & Women Combined)	All Afro-Latinas
Management	13.7%	16.8%	13.1%	8.4%	9.0%
Business Operation Specialists	3.1%	2.7%	4.1%	2.8%	3.7%
Financial Specialists	2.8%	2.5%	3.7%	1.9%	2.5%
Computer & Mathematical	3.6%	4.5%	2.0%	2.8%	2.0%
Architecture & Engineering	2.4%	3.9%	0.8%	1.1%	0.6%
Life, Physical & Social Science	1.1%	1.0%	1.1%	0.4%	0.5%
Community & Social Service	1.9%	1.3%	2.7%	3.2%	4.8%
Legal	1.3%	1.5%	1.6%	1.1%	1.8%
Education, Training, & Library	1.0%	0.9%	1.1%	4.6%	0.7%
Arts, Entertainment, Sports, & Media	1.7%	1.9%	1.9%	1.3%	0.9%
Healthcare Practitioners	6.3%	3.1%	11.2%	4.9%	7.8%
Healthcare Support	1.8%	0.3%	2.9%	4.3%	7.7%
Protective Services	2.4%	3.3%	0.8%	3.4%	1.7%
Food Prep & Serving	2.7%	1.5%	2.6%	4.4%	4.1%
Building/Grounds Cleaning & Maintenance	2.8%	2.5%	1.2%	4.3%	3.3%
Personal Care & Service	2.3%	0.8%	3.4%	3.9%	5.0%
Sales & Related	9.2%	10.5%	8.8%	7.9%	8.6%
Office & Administrative Support	12.9%	5.7%	22.4%	15.9%	22.0%
Farming, Fishing, & Forestry	0.7%	0.8%	0.2%	0.5%	0.4%
Construction & Extraction	4.8%	7.8%	0.3%	4.9%	0.5%
Installation, Maintenance, & Repair	3.7%	6.7%	0.3%	3.4%	0.3%
Production	5.8%	7.5%	2.7%	4.7%	3.0%
Transportation & Material Moving	5.8%	8.0%	1.4%	7.0%	2.0%
Military-Specific	0.5%	0.7%	0.1%	1.5%	0.6%

Data Source: Author analysis of 2015 American Community Survey data obtained from Steven Ruggles, Katie Genadek, Ronald Goeken, Josiah Grover, and Matthew Sobek. Integrated Public Use Microdata Series, Version 6.0 [dataset]. Minneapolis, University of Minnesota, 2015. http://doi.org/10.18128/D010.V6.0.

NOTE: Numbers may not round to 100%

Table 3.2. Median Annual Wages for Full-Time Workers 18+ Years Old, Select Demographic Groups in the U.S., 2015

All	$42,000
All White Non-Latinxs	$45,000
White Non-Latinx Men	$50,000
White Non-Latinx Women	$40,000
African Americans	$35,000
African American Men	$36,000
African American Women	$33,000
Asians	$50,000
Asian Women	$48,000
Native Americans	$31,000
Native American Women	$30,000
All Latinxs	$30,000
All Latinas	$28,000
Latinx Men Who Identify as Black	$32,000
Latinas Who Identify as Black	$33,000
Latinx Men Who Identify as White	$32,000
Latinas Who Identify as White	$29,000
All Latinxs Citizens	$35,000
All Latinas Citizens	$31,200
Latinx Men Who Identify as Black Citizens	$35,000
Latinas Who Identify as Black Citizens	$35,000
Latinx Men Who Identify as White Citizens	$38,000
Latinas Who Identify as White Citizens	$32,000

Data Source: Author analysis of 2015 American Community Survey data obtained from Steven Ruggles, Katie Genadek, Ronald Goeken, Josiah Grover, and Matthew Sobek. Integrated Public Use Microdata Series, Version 6.0 [dataset]. Minneapolis, University of Minnesota, 2015. http://doi.org/10.18128/D010.V6.0.
NOTE: The categories "white non-Latinx" and "Asian" are restricted to U.S. citizens.

as well as differences in occupational distribution between the two groups. However, in the case of Latinxs who are citizens, white Latinx men tend to earn more than their Afro-Latinx counterparts. In addition, Latinxs who are citizens earn higher wages than Latinxs overall.

THE CONTRADICTION OF HIGHER EDUCATIONAL ATTAINMENT AND HIGHER UNEMPLOYMENT AMONG AFRO-LATINXS

Employment-related statistics in the U.S. show a strong inverse relationship between educational attainment and unemployment; within demographic groups, higher levels of educational attainment are generally associated with lower levels of unemployment—see table 3.3. However, in the U.S., both African Americans and Afro-Latinxs have higher rates of educational attainment when compared to Latinxs overall, but higher rates of unemployment as well. What might explain these seeming anomalies? In comparing African Americans and non-Latinx whites, the gap in the unemployment rate between the two groups, with whites holding the more favorable position, has typically been explained by differences in human capital and occupational distribution as well as racial discrimination in the American labor market.[9] However, these explanations cannot be applied in *exactly* the same way to explain why Afro-Latinxs have higher educational attainment rates yet higher unemployment rates than Latinxs overall. Because Afro-Latinxs in the U.S. identify with African Americans (see chapter 1), and a higher proportion of the former group is native-born when compared to Latinxs overall, one avenue to explore is what role, if any, the "immigrant experience" may play in this phenomenon, since a higher proportion of Latinxs overall, compared to Afro-Latinxs, are immigrants.

Table 3.3.   Educational Attainment and Unemployment Status for the U.S. Population, 25–64 Years Old, 2015

Less than High School	9.6%
High School Graduate (incl. Equivalency)	6.8%
Some College	5.2%
Bachelor's Degree or Higher	2.9%

Data Source: U.S. Census Bureau American Community Survey data for 2015.

Luthra and Waldinger conducted empirical analysis to assess the saliency of neo-assimilationist, pluralist, and segmented assimilationist theories in explaining the labor market experiences of Mexican-origin workers; neo-assimilationists posit that subsequent generations of immigrants will enjoy better employment opportunities than the initial generation, while segmented assimilationists theorize almost the opposite—that these subsequent generations will remain trapped in low-wage, low-mobility jobs.[10] Luthra and Waldinger found the strongest evidence for the pluralist hypothesis, which indicates that second-generation workers will experience better labor market outcomes than their parents without having to extensively rely on self-employment, but these outcomes are the result of employment in "niche" sectors, such as the public sector, where members of the group are concentrated.[11] According to the pluralist hypothesis, concentration of second and subsequent immigrant generations in niche sectors is the result of "distinctive ethnic social structures put in place by migration" and they "persist even as immigrants and their descendants move ahead in the labor market."[12] These "ethnic social structures" are networks. However, networks which help facilitate job acquisition certainly exist in the African American community (the latter of which Afro-Latinxs, as noted in chapter 1, strongly identify with), but networks among Latinxs are characterized more heavily by the immigrant experience. As outlined below, networks heavily defined by the immigrant experience can produce ethnically and/or racially homogeneous workplaces.

Theories of social capital indicate that social networks, primarily created for non-economic reasons, can nevertheless help members of the network gain access to job information.[13] Granovetter writes about the importance of networks in job acquisition, noting, "the denser the network, the more unique paths along which information, ideas, and influence can travel between two nodes."[14] Importantly, other researchers have pointed out that networks can serve to maintain racially or ethnically segregated labor markets since job information is shared through presumably homogeneous networks, and thus prospective employers are drawing candidates from racially or ethnically homogeneous pools.[15] Sociologist Stephen Steinberg has stressed this point, arguing that "ethnic queues" and "ethnic niches" can maintain hierarchies that discriminate against Blacks.[16] In his words, "networking hiring is a device that employers use to prevent Blacks from getting their foot in the door. This is racism, plain and simple! Networking hiring is a mechanism of discrimination, and one that employers use precisely because it insulates them from allegations of racism since they are not directly implicated in the recruitment of workers."[17]

It has been estimated that about half of jobs in the U.S. are filled through social contacts.[18] One potential explanation for this is such a process for filling jobs can be beneficial for, primarily, employers at no added human resource cost; Roberto M. Fernandez, Emilio J. Castilla, and Paul Moore conceptualized the "richer pool" theory which indicates that, by tapping its employees for referrals for company vacancies, employers obtain a better and larger pool of candidates for job openings.[19] In addition, employers can reap other benefits from hiring individuals who were referred to the firm by incumbent employees, including referrals of candidates trusted by employees since incumbents presumably place their "reputation on the line," incumbents' willingness to provide other information about candidates not easily assessed during the hiring process, as well as incumbents' willingness to help acclimate referral hires to their new work environment.[20]

Research has shown that recent Latinx immigrants rely extensively, more so than native-born whites and Blacks as well as native-born Latinxs, on informal job referrals.[21] In a critique of prior research that examined ethnic group concentrations in specific industries and occupations where inferences were drawn about the role of informal networks or racial and ethnic differences in the use of networks, James R. Elliott, utilizing data from the Multi-City Survey of Urban Inequality, found evidence that "recent" Latinx immigrants were the group most likely, when compared to native-born whites, Blacks, and Latinxs, to obtain jobs through an "insider referral."[22] Elliott defines "recent" immigrants as those who have been in the U.S. five years or less.[23] According to Elliott, looking at the role of networks in the position of Latinxs in the labor market is important because "social networks tend to be homogenous, which means that there is a high probability that same-race candidates will be referred and hired through incumbent networks."[24] In addition, Elliott's quantitative research showed that native-born Blacks and native-born Latinxs appear to share more in common with regard to the degree of racial and/or ethnic homogeneity in their workplaces than do native-born Latinxs and recent Latinx immigrants.[25]

Alternatively, research shows that African Americans (who, again, Afro-Latinxs identify with) tend to rely on more formal routes to employment.[26] Harry J. Holzer argues that Blacks are more likely to rely on formal routes to employment because the role ascriptive characteristics can play in hiring, given the professionalization of the human resources occupation, is given more scrutiny.[27] If, as per the pluralist hypothesis of Latinx immigrant integration into the U.S. workforce, immigrant Latinx communities create and maintain social networks that can assist in job acquisition, and these networks are more efficiently utilized than networks in the African American community with regard to employment outcomes, this may partly explain the contradiction of higher educational attainment rates among Afro-Latinxs compared to all Latinxs, yet higher unemployment rates among the former group.

AFRO-LATINXS AND EMPLOYER DISCRIMINATION

Another avenue to explore regarding higher unemployment rates among Afro-Latinxs when compared to Latinxs overall, despite higher educational attainment rates among the former when compared to the latter, would be employer discrimination. However, neoclassical economic theory has been unable to explain the persistence of discrimination in the labor market. Indeed, a major assumption in mainstream economic theory is that biased behavior on the part of employers cannot be sustained in the long run because competitive markets will chip away at such behavior. Yet, discrimination in the U.S. labor market still exists according to both empirical as well as audit studies. Neoclassical economic theory posits that discrimination in labor markets occurs in primarily two ways: (1) employers gain some utility from bigoted behavior, and thus exhibit a "preference" for discrimination, or; (2) employers engage in "statistical discrimination" in which they ascribe average group characteristics to individual group members in making employment decisions. However, economists like William Darity Jr., Patrick Mason, and Darrick Hamilton have pointed out that both forms of discrimination would not be sustainable in the long run because enterprising, non-discriminatory employers will exploit the arbitrage opportunities created by biased employers by hiring excluded group members at lower wages. Taking into account this critique, Human Capital Theory (HCT) subsequently posited that if some groups experience higher unemployment rates it is because these groups have lower levels of human capital endowments. But in the case of Afro-Latinxs, this is clearly not applicable given this group's higher relative levels of educational attainment which normally has a strong correlation with low unemployment in the U.S. The question that naturally arises, therefore, is what other factors are happening that nullify the effect higher educational attainment levels should normally have on employment outcomes for Afro-Latinxs?

Research conducted on employer discrimination involving Blacks has shown the key role of employers' perceptions about Black productivity; Blacks are perceived to be less productive because employers assume Black applicants possess poorer educational training or lack strong work ethics along with negative associations employers make about the areas where African Americans typically reside or the presumption of criminal proclivity given higher average incarceration rates among Blacks. This research typically examines employers' preference for white job applicants over similarly qualified Black applicants. However, some research does exist looking at employer preference for Latinxs over Blacks.[28] But, in the context of this research, applying the finding of employer preference for Latinx applicants over Black applicants to the case of higher unemployment rates of Afro-Latinxs compared to Latinxs overall is obviously not straightforward; Afro-Latinxs are both Black and Latinx. One main difference, though, between Afro-Latinxs and Latinxs is that Afro-Latinxs identify as Black, and thus may be subject to race-based employment discrimination in addition to ethnicity-based employer preferences. So while it is problematic to assume that the findings of research on employer preference for Latinxs over Blacks can be used to infer similar patterns of discrimination for Afro-Latinxs compared to Latinxs overall, at a minimum that research can provide insight into the differential labor market statuses of Afro-Latinxs versus all Latinxs in the U.S.

CONCLUSION

Labor force indicators for Afro-Latinxs in the U.S. suggest experiences that bear a greater degree of similarity to Blacks overall than to Latinxs overall; even though Afro-Latinxs have higher educational attainment levels than Latinxs, the former group's unemployment rates are also higher than the latter group's. One factor that may play a role here is networks, which may be stronger among Latinxs than Afro-Latinxs given the latter group's affinity with the Black community, who tend to rely on more formal routes to employment. Another factor which may be of importance in the differential labor force statuses of Afro-Latinxs and all Latinxs is employer discrimination against Blacks as well as research that suggests employer preferences for (presumably non-Black) Latinxs over Blacks. In addition, employment data shows that Afro-Latinxs are overrepresented in low-wage major occupational categories, while underrepresented in higher wage occupations such as architecture/engineering and management, similar to both Latinxs overall as well as African Americans. Taken together, these indicators suggest a less than favorable position for Afro-Latinxs in the U.S. labor market compared to not only non-Latinx whites but also Latinxs overall. This is particularly problematic since Afro-Latinxs have sought to increase their overall human capital endowments through higher relative educational attainment than their non-Black Latinx counterparts.

NOTES

1. Christopher Rugaber, "AP Fact Check: Trump on Unemployment for Blacks, Latinos," *AP News*, February 5, 2019, www.apnews.com/article/e1afa3f19a054540 a7c34ca193bdd9ae.

2. See Valerie Wilson, "Before the State of the Union, a Fact Check on Black Unemployment," *Economic Policy Institute* (blog), February 1, 2019, https://www .epi.org/blog/before-the-state-of-the-union-a-fact-check-on-black-unemployment/. See Darrick Hamilton, "The Federal Job Guarantee: A Step Toward Racial Justice," *Dissent Magazine*, November 9, 2015, www.dissentmagazine.org/online _articles/federal-job-guarantee-racial-justice-darrick-hamilton; Janelle Jones and John Schmitt, "A College Degree Is No Guarantee," Center for Economic and Policy Research, May 2014. Also see Mark Paul, William Darity Jr., and Darrick Hamilton, "The Federal Job Guarantee—A Policy to Achieve Permanent Full Employment," Center on Budget and Policy Priorities, March 8, 2018, https://www.cbpp.org /research/full-employment/the-federal-job-guarantee-a-policy-to-achieve-permanent -full-employment.

3. Hamilton's important and critical essay is written in the context of the Obama administration's attempt to implement neoliberal reforms (like "My Brother's

Keeper") that stress individual to group-level deficiencies as determinant in labor market experiences for Black Americans. He argues that these policies, which perpetuate austerity, ignore "the plight of young black women altogether and [attempt] to incentivize so-called defective black men to be more employable rather than addressing the discriminatory labor market conditions they face." See Hamilton, "The Federal Job Guarantee."

4. Author analysis of American Community Survey data for 2011–2015 from IPUMS.

5. Author analysis of American Community Survey data for 2011–2015 from IPUMS.

6. Among several findings, Jones and Schmitt underscored in 2014 that Black college graduates of ages 22–27 were more than twice as likely to be unemployed as compared to all college graduates of same age range. They also found disturbing unemployment figures pre- and post–Great Recession, in that the unemployment rate for black college graduates tripled from 2007 to 2013. Given their findings, they concluded: "That black college graduates of all ages consistently have higher unemployment rates, higher underemployment, and lower wages than their white counterparts, even when black students complete STEM majors, reinforces concerns that racial discrimination remains an important factor in contemporary labor markets." See Jones and Schmitt, "A College Degree Is No Guarantee," 13.

7. Timothy M. Diette et al., "Race, Unemployment, and Mental Health in the USA: What Can We Infer About the Psychological Cost of the Great Recession Across Racial Groups?," *Journal of Economics, Race, and Policy* 1, no. 2 (September 1, 2018): 75–91, https://doi.org/10.1007/s41996-018-0012-x, for example, use descriptive statistics and regression techniques from a national survey to argue that the Great Recession had greater detrimental effects on the mental health of Black Americans relative to other groups. Given their findings, they further stress the importance of psychological and monetary costs of unemployment, with anti-Black racism centered, as crucial for policymakers. This is especially important as we consider the role of a federal job guarantee for Afro-Latinxs (see chapter 6) as key policy recommendation.

8. Michelle Holder, *African American Men and the Labor Market during the Great Recession* (New York: Palgrave Macmillan US, 2017), 9–12, https://doi.org/10.1057/978-1-137-56311-8.

9. For background literature and critiques, see Holder, *African American Men and the Labor Market during the Great Recession*; Paul, Darity Jr., and Hamilton, "The Federal Job Guarantee—A Policy to Achieve Permanent Full Employment"; William A. Darity Jr. and Patrick L. Mason, "Evidence on Discrimination in Employment: Codes of Color, Codes of Gender," *Journal of Economic Perspectives* 12, no. 2 (June 1998): 63–90, https://doi.org/10.1257/jep.12.2.63.

10. Renee Reichl Luthra and Roger Waldinger, "Into the Mainstream? Labor Market Outcomes of Mexican-Origin Workers," *International Migration Review* 44, no. 4 (2010): 830–68, https://doi.org/10.1111/j.1747-7379.2010.00827.x.

11. Luthra and Waldinger, 834.

12. Luthra and Waldinger, 831.

13. George J. Borjas, "Ethnic Capital and Intergenerational Mobility," *Quarterly Journal of Economics* 107, no. 1 (1992): 123–50, http://www.jstor.org /stable/2118325; Nan Lin, *Social Capital: A Theory of Social Structure and Action*, Structural Analysis in the Social Sciences (Cambridge: Cambridge University Press, 2001), https://doi.org/10.1017/CBO9780511815447.

14. Mark Granovetter, "The Impact of Social Structure on Economic Outcomes," *Journal of Economic Perspectives* 19, no. 1 (March 2005): 34, https://doi.org /10.1257/0895330053147958.

15. Kevin Stainback, "Social Contacts and Race/Ethnic Job Matching," *Social Forces* 87, no. 2 (December 1, 2008): 857–86, https://doi.org/10.1353/sof.0.0123.

16. Stephen Steinberg, "Immigration, African Americans, and Race Discourse," *New Politics* 10, no. 3 (Summer 2005); Stephen Steinberg, *Turning Back: The Retreat from Racial Justice in American Thought and Policy* (Boston, M.A.: Beacon Press, 1995).

17. Steinberg, "Immigration, African Americans, and Race Discourse," 2.

18. Mark Granovetter, *Getting a Job: A Study of Contacts and Careers* (Chicago, I.L.: University of Chicago Press, 1995).

19. Roberto M. Fernandez, Emilio J. Castilla, and Paul Moore, "Social Capital at Work: Networks and Employment at a Phone Center," *American Journal of Sociology* 105, no. 5 (2000): 1288–1356, https://doi.org/10.1086/210432.

20. James R. Elliott, "Referral Hiring and Ethnically Homogeneous Jobs: How Prevalent Is the Connection and for Whom?," *Social Science Research* 30, no. 3 (September 1, 2001): 401–25, https://doi.org/10.1006/ssre.2001.0704; Fernandez, Castilla, and Moore, "Social Capital at Work"; Granovetter, "The Impact of Social Structure on Economic Outcomes."

21. Elliott, "Referral Hiring and Ethnically Homogeneous Jobs."

22. Elliott, "Referral Hiring and Ethnically Homogeneous Jobs."

23. Elliott, 402.

24. Elliott, 404.

25. Elliott, 412–13.

26. Harry J. Holzer, "Informal Job Search and Black Youth Unemployment," *American Economic Review* 77, no. 3 (1987): 446–52; Elliott, "Referral Hiring and Ethnically Homogeneous Jobs."

27. Holzer, "Informal Job Search and Black Youth Unemployment."

28. Kathryn M. Neckerman and Joleen Kirschenman, "Hiring Strategies, Racial Bias, and Inner-City Workers," *Social Problems* 38, no. 4 (1991): 433–47, https:// doi.org/10.2307/800563; Roger Waldinger, "Black/Immigrant Competition Re-Assessed: New Evidence from Los Angeles," *Sociological Perspectives* 40, no. 3 (September 1997): 365–86, https://doi.org/10.2307/1389448; also see Roger Waldinger and MI Lichter, *How the Other Half Works: Immigration and the Social Organization of Labor* (Berkeley: University of California Press, 2003).

Chapter Four

Afro-Latinas in the U.S.

African American female scholar and critical race theorist Kimberlé Crenshaw was part of a vanguard of scholars in the 1990s proposing "intersectionality" or "intersectional theory," which posits that while marginalized groups share disenfranchisement in common, forms of discrimination and marginalization differ depending on race, class, ethnicity, gender, sexual orientation, ancestry, and so on.[1] Afro-Latinas in the U.S. are a group where multiple forms of marginalization crosshatch, such as gender, race, ethnicity, immigration status, language barriers, and caregiving status. When intersectionality theory was conceptualized, part of the impetus was the recognition that a "one size fits all" approach could not be applied to the kinds of discrimination *all* women face because while both white and Black women can encounter gender bias, Black women can also encounter racial bias. However, if African American women are a "double-minority," then, arguably, Afro-Latinas are a "triple minority."

In his explanation of "Afro Latinidades," Agustín Laó-Montes wrote about the "subalternized histories of African diasporic subjects within and beyond the borders of its definition."[2] In the same article, Laó-Montes pointed out the "missing narratives" of Afro-Latinxs in notions of what "African-ness" and Blackness mean. The debates about the marginalization of Latinidad in perceptions of Blackness, along with the marginalization of African-ness in ideas about Latinx identity, crosshatched with the subordinate status of women in most economies, sheds light on why Afro-Latinas are virtually invisible in economic literature. Even when these identities are brought together, popular assumptions about who Afro-Latinas are, and what their productive capacities are, have been highly stereotyped. Maritza Quiñones Rivera noted that in Puerto Rico, a territory of the U.S. where hundreds of thousands migrated to the U.S. mainland (primarily New York City) after

World War II, Afro-Latinas (or "Negras") are stereotyped as women engaged in illegal or low-wage work (cleaning, selling food at roadsides, prostitution) who live in impoverished, predominantly Black areas such as Loíza.[3] This imagery of Afro-Latinas in Puerto Rico is disturbingly similar to the iconic "mammy" figure in early twentieth-century American culture—a Black woman perceived as having low productive capacities in the U.S. economy, relegated to low-wage care work and/or housekeeping jobs; the mammy figure arose within slave society in the American South. It's noteworthy to point out, however, that the iconic, caricatured figures of "Mama Inés" in Puerto Rico and mammy in mainland U.S. also share something else in common— they are, indeed, *working women.*

Marta I. Cruz-Janzen gives a poignant first-person account of her experiences being Afro-Latina in Puerto Rico and the U.S.:

> Latinegras are women who cannot escape the many layers of racism, sexism, and inhumanity that have marked their existence. Painters, poets, singers and writers have exalted their beauty, loyalty, and strength, but centuries of open assaults and rapes have turned them into concubines, prostitutes, and undesirable mothers, daughters, sisters and wives. . . . I am a Latinegra, born to a world that denies my humanity as a Black person, a woman, and a Latina; born to a world where other Latinos reject me and deny my existence even though I share their heritage.[4]

These perceptions of Afro-Latinas also bear a striking resemblance to another doomed female figure in American twentieth-century literature and film— the "tragic mulatto," a beautiful, often hypersexualized, light-complexioned mixed-race Black women who is unable to successfully navigate either white or Black societies in an era of discrimination and segregation, with unfortunate consequences. In early and mid-twentieth-century American films like *Pinky, Imitation of Life,* and Oscar Micheaux's *God's Stepchildren* the mulatto ("mulatta" would be the more accurate term, but mulatto was the widely used term) is presented as a woman who is sexually desirable yet deeply flawed because of her desire to deny her Blackness and gain acceptance into racist white American society where she will not experience racial discrimination, though, ironically, she will be subject to gender oppression.

An Afro-Latina counterpart to the American "tragic mulatto" figure is that of the fictional character Cecilia Valdés in Cirilo Villaverde's nineteenth-century work *Cecilia Valdés o La Loma del Angel.* The central character is someone who wants to enter white society, with unfortunate consequences. These cultural representations of Afro-Latina and mixed-race women reflect the still lingering perceptions of the aspirations of Black Latinas—that in order to succeed in society associations with Blackness/African-ness must ultimately be shed. Because only a few self-affirming Afro-Latinas have achieved recognition and some measure of success in popular American culture, including women like the late great singer Celia Cruz, actor Rosie Perez, singer Amara La Negra, and rapper Cardi B (who has vigorously defended the validity of her Blackness as well as Latinidad), there is not a weighty-enough counter-narrative to combat degrading notions about Afro-Latinas. In addition, as Dr. Marta Moreno Vega, founder in 1976 of the Caribbean Cultural Center African Diaspora Institute, pointed out in 2006, the major problem that feeds the racism and sexism Afro-Latinas face is *poverty*, an enemy of individual and collective agency. Dr. Moreno Vega noted:

> Poverty. Absolutely. Look at the South Bronx, Bed-Stuy, Brazil's favelas, Colombia's slums. . . . Most of what you'll find are people of African descent.[5]

THE INVISIBLE AFRO-LATINA

In U.S. popular media, movies, and television shows it is rare to find Afro-Latinas represented as such. Black women are presented as either African American or African, and Latinas are typically depicted as non-racialized, as the "spicy mama" (a contemporary example of this is actor Sofía Vergara's character in the American television series *Modern Family*), or as possessing European phenotypical attributes. Yvette Modestin, a Panamanian Afro-Latina activist, pointedly noted her disappointment with the extreme lack of Black women in both Spanish-language programming on the channels Telemundo and Univision as well as in the magazine *Latina*.[6] If you are a young Afro-Latina growing up in the U.S. you have to look for role models that look like you in your family, your community, or in books, including graphic novels such as *La Borinqueña*, because you will have to look hard to find them in popular American culture *presented as Afro-Latinas*, especially if you are a gay, queer, or transgender Afro-Latina; the rapper Young M.A is, to our knowledge, the only openly gay Afro-Latina who has gained some measure of success in American hip-hop culture, and the television series *Pose* is the only one in history on a major station in the U.S. to have featured and elevated transgender Afro-Latina actors. Ironically, however, if one were to go by the sheer number of (sometimes derogatory) terms used to refer to Black or dark-complected Latinas—negra, prieta, trigueña, chola, mulatta, morena, etc.—it's clear that these women are visible, but in a diminished or "color-stratified" manner. Angela Jorge pointed out that many of these terms relate specifically to skin-tone gradations, with the degree of degradation of a term correlated with the degree of skin-tone darkness the term may suggest.[7] Where the Afro-Latina fits in American culture is, thus, a complicated question. The writer Spring Redd detailed her experience growing up as a Black Puerto Rican in Massachusetts; because there weren't many Puerto Ricans where her family lived, they chose to assimilate into the Black community.[8] (Redd's family choice underscores a theme of our book delineated in chapter 1 —"choosing Blackness.")

Some economics literature has been devoted to the status of African American women as well as Latinas.[9] However, published economic research on Afro-Latinas in the U.S. is significantly lacking. With this dearth in the economics literature as background, the next section considers Afro-Latinas with regard to educational attainment, unemployment, and occupational distribution. A reminder to the reader that, in previous chapters, we documented the relationship between education and economic outcomes for the Afro-Latinx community. We found that, similar to the African American community, returns to educational attainment are lower for Afro-Latinxs than for white non-Latinxs. How does this unequal reality look when gender is centered?

EDUCATIONAL ATTAINMENT AND
UNEMPLOYMENT FOR AFRO-LATINAS

Unemployment rates for Afro-Latinas tend to be higher than for other Latinas, which follows a similar pattern of higher unemployment rates for African American women when compared to Latinas in general—see table 4.1. Indeed, Afro-Latinas appear to have the highest unemployment rate of all major female demographic groups in the U.S., with the possible exception of Native American women.

High unemployment rates for Afro-Latinas are in stark contradiction to their higher educational attainment compared to other groups, as can be seen in table 4.2. Afro-Latinas born in the U.S., or who obtain U.S. citizenship, have the same median educational attainment as that of white non-Hispanic men or women—one or more years of college (no degree)—yet a higher unemployment rate than the latter two groups. In addition, Afro-Latina citizens' median educational attainment level exceeds that of all Latinas born in the U.S. or who possess citizenship, as well as that of African American and Native American women. Table 3.3 in chapter 3 illustrates a clear inverse relationship between education and unemployment; the higher the educational attainment, the lower the unemployment rate. However, this pattern does not hold for Afro-Latinas. This is problematic, since Afro-Latinas also appear to have the highest labor force participation rate of all major female demographic groups.

Table 4.1. Average Annual Female Unemployment Rate by Select Demographic Group, 16 Years of Age & Over, 2011–2015

White Non-Latinx	6.1%
African American	13.8%
Asian	5.9%
Native American	14.2%
All Latinas	11.2%
Latinas Who Identify as Black	14.4%
Latinas Who Identify as White	10.6%
All Latina Citizens	10.6%
Latina Citizens Who Identify as Black	14.1%
Latina Citizens Who Identify as White	9.8%

Data Source: Author analysis of 2011–2015 American Community Survey 5-Year data obtained from Steven Ruggles, Katie Genadek, Ronald Goeken, Josiah Grover, and Matthew Sobek. Integrated Public Use Microdata Series, Version 6.0 [dataset]. Minneapolis, University of Minnesota, 2015. http://doi.org/10.18128/D010.V6.0.
NOTE: The categories "white non-Latinx" and "Asian" are restricted to U.S. citizens.

Table 4.2. Median Educational Attainment for Select Female Demographic Groups in the U.S., 25 Years of Age & Over, 2011–2015

White Non-Latinx	1 or More Years of College, No Degree
African American	Some College, but Less than 1 Year
Asian	Associate's Degree
Native American	H.S. Graduate or Equivalent
All Latinas	H.S. Graduate or Equivalent
Latinas Who Identify as Black	Some College, but Less than 1 Year
Latinas Who Identify as White	H.S. Graduate or Equivalent
All Latina Citizens	Some College, but Less than 1 Year
Latina Citizens Who Identify as Black	1 or More Years of College, No Degree
Latina Citizens Who Identify as White	Some College, but Less than 1 Year

Data Source: Author analysis of 2011–2015 American Community Survey 5-Year data obtained from Steven Ruggles, Katie Genadek, Ronald Goeken, Josiah Grover, and Matthew Sobek. Integrated Public Use Microdata Series, Version 6.0 [dataset]. Minneapolis, University of Minnesota, 2015. http://doi.org/10.18128/D010.V6.0.
NOTE: The categories "white non-Latinx" and "Asian" are restricted to U.S. citizens.

OCCUPATIONAL DISTRIBUTION AND WAGES OF AFRO-LATINAS

Women overall, including Afro-Latinas, tend to be overrepresented, or "crowded," into low-wage occupations when compared to men, especially non-Latinx white men. According to some economists, occupational crowding is an important contributing factor to both the "racial wage gap" and the "gender wage gap" in that any comparison of earnings between Blacks and whites, or men and women, will be impacted if some demographic groups are overrepresented in low-paying jobs.[10] Such is the case when examining the occupational distribution of Afro-Latinas.

Why are women crowded into low-wage occupations in the first place? Feminist economics has addressed the reasons behind the crowding of women into low-wage occupations. One of the most prominent thinkers on this topic, Heidi Hartmann, wrote in 1976 that patriarchal systems in public (societal) and private (household) domains were the predominant forms of organizing political and economic activity prior to the rise of industrialization in the U.S., and these forms influenced the occupational distribution of women upon mass entry into paid work.[11] In addition, she noted that it wasn't simply prevailing societal norms that dictated the kinds of work women should do—there were also economic motives on the part of men to prevent women from becoming competing sources of labor for well-paying jobs. To accomplish this, male employers could refuse to hire women, and white male-dominated unions were free to establish rules that discouraged or prevented women from joining. Hartmann's 1976 analysis of women's position in the U.S. labor market fell squarely within the Marxist-Feminist paradigm. So did Marilyn Power's, whose 1983 analysis of the movement of (married) women into the U.S. workforce posited that the capitalist system of production eroded the amount of time women were laboring in the household, pushing women to join the ranks of the "latent reserve army of labor" who would enter the workforce in larger numbers in the 1970s initially as low-wage clerical workers. Cecilia Conrad, restricting her analysis to Black women, also noted that, prior to the passage of the 1964 Civil Rights Act in the U.S., including Title VII of the act, which prohibited race- and gender-based discrimination in employment, the occupation employing the highest share of Black women in the U.S. (38 percent in 1960) was private households (i.e., domestic servants).[12] Conrad pointed out that by 1980, the occupation employing the highest share of Black women had changed from the private household occupation to the clerical occupation.

Table 4.3 shows the occupational distribution of Afro-Latinas in 2015 compared to other demographic groups in the U.S., including Latinas who identify as white. Some of the distributional similarities between Afro-Latinas and other female demographic groups, including white and African American women, include "pink-collar job" crowding: occupations in which both African American and white women are crowded, as evidenced by these groups' higher share in an occupation compared to the share of the overall workforce in the same occupation, are the same occupations in which Afro-Latinas are crowded. These occupations include community and social services, healthcare practitioners (including nurses), and office and administrative support. Similarly, occupations dominated by white non-Hispanic men are the same occupations in which women generally, including Afro-Latinas, are underrepresented; these occupations include management, architecture and engineering, construction and extraction, and installation and repair.

Table 4.3. Occupational Distribution of Select Groups of Full-Time Workers, 18+ Years Old, U.S., 2015

	White Non-Latinx Men	White Non-Latinx Women	African American Women	All Afro-Latinas	All White Latinas
Management	16.8%	13.1%	9.1%	9.0%	9.2%
Business Operation Specialists	2.7%	4.1%	3.6%	3.7%	2.7%
Financial Specialists	2.5%	3.7%	2.9%	2.5%	2.5%
Computer & Mathematical	4.5%	2.0%	1.7%	2.0%	1.2%
Architecture & Engineering	3.9%	0.8%	0.4%	0.6%	0.6%
Life, Physical, & Social Science	1.0%	1.1%	0.5%	0.5%	0.7%
Community & Social Service	1.3%	2.7%	4.3%	4.8%	2.6%
Legal	1.5%	1.6%	0.9%	1.8%	1.2%
Education, Training, & Library	0.9%	1.1%	0.6%	0.7%	0.6%
Arts, Entertainment, Sports, & Media	1.9%	1.9%	0.7%	0.9%	1.3%
Healthcare Practitioners	3.1%	11.2%	9.8%	7.8%	6.2%
Healthcare Support	0.3%	2.9%	7.3%	7.7%	4.2%
Protective Services	3.3%	0.8%	2.5%	1.7%	1.2%
Food Prep & Serving	1.5%	2.6%	3.4%	4.1%	5.5%
Building/Grounds Cleaning & Maintenance	2.5%	1.2%	3.1%	3.3%	6.2%
Personal Care & Service	0.8%	3.4%	4.8%	5.0%	4.5%
Sales & Related	10.5%	8.8%	6.9%	8.6%	9.2%
Office & Administrative Support	5.7%	22.4%	22.0%	22.0%	22.4%
Farming, Fishing, & Forestry	0.8%	0.2%	0.1%	0.4%	1.0%
Construction & Extraction	7.8%	0.3%	0.3%	0.5%	0.5%
Installation, Maintenance, & Repair	6.7%	0.3%	0.4%	0.3%	0.3%
Production	7.5%	2.7%	4.0%	3.0%	5.3%
Transportation & Material Moving	8.0%	1.4%	2.8%	2.0%	2.8%
Military-Specific	0.7%	0.1%	0.3%	0.6%	0.2%

Data Source: Author analysis of 2015 American Community Survey data obtained from Steven Ruggles, Katie Genadek, Ronald Goeken, Josiah Grover, and Matthew Sobek. Integrated Public Use Microdata Series, Version 6.0 [dataset]. Minneapolis, University of Minnesota, 2015. http://doi.org/10.18128/D010.V6.0.

NOTE: Numbers may not round to 100%.

Narrowing the analysis to differences among female demographic groups, there appear to be several higher-paying, higher-status occupations in which non-Latinx white women are better represented than African American women and Latinas, including Afro-Latinas and Latinas who identify as white; these occupations include management, life and social science, and education and library. Occupations in which African American women and Latinas, whether Black- or white-identified, were overrepresented to a greater degree than non-Latinx white women include food preparation and serving, healthcare support (including home health aides), building and grounds cleaning (including housekeepers), and personal care (including hairdressers and childcare workers).

Where wages are concerned, even though Afro-Latinas are overrepresented in low-wage occupations, they tend to earn more than white Latinas—see table 3.2 in chapter 3. This may be due to more human capital endowments in the form of increased educational attainment on the part of Afro-Latinas compared to white Latinas—see table 4.2. The difference in median wages between Afro-Latinas and white Latinas could also be attributable to the differences in occupational distribution—see table 4.3. Afro-Latinas are *better* represented (though still not *proportionally* represented) than white Latinas in higher-wage occupations such as business operations specialists as well as computer and mathematical. In addition, white Latinas are overrepresented to a greater degree than Afro-Latinas in low-wage occupations such as food preparation and serving as well as building and grounds cleaning.

Special Topic: School Desegregation in the U.S. and the Critical yet Hidden Role of the Afro-Latina

In 1947, one of the most important federal court cases regarding school desegregation was won, setting the legal context for larger-scale school desegregation (e.g., *Brown v. Board of Education* 1954). In *Mendez v. Westminster*, a California Latinx family argued that because their children were deemed "white" by the state, as Mexican Americans were declared by the federal government in 1940, they should not be sent to segregated "all-Mexican" schools. The judge in the case, however, didn't buy the racial classification argument, ruling instead that segregated schools were violating the Equal Protection Clause (14th Amendment) by not offering equitable resources, and therefore they should be available to all children "regardless of lineage."

For the most part, the conventional narrative surrounding *Mendez v. Westminster* has held that Latinxs, primarily Mexicans, helped lead the way for school desegregation for African Americans, especially when *Brown v. Board* was won seven years later.[13] In fact, a young Thurgood Marshall, on behalf of the NAACP, argued on appeal and won the *Mendez* case, viewed as a litmus test and strategic argument for the eventually monumental *Brown*. But there's more to the story, one that, when applying an intersectional analysis, makes more visible the role of gender, race, class, and "coloniality" within the context of Afro-Latinidad. The plaintiff, Felicita Mendez, was indeed of Mexican ancestry, but also Afro-Puerto Rican. Known as "prieta" (dark-skinned) in Puerto Rico, Felicita's family migrated from Puerto Rico to the southwest U.S., having been recruited as low-wage workers; the family underwent different processes of racialization, one that ultimately deemed her as both Mexican and Black. Jennifer McCormick and Cesar Ayala's illuminating piece in *Centro* journal argues that the Black-white binary doesn't exactly explain the case's racialized undercurrents; instead, a "complex system of gradated exclusion" better describes what occurred, one of "partial exclusion and partial enfranchisement."[14] Put differently, it wasn't just Mexican ancestry that played a role in Felicita's experience of exclusion (though this was arguably a large factor), it was also the role of color, of Blackness, given that her own lighter-skinned family members weren't treated the same way.[15] McCormick and Ayala go on to write:

> Felicita herself experienced several forms of "bordering" in her own lifetime: as a colonial subject on the island of Puerto Rico, as a disenfranchised "black" in Arizona, and as a "Mexican" with partial rights, where her first husband was deported. Her own conclusion was that the struggle had to be for "all our children, bronceados, negros y blancos." Her memory can thus be honored in many ways under different rubrics: as a Puerto Rican, as a Chicana, as a woman of color.[16]

The experience and treatment of Felicita Mendez in the larger educational sphere pose a set of largely unexamined questions in the vast economic literature, especially when considering the intersections of gender, race, ethnicity, immigration, colonial status, and other interacting, if not compounding, variables.

CONCLUSION

Afro-Latinas in the U.S. are situated within a complex and contradictory intersectional web consisting of multiple forms of American bigotries, disenfranchisement, and misperceptions. On the one hand, the Afro-Latina is exoticized, and, on the other, made to believe her phenotypical attributes are deviations from accepted and encouraged standards of beauty. Afro-Latinas excel educationally compared to most other major female demographic groups, including Latinas overall, yet this excellence is not reflected in a higher status of the Afro-Latina in the American workforce. Self-identified Afro-Latinas may "choose Blackness" in addition to "Latin-ness," even though: (a) they could choose only the latter, and (b) "Blackness" in America is associated with poor economic outcomes overall. It is unfortunate and a missed opportunity that the American culture at large has neither recognized nor embraced the unique attributes Afro-Latinas embody that represent the best our *collective* American culture has to offer—their ancestries, their race, their language, their cultures, their histories, their gender. The good news is that we, Afro-Latinas, will continue to recognize and embrace that in each other—our mothers, daughters, sisters, *y amigas*. Hopefully soon, America will catch on to the true beauty, in every sense, that it has overlooked in us.

NOTES

1. Kimberlé Crenshaw, "Mapping the Margins: Intersectionality, Identity Politics, and Violence against Women of Color," *Stanford Law Review* 43, no. 6 (1991): 1241–99, https://doi.org/10.2307/1229039.

2. Agustín Laó-Montes, "Afro-Latinidades and the Diasporic Imaginary," *Iberoamericana* 5, no. 17 (2005): 118, http://dx.doi.org/10.18441/ibam.5.2005.17.117–130.

3. Maritza Quiñones Rivera, "From Trigueñita to Afro-Puerto Rican: Intersections of the Racialized, Gendered, and Sexualized Body in Puerto Rico and the U.S. Mainland," *Meridians* 7, no. 1 (2006): 162–82, https://doi.org/10.2979/MER.2006.7.1.162.

4. Marta I. Cruz-Janzen, "Latinegras: Desirable Women—Undesirable Mothers, Daughters, Sisters, and Wives," in *The Afro-Latin@ Reader: History and Culture in the United States*, ed. Miriam Jiménez Román and Juan Flores (Durham, NC: Duke University Press, 2010), 282.

5. Joe Cunningham, "Center of Attention: Afro Latino Institution Celebrates 30 Years in the Big Apple," *New York Post*, March 22, 2006, https://nypost.com/2006/03/22/center-of-attention-afro-latino-institution-celebrates-30-years-in-the-big-apple/.

6. Yvette Modestin, "An Afro-Latina's Quest for Inclusion," in *The Afro-Latin@ Reader: History and Culture in the United States*, ed. Miriam Jiménez Román and Juan Flores (Durham, NC: Duke University Press, 2010), 420.

7. Angela Jorge, "The Black Puerto Rican Woman in Contemporary American Society," in *The Afro-Latin@ Reader: History and Culture in the United States*, ed. Miriam Jiménez Román and Juan Flores (Durham: Duke University Press, 2010), 269.

8. Spring Redd, "Something Latino Was Up with Us," in *Home Girls: A Black Feminist Anthology*, ed. Barbara Smith (New York: Kitchen Table: Women of Color Press, 1983), 52–56.

9. Cecilia A. Conrad, "Changes in the Labor Market Status of Black Women, 1960–2000," in *African Americans in the U.S. Economy*, ed. Cecilia Conrad et al. (Lanham, MD: Rowman & Littlefield Publishers, 2005), 157–62; Redd, "Something

Latino Was Up with Us"; Carmen Teresa Whalen, "Sweatshops Here and There: The Garment Industry, Latinas, and Labor Migrations," *International Labor and Working-Class History*, no. 61 (2002): 45–68, https://doi.org/10.1017/S0147547902000054.

10. See for example Patrick L. Mason, "Male Interracial Wage Differentials: Competing Explanations," *Cambridge Journal of Economics* 23, no. 3 (1999): 261–299, https://doi.org/10.1093/cje/23.3.261.

11. Heidi Hartmann, "Capitalism, Patriarchy, and Job Segregation by Sex," *Signs* 1, no. 3 (1976): 137–69, https://doi.org/10.1086/493283.

12. Conrad, "Changes in the Labor Market Status of Black Women, 1960–2000."

13. See for example Lesli A. Maxwell, "Sylvia Mendez and California's School Desegregation Story," *Education Week*, 2014, http://blogs.edweek.org/edweek/learning-the-language/2014/05/sylvia_mendez_and_californias_.html?cmp=SOC-SHR-FB; Antonio Tijerino, "As We Celebrate Brown vs. BOE, Let's Remember Mendez vs. Westminster," May 16, 2014, https://www.huffpost.com/entry/as-we-celebrate-brown-vs-_b_5340165. In both pieces, Mendez's Puerto Rican heritage, or Afro-Latinx roots, are not mentioned.

14. Jennifer McCormick and César J. Ayala, "Felícita 'La Prieta' Méndez (1916–1998) and the End of Latino School Segregation in California," *CENTRO Journal* 19, no. 2 (2007): 13–35.

15. See McCormick and Ayala.

16. McCormick and Ayala, 2007: 30.

Chapter Five

Afro-Latinxs and Incarceration

In the last five decades, national criminal justice policies have had a devastating impact on African Americans, and thus the bulk of research on "mass incarceration" (a term coined by sociologist David Garland) has focused on the Black community. But in many of the country's urban centers, disproportionately high incarceration rates impact Latinxs as well. Incarceration is associated with poorer employment and earnings outcomes post-imprisonment. Disparities in incarceration rates based on race and ethnicity, therefore, can exacerbate racial and ethnic disparities in labor market experiences. In addition, such disparities can affect political representation since imprisonment can result in the denial of voting rights in some states.[1]

Unfortunately, federal statistics on incarceration don't categorize Afro-Latinxs separately. Thus, it's difficult to determine with accuracy how prevalent incarceration is among this group. What we do know is that the majority of the incarcerated in the U.S. are men in state prisons. We also know, as will be outlined below, that Black and Latinx male incarceration rates are disproportionately higher than the white male incarceration rate. It would not be unreasonable, therefore, to suspect that the incarceration rate of Afro-Latinx men is likely disproportionately high as well. Because much of the literature on high imprisonment rates in the U.S. has focused on the African American community, below we briefly outline how mass incarceration has impacted Latinxs. We then examine risk factors for incarceration among the Latinx subgroup who, according to our data, accounts for the largest number of Afro-Latinxs in the U.S.—Puerto Ricans. Note that 40 percent of Puerto Ricans living within the continental U.S. (i.e., not residing in Puerto Rico) are in New York City.[2]

BACKGROUND—THE RISE IN IMPRISONMENT IN THE U.S.

The United States is an outlier compared to the rest of the world regarding the degree to which it imprisons its residents; as of 2017, it had the largest absolute number of people imprisoned in the world (1.6 million in federal and state prisons and local jails[3]) as well as the highest relative incarceration rate—440 inmates in federal and state prisons per 100,000 residents.[4] Where the U.S. stands regarding high incarceration rates did not occur by chance, nor was it related to sudden shifts in crime trends.[5] Instead, significant changes in national criminal justice policies over the last five decades resulted in an exponential increase in the prison population. In 1977 there were 289,563 federal and state prisoners in the U.S.,[6] and the total U.S. population was about 220 million.[7] By 2009, three decades later and the year in which the number of prisoners (excluding county and local inmates) reached a peak before starting a downward trend after the Great Recession, the federal and state prison population totaled 1.62 million,[8] a nearly 600 percent increase, while the country's population reached 307 million, a 40 percent increase—see figure 5.1.[9] This massive increase shows disparities by race: combined federal and state prison data for 2017[10] show that among men (over 90 percent of the imprisoned in the U.S. are male) the incarceration rate of Blacks was 2,336 prisoners per 100,000 U.S. residents, Latinxs, 1,054 prisoners per 100,000 U.S. residents, and whites, 397 prisoners per 100,000 U.S. residents—see figure 5.2.[11] Disaggregating the U.S. population by demographic group, in 2001 approximately 22 percent of Black non-Hispanic men ages 35 to 44 had been incarcerated at some point in federal or state prison compared to 10 percent of Latinx men and 3.5 percent of white non-Hispanic men, in the same age group.[12] These statistics alone are disturbing, but the implications of these statistics for labor market outcomes are striking; as noted at the beginning of this chapter, a large body of literature exists showing that incarceration leads to poorer employment and earnings outcomes.[13]

One of the reasons for this, among several, is prospective employer discrimination against individuals with a criminal record, and the National Employment Law Project has estimated that 65 million adults in the U.S. have an arrest record.[14] Criminal justice policy changes at the national level, therefore, have the potential to have an indirect but significant impact in labor market outcomes in the U.S., varying by race and ethnicity.[15] Changes in national criminal justice policies have had the largest relative impact on African Americans, then Latinxs, followed by whites, in that order. While most of the attention of the disparate impact of mass incarceration in the U.S. has been focused on African Americans, *unequivocally, the next most affected demographic group are Latinxs, whose share of the U.S. population is projected to nearly double over the next four decades.*[16]

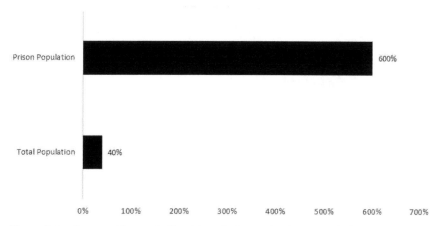

Figure 5.1. Percent Change in Total Population and Prison Population, U.S., 1977–2009. *Data Source*: For incarceration data U.S. Department of Justice Bureau of Justice Statistics; for population data U.S. Department of Commerce Bureau of the Census.

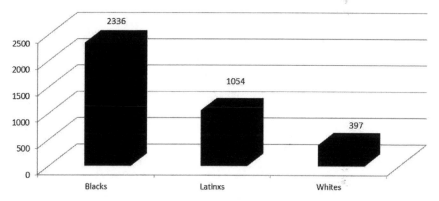

Figure 5.2. Male Incarceration Rate per 100,000 Residents by Demographic Group in the U.S., 2017. *Data Source*: U.S. Department of Justice, Bureau of Justice Statistics "Prisoners in 2017" report, Table 5, p. 9.

DRIVING FORCES BEHIND THE RISE IN INCARCERATION

To illustrate again the dramatic increase in imprisonment in the U.S., an examination of the increase in incarceration rates, along with the country's population growth, during the period of the *sharpest* rise in imprisonment might be instructive: (a) in 1977, the combined federal and state incarceration rate was 129 prisoners per 100,000 residents,[17] and the total U.S. population was about 220 million;[18] (b) by 1998, just over 20 years later, the federal and state incarceration rate was 460 prisoners per 100,000 residents, a 400 percent increase, while the population rose to approximately 270 million, an increase of 23 percent.

A starting point for examining potential factors in the disproportionate rise in Latinx incarceration rates would be to examine what changes occurred in national criminal justice policies that led to the exponential increase in the U.S. prison population overall, and then to examine risk factors that made Latinxs vulnerable to high relative incarceration. A widely held belief is that the "War on Drugs," which began in earnest under President Richard Nixon, pushed full-throttle under President Ronald Reagan (who often gets credited with this "War"), and carried out enthusiastically under President Bill Clinton, and which included mandatory minimum sentencing for drug offenses, was largely responsible for the significant increase in incarceration rates of Americans. The statistics support this hypothesis: according to state correctional data on persons in custody by type of serious offense, from 1980 to 2003 the number of persons in custody for violent crime increased 275 percent, property offenses (e.g., burglary) 193 percent, public order (e.g., drunk driving) 596 percent, and drugs (including possession, manufacturing, and trafficking) a whopping 1,220 percent—see figure 5.3.[19] Research exists that supports the proposition that the likelihood of receiving a prison sentence after arrest increased for drug-related as well as other crimes, and this has been posited as a significant driving factor in rising incarceration rates.[20] However, increases in arrests due to drug-related offenses left increases in arrests for most other categories of offenses far behind during the heyday of the War on Drugs, illustrating a marked redirection of law enforcement resources.

Factors that made Latinxs vulnerable to higher relative incarceration when compared to non-Latinx whites during the last five decades are strikingly similar to the factors that made African Americans vulnerable to rising incarceration over the same time period. The War of Drugs was a significant contributing factor; according to a 2004 report by the National Council of La Raza (NCLR), while Latinxs are no more likely than non-Latinx whites to use illegal drugs, the former group was more likely to be arrested for drug-related offenses, similar to African Americans.[21] In addition, like African Americans, Latinxs were noted in the 2004 NCLR report to experience disparate outcomes, when compared to non-Latinx whites, at each level of involvement in the criminal justice process; bias occurs at every step from search, arrest, prosecution, and sentencing, and the cumulative impact of such treatment contributes to the higher relative incarceration rate of Latinxs compared to non-Latinx whites.[22] Educational attainment also plays a role in the risk for incarceration; Western noted that the lack of a high school diploma is a risk factor for imprisonment, and among major demographic groups Latinxs have

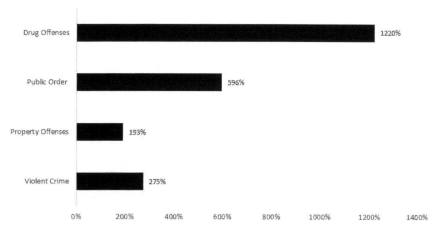

Figure 5.3. Percent Change in Number of Persons in State Custody by Type of Offense, 1980–2003. *Data Source*: U.S. Department of Justice, Bureau of Justice Statistics, "Table—Number of Persons in Custody of State Correctional Authorities by Most Serious Offense, 1980–2003."

lower levels of high school completion compared to non-Latinx whites.[23] Finally, there is the role of arrest and detention of undocumented immigrants, and according to a Brookings Institution 2019 report there were an estimated 7 million undocumented immigrants from Mexico and Central America in the U.S. in 2017.[24]

Special Topic: Are Young Puerto Rican Men at Increased Risk?

Research has shown that incarceration has become a common experience for male high school dropouts.[25] In the late 1990s, an estimated 68 percent of state prisoners in the U.S. did not have a high school diploma.[26] According to data from the Census Bureau, high school non-completion rates for Latinxs are higher than that of whites.[27] And in a report from the Community Service Society of New York (CSS) examining sociological trends among Latinx youth in New York City using data from 2006–2008[28] it was found that the percentage of native-born Latinxs ages 16–24 with less than a high school diploma or "General Equivalency Diploma" (GED) was 34 percent compared to 10 percent of native-born whites and 29 percent of African Americans, in the same age group. This report not only examined Latinx youth, whether native- or foreign-born, in New York City as a whole, but also looked at indicators like school enrollment, educational attainment, and labor force participation rates among Latinx subgroups, specifically Puerto Ricans, Mexicans, and Dominicans. A troubling finding that emerged from the report was educational attainment and employment levels among young Puerto Rican men were lower when compared to the other Latinx subgroups as well as young Black men. In examining both school enrollment and labor force participation, while 14 percent of Black men 16–24 years of age in New York City were neither in school nor in the labor force (being out of the labor force means a person is neither working nor looking for work), the comparable figure for young Dominican men was 9 percent, for young Mexican men 8 percent, but for young Puerto Rican men 17 percent—nearly one in five. Both high unemployment and the lack of a high school diploma are factors associated with an increased risk for incarceration.[29]

In looking at the case of Black men, educational attainment, and incarceration, research found that an estimated 50 percent of Black men born between 1965 and 1969 who did not obtain a high school diploma had a prison record by 1999.[30] Does a higher rate of "disconnection" from school and the labor force, similar to that for young African American men, also place young Puerto Rican men at an increased risk for involvement in the criminal justice system? This is not an unreasonable question to ask. In one of the few localized reports that teased out data regarding criminal justice involvement among Afro-Latinxs, a 2018 report from the American Civil Liberties Union in Florida examined criminal justice outcomes for Black non-Hispanics, white non-Hispanics, white Latinos, and Afro-Latino men in Miami-Dade County from 2010 to 2015.[31] A key finding of the report was that Afro-Latinx men were found to have the worst criminal justice outcomes, compared to the other male demographic groups, from arrest and detention to conviction and imprisonment.

The Puerto Rican community in New York City, like the African American community, is native—Puerto Ricans are U.S. citizens, and the majority of Puerto Ricans in the city were born on the mainland U.S., including 91 percent of Puerto Rican youth.[32] Both communities have similar experiences; they live side by side given similar residential patterns, share intertwined cultures —Puerto Ricans and African Americans together birthed hip-hop culture in the Bronx, New York—and have been subject to similar historical patterns of ethnic and racial discrimination as well as "profiling" policing practices in their neighborhoods. In a report from the Center for Constitutional Rights, 84 percent of the 576,384 individuals subjected to "stop and frisks" in 2009 in New York City were either Latinx, including Puerto Ricans, or Black[33] though these two demographic groups represent roughly half of New York City residents. However, it may be simplistic to posit that because the Puerto Rican community in New York City may share more in common with the African American community than other Latinx subgroups then young men in both communities also have similar patterns of exposure to the criminal justice system. But given that young men in both communities experience similar levels of disconnection from school and work, factors that research suggests put one at increased risk for incarceration, then the inquiry of whether young Puerto Rican men are at increased risk for incarceration should be raised because the future well-being of the Puerto Rican community in New York City is at stake.

The difficulty in discovering an answer to this question is that demographic data on Latinxs in prison available from the New York State Department of Correctional Services is not broken down by subgroup, that is, Dominican, Mexican, and Puerto Rican. Therefore, if there is a potential public policy issue of young Puerto Rican men being at increased risk for involvement in the criminal justice system compared to other Latinx subgroups then it is a *hidden* public policy issue given the lack of available data from criminal justice agencies. However, there may be viable alternative approaches to pursuing this question, such as conducting a sample survey among the Puerto Rican community in New York City. For the moment, however, such a strategy is beyond the scope of this chapter.

CONCLUSION

Answering the question about whether mass incarceration has also disproportionately affected the Afro-Latinx community in the U.S. may, at first glance, appear to have an intuitive answer—yes, since Afro-Latinxs are Black, and disproportionately high incarceration rates have marred the Black community in the U.S. for decades. However, upon closer examination, the answer to this question is not straightforward, because while there are many overlaps between the African American and Afro-Latinx communities in the U.S. there are still some differences, including nativity, ancestry, culture, and language. Differences in incarceration rates between Blacks and Latinxs in the U.S. suggest that while some of the forces at play may be similar, some are likely different. Is it the case, therefore, that the impact of mass incarceration has been compounded in the Afro-Latinx community because of the higher exposure to incarceration for both African Americans and Latinxs? While the answer to this question cannot be obtained with existing publicly available data on incarceration in the U.S., such a question could be critical to the future well-being of the Afro-Latinx community in the U.S., which will likely grow proportionally larger, as the U.S. Latinx community in general will.

NOTES

1. Juan Cartagena, "Lost Votes, Lost Bodies, Lost Jobs: The Effect of Mass Incarceration on Latinx Civic Engagement," in *Behind Bars: Latino/as and Prison in*

the United States, ed. Suzanne Oboler (New York: Palgrave Macmillan US, 2009), 133–48, https://doi.org/10.1057/9780230101470.

2. U.S. Department of Commerce, Bureau of the Census American Community Survey (ACS) 2013–2017 estimates.

3. Jennifer Bronson and E. Ann Carson, "Prisoners in 2017," U.S. Department of Justice, Bureau of Justice Statistics, April 25, 2019, p. 3, table 1, and p. 27, table 17, https://www.bjs.gov/index.cfm?ty=pbdetail&iid=6546.

4. Bronson and Carson, p. 9, table 5.

5. Bruce Western, "The Impact of Incarceration on Wage Mobility and Inequality," *American Sociological Review* 67, no. 4 (August 2002): 526–46, https://doi.org/10.2307/3088944.

6. George Hill and Paige Harrison, "Table—Prisoners in Custody of State or Federal Correctional Authorities, 1977–1998," U.S. Department of Justice, Bureau of Justice Statistics, December 6, 2005, https://www.bjs.gov/content/dtdata.cfm.

7. Population Estimates Program, Population Division, U.S. Census Bureau, "Table—Historical National Population Estimates: July 1, 1900—July 1, 1999" (U.S. Census Bureau, June 28, 2000), https://www2.census.gov/programs-surveys/popest/tables/1900-1980/national/totals/popclockest.txt.

8. Bronson and Carson, "Prisoners in 2017," p. 3, table 1.

9. http://factfinder.census.gov/servlet/SAFFPopulation?_submenuId=population_0&_sse=on.

10. Note that throughout this chapter some imprisonment statistics include jail data while others do not depending on the data source.

11. Bronson and Carson, "Prisoners in 2017," p. 17, table 9.

12. Thomas P. Bonczar, "Prevalence of Imprisonment in the U.S. Population, 1974–2001," U.S. Department of Justice, Bureau of Justice Statistics, August 2003, 1, bjs.gov/content/pub/pdf/piusp01.pdf.

13. Patricia M. Harris and Kimberly S. Keller, "Ex-Offenders Need Not Apply: The Criminal Background Check in Hiring Decisions," *Journal of Contemporary Criminal Justice* 1, no. 21 (February 1, 2005): 6–30, https://doi.org/10.1177/1043986204271678; Harry J. Holzer, Steven Raphael, and Michael A. Stoll, "Perceived Criminality, Criminal Background Checks, and the Racial Hiring Practices of Employers," *Journal of Law & Economics* 49, no. 2 (2006): 451–80, https://doi.org/10.1086/501089; Western, "The Impact of Incarceration on Wage Mobility and Inequality."

14. Michelle Natividad Rodriguez and Maurice Emsellem, "65 Million 'Need Not Apply'—The Case for Reforming Criminal Background Checks for Employment," The National Employment Law Project, March 2011, 5, https://www.nelp.org/wp-content/uploads/2015/03/65_Million_Need_Not_Apply.pdf.

15. While beyond the scope of this chapter given data limitations, Michelle Alexander (author of *The New Jim Crow: Mass Incarceration in the Age of Colorblindness* speaks to the larger prospects for African Americans once they are criminalized. She writes in the *American Prospect*: "Once you're labeled a felon, depending on the state you're in, the old forms of discrimination—employment discrimination, housing discrimination, denial of the right to vote, and exclusion of jury service—are

suddenly legal." Accessed at: Michelle Alexander, "The New Jim Crow," *American Prospect*, December 6, 2010, https://prospect.org/api/content/405622bc-f188-5d86-af10-ea51957607e0/.

16. Jennifer Cheeseman Day, "Population Projections of the United States by Age, Sex, Race, and Hispanic Origin: 1995 to 2050," U.S. Bureau of the Census, Current Population Reports, February 1996, 12, table I, Population by Race and Hispanic Origin: 1990 to 2050, https://www.census.gov/prod/1/pop/p25-1130/p251130.pdf.

17. Paige Harrison, "Table—Incarceration Rates for Prisoners Under State or Federal Jurisdiction per 100,000 Residents," U.S. Department of Justice, Bureau of Justice Statistics, March 28, 2011, https://www.bjs.gov/content/dtdata.cfm.

18. Population Estimates Program, Population Division, U.S. Census Bureau, "Table—Historical National Population Estimates: July 1, 1900–July 1, 1999."

19. U.S. Department of Justice, Bureau of Justice Statistics, "Table—Number of Persons in Custody of State Correctional Authorities by Most Serious Offense, 1980–2003."

20. Alfred Blumstein and Joel Wallman, *The Crime Drop in America* (Cambridge, UK: Cambridge University Press, 2000); Patrick A. Langan, "America's Soaring Prison Population," *Science* 251, no. 5001 (March 29, 1991): 1568–73, https://doi.org/10.1126/science.251.5001.1568.

21. Nancy E. Walker et al., "Lost Opportunities: The Reality of Latinos in the U.S. Criminal Justice System," National Council of La Raza, September 21, 2004, http://publications.nclr.org/handle/123456789/1213.

22. Patrick L. Mason, "The Janus Face of Race: Rhonda M. Williams on Orthodox Economic Schizophrenia," *The Review of Black Political Economy* 29, no. 4 (March 1, 2002): 63–75, https://doi.org/10.1007/BF02717296.

23. Western, "The Impact of Incarceration on Wage Mobility and Inequality."

24. Elaine Kamarck and Christine Stenglein, "How Many Undocumented Immigrants Are in the United States and Who Are They?," *Brooking Institution—Vital Voters* (blog), November 12, 2019, https://www.brookings.edu/policy2020/votervital/how-many-undocumented-immigrants-are-in-the-united-states-and-who-are-they/.

25. Bruce Western, Jeffrey R. Kling, and David F. Weiman, "The Labor Market Consequences of Incarceration," *Working Papers*, Working Paper 829 (Princeton, NJ: Princeton University, Department of Economics, Industrial Relations Section, January 2001), https://ideas.repec.org/p/pri/indrel/450.html; Bruce Western, Becky Petit, and Josh Guetzkow, "Black Economic Progress in the Era of Mass Imprisonment," in *Invisible Punishment: The Collateral Consequences of Mass Imprisonment*, ed. Meda Chesney-Lind and Marc Mauer (New York: New Press, 2011), 165–80.

26. Bruce Western, Vincent Schiraldi, and Jason Ziedenberg, "Education & Incarceration," Justice Policy Institute, August 28, 2003, 6, http://www.justicepolicy.org/images/upload/03-08_REP_EducationIncarceration_AC-BB.pdf.

27. U.S. Department of Labor, Bureau of Labor Statistics, Tables: "Educational Attainment of the Population 25 Years and Over by Sex, for Black Alone and White Alone, Not Hispanic, March 2004" and "Educational Attainment of the Population 18 Years and Over by Age, Sex, Race and Hispanic Origin 2009."

28. Lazar Treschan, "Latino Youth in New York City: School, Work and Income Trends for New York's Largest Group of Young People," Policy Brief, Community Service Society of New York, October 2010, https://www.cssny.org/publications/entry/latino-youth-in-new-york-cityoct2010.

29. Western, "The Impact of Incarceration on Wage Mobility and Inequality," 526; Western, Petit, and Guetzkow, "Black Economic Progress in the Era of Mass Imprisonment," 169–70.

30. Western, Petit, and Guetzkow, "Black Economic Progress in the Era of Mass Imprisonment," 170.

31. Nick Petersen et al., "Unequal Treatment: Racial and Ethnic Disparities in Miami-Dade Criminal Justice," ACLU of Florida, 2018.

32. Treschan, "Latino Youth in New York City: School, Work and Income Trends for New York's Largest Group of Young People," 6.

33. Center for Constitutional Rights, "NYPD Stop-and-Frisk Statistics 2009 and 2010," Center for Constitutional Rights, n.d., https://ccrjustice.org/files/CCR-Stop-and-Frisk-Fact-Sheet-2010.pdf.

Chapter Six

Afro-Latinxs, Discrimination, and the Need for Bold Policies and Movements

In 2016, the Movement for Black Lives released a comprehensive platform in response to the "sustained and increasingly visible violence against Black communities in the U.S. and globally."[1] The platform was drawn up by a large coalition of grassroots organizations and advocacy groups so as to "articulate a common vision and agenda," calling specifically for a "remaking" of discriminatory U.S. institutions.[2] Central to the host of demands, including the call for sweeping overhauls of criminal justice and electoral systems, were a series of intersecting economic justice-based reforms and recommendations. Tax code restructuring, federal and state job programs, worker protections, support for cooperative economies, and other recommendations were all listed as central to empowering and improving the lives of Black Americans.[3]

"Black Lives," the writers of the platform made clear, pertained to all Blacks in America inclusive of origin, with recognition of global and domestic anti-Blackness.[4] In this chapter, we use the recent visible resurgence of anti-racist activism as sociopolitical context, with the goal of highlighting and discussing discrimination against U.S. Afro-Latinxs. Our goal is not only to challenge the prevailing economics literature that perpetually obfsucates the role of race and racism in everday life, but also to empirically validate the claims Black Americans, with a spotlight on Afro-Latinxs, have made with regard to their lived discriminatory experiences. This final chapter is largely informed by our findings in previous chapters (and supported by interdisciplinary literature across the social sciences). We first underline how discrimination can be measured in economics, and provide explanations for our findings by revisiting a structural or "stratification economics" approach in understanding Afro-Latinx discrimination.[5] We discuss the challenges and limitations of our findings, and then go on to call for more robust data

collection. Finally, we end with bold policy recommendations intended to inform social movements and policymakers from the local to the national level.

UNDERSTANDING DISCRIMINATION

Economists typically address discrimination in the context of markets and
market transactions, including labor, housing, and capital/credit markets.
Discrimination in markets can take the form of excluding a group or groups
from equitable access, and can occur for reasons such as simple bigotry (what
economists classify as exhibiting a "taste" or "preference" for discrimination),
assumptions about the productive ability or credit-worthiness of certain groups
given average group characteristics (what economists classify as "statistical
discrimination"), or collusive behavior on the part of employers or unions.

To begin with a general textbook definition, discrimination in the labor
market can occur either as "pre-market" or "in-market." These occurrences
are explained through a set of theories:[6] labor quality, statistical discrimination, and taste for discrimination theories.

The labor quality theory can be characterized as "pre-market:" this theory
posits that subaltern groups (in this case the U.S. Afro-Latinx community)
enter the labor market with inferior abilities due to "culture" (group deficiencies, lack of motivation, self-sabotaging behaviors), biology (innate differences, a belief that continues to be maintained despite "post-racial" rhetoric
in scholarship), or pre-market structural racism (see "stratification economics" discussion in chapter 2).[7] This theory may be depicted by the following
equation:[8]

$$\ln(\text{wage}) = \beta_0 + \Sigma\beta_i X_i + \beta_r R + \beta_t \text{Unobserved Ability} + \varepsilon$$

where X is a vector of productivity characteristics (e.g., experience, training,
educational attainment), R is a dummy variable for race, and the variable
"Unobserved Ability" represents what is assumed to be: (1) an omitted variable; (2) the source of unexplained residuals; (3) was previously attributed
to racial discrimination; and (4) now stands in for some characteristic of the
subaltern group that lowers their productivity relative to another group. Labor
quality theorists argue that there are no unexplained residuals attributable to
racism in this formulation.

Concordantly, taste for discrimination and statistical discrimination can be
characterized as "in-market" theories. The statistical discrimination model
posits that employers use perceived group characteristics in employment
decisions (see discussion in chapter 3).[9] This theory may be depicted by the
following equation:[10]

$$y = q + u$$

In this equation, y is a measure of productive ability, q is an indicator of productive ability, and u is an error term. Applying this model to the differing labor market experiences of Blacks and whites, while the presumption is that u is normally distributed for whites and Blacks, q is not; the variance of q is larger for Blacks than whites, and thus y is a less accurate predictor of ability for Blacks than it is for whites. Employers assume the accuracy of y as a predictor of productivity for Blacks is less than that for whites due to characteristics possessed by Blacks that presumably: (1) lower their productivity and (2) cannot be effectively captured by q.

As underscored throughout this book, we take strong issue with economics literature that ignores empirical studies which control for a host of productivity-related characteristics yet still show unexplained residual differences in wages or employment between Blacks and whites; discrimination, therefore, must be front and center in explaining economic disparities among subaltern groups, especially Black Americans.[11] We also maintain that our findings for the typical Afro-Latinx in the U.S. are best viewed through a "stratification economics" lens, which challenges the neoclassical economic position that the free market results in an equitable allocation of resources.[12] Through this theoretical lens, as Darrick Hamilton and William Darity Jr. wrote, we actually "presume a *rationality* of discrimination," in that structural factors have allowed dominant groups to preserve (and transfer to their children) their wealth-based privilege at the exclusion of subaltern groups, specifically Black Americans and Latinxs alike.[13] This is evident in data presented throughout this book; for example, despite the presence of relatively higher educational attainment, economic returns were not evident for Afro-Latinxs, whether measured by wages or wealth.

CONSIDERATIONS IN MEASURING AFRO-LATINX DISCRIMINATION

Before we highlight policy recommendations, we must first provide some recommendations for scholars, researchers, and advocates who seek to better understand the U.S. Afro-Latinx economic condition. One of the challenges we have highlighted in our book is embedded in a "collective passing" among the Latinx community based on anti-Blackness.[14] Recent demographic data, along with empirical evidence from numerous disciplinary fields, explores the intra-group phenomenon of preferring a white (or non-Black) identity given coloristic treatment at the everyday level.[15] This disjuncture between

the way one self-reports versus how one is perceived, hence treated by society at the material level, provides challenges for researchers in measuring
everyday labor market and other forms of institutional discrimination against
Blacks, whether of Latin American, Caribbean, or U.S.-based ancestry, or
from African continent migrations. This suggests that our own estimates,
which make use of largely self-reported data, only scratch the surface of the
quantitative evidence of persistent anti-Black discrimination in the U.S. Legal scholar Tanya K. Hernández's crucial work helps us understand why this
is, with lessons for economists who rely on data under the broader umbrella
term "Hispanic" (or Latina/o/x).[16] Her research on intra-group discrimination, particularly in the workplace, is based on surveyed legal cases, and
Hernández found that while Black Latinxs experienced intra-group "colorism" by their fellow Latinx peers, the legal system itself played a role—it
wasn't fully prepared to capture the complexities of intra-group hierarchy and
discrimination.[17] As context, in chapter 1 we summarized the growing quantitative, qualitative, and mixed-method interdisciplinary literature that seeks
to place anti-Black discrimination as endemic across institutional spheres.[18]
Yet as Hernández outlined, the role of the state was crucial and determinant
in that, under blanket legal definitions (e.g., "Hispanic"), all Latinxs were
interchangeable, viewed collectively as underrepresented under the law, and
not within racialized hierarchies that exist in Latin America and the U.S.
Hernández explains:

> This is in part because the federal employment discrimination legislation of
> Title VII of the Civil Rights Act of 64 provides separate categories of "race,"
> "color," and "national origin" for what is viewed as impermissible discrimina-
> tion. As a result, judges have fallen prey to the notion that the categories are
> mutually exclusive and do not relate to or reinforce each other, despite the fact
> that the statutes do not provide definitions of what race, color, and national-
> origin discrimination are or how they differ. This tunnel vision hampers judges
> from understanding intersectional claims where the various categories overlap
> in one person's experience of discrimination.[19]

Hernández's important claim that "intersectional discrimination" is layered
is a point we repeatedly emphasized in this book. Afro-Latinxs, as a collectivity, experience discrimination in institutional spheres in ways that are
different from their lighter-skinned, or white/white-passing peers. In fact,
Juliana M. Horowitz, Anna Brown, and Kiana Cox of the Pew Research
Center released a comprehensive report finding that while nearly 60 percent
of U.S. Latinxs say they experienced discrimination or were treated unfairly,
those with darker complexions were much more likely to report discriminatory treatment compared to their lighter-complexioned peers—64 percent to

50 percent, respectively.[20] And within the larger collectivity discrimination is layered, with sometimes additive or multiplicative effects based on gender, sexual orientation, immigration status, and other group-based identities. For economists, one lesson here is that the catchall, commonly used term "Hispanic," predominant in economics literature, is a problematic term itself in definition and analytical category. And even examining Latinxs by ancestral subgroups, however helpful in assessing intra-group differences, can hide settler-colonialist histories and present manifestations of economic discrimination against Afro-Latinxs if attention is not paid to important socio-historical contexts.[21]

Thus, to inform policies as well as social movements, we must confront the ways in which data is collected to more accurately assess the U.S. Afro-Latinx condition. As explained in chapter 1, the process of "passing on Blackness" poses a challenge for researchers, advocates, and policymakers, leaving us to rely on nuanced methodologies to assess the lived material experience for Afro-Latinxs. One recent recommendation by researchers and policymakers is to view Latinxs as asserting an identity outside the boundaries of the typical Black-white frame; quantitative surveys (such as those conducted by the Census Bureau) should reflect this. Other recommendations include counting Hispanics/Latino/a/xs as a racial category alongside whites, Blacks, Asians, and Native Americans.[22] This is a highly problematic approach without nuanced methodological technique, given that "race" and "ethnicity" can have different social meanings. A Latinx person can belong to multiple groups by ancestry and thus should not be conflated or merged numerically into one category. Take sociologist Nancy López, for example, who provides clear reasoning:

> To understand why such arguments are problematic, we must first understand that achieving equity requires different treatment. In the United States, the enslavement of Africans and colonization of Native American sovereign groups created systems of racialized inequality, with reverberations in employment, poverty, and many social spheres. Visual markers such as skin color, hair texture, and other racial features are imbued with historically embedded social meanings that map onto many societal inequalities. This means that darker-skinned Latin-origin people often experience more discrimination than their lighter-skinned kin.[23]

Long-standing separate questions detailing Hispanic origin (as proxy for ethnicity) and race (as proxies of racialization), whatever their limitations, should be kept separate, so as to ensure the right of Afro-Latinxs to declare BOTH their ethnic origin, specifically their ancestry, and their "social" race.[24] In fact, the respected research-advocacy group Afro-Latin@ Forum, based out of New York City, engaged in a concerted public education campaign before the 2010 U.S. Census to "Check Both!/Chequea los dos!" so as to increase the numerical count of U.S. Afro-Latinxs, and are doing so again in the wake of the 2020 U.S. Census.[25] Other data-collection strategies could also include more meaningful terms for Afro-Latinx individuals, such as more recent immigrants who may not identify and resonate with the term "African American." National Black movements in Latin America during the 1970s, for example, spurred a wave of internal and external pressure on governments to more directly capture the Afro-descendant experience through more appropriate terms in national censuses.[26] In the U.S., inspired by the Afro-Latin@ Forum's crucial work, a recent collaboration between The Black Futures Lab and Mijente included a Spanish-language version of the independent "Black Census Project," so as to directly ensure participation by Afro-Latinxs.[27]

In addition, surveys that ask respondents to assess their skin shade (dark, medium, light) are important but incomplete, given the evidence respondents may incorrectly self-report their skin shade at similar rates as they self-report their race. Thus, providing a scale for the observer-researcher in conjunction with self-reporting methods is crucial.[28] This could also include Nancy López and colleagues' mixed-method approach of asking people not just how they self-identify, but how they believe others view or identify them (called "street race-gender") at the everyday level.[29] "Race-gender profiling," López explains, "whether in housing, employment, law enforcement, educational institutions or even when accessing health care, voting, or traveling in an airport, takes place according to one's 'street race-gender.'" Field experiments and labor market audit studies, which continue to identify persistent patterns of hiring discrimination against African Americans and Latinxs measured independently (see chapter 3), could be applied to the group where both of these demographics intersect: Afro-Latinxs.[30] Text analyses, archival research, intensive interviewing techniques, and surveys of interdisciplinary research have all already provided us a window into the U.S. Afro-Latinx economic condition, placing anti-Blackness, regardless of ancestry and origin, as a central, recurring theme.

POLICY IMPLICATIONS

For the average Afro-Latinx in the U.S., discrimination is omnipresent. Despite economic theories that posit market-level competition will essentially bleed out discriminatory practices among employers (see chapter 3), there is no evidence this is the case for Afro-Latinxs and other Blacks, broadly speaking. As we underscored in our data, Afro-Latinxs are a well-educated group, and while education is viewed as a predictor for labor market success, there is no evidence that a comparatively higher educational attainment level is shielding this group from discrimination (as it doesn't for Black/African Americans overall).[31] Indeed, as we outlined in chapter 2, recent research on educational credentialing and wealth inequality finds that whites are more likely to experience long-term beneficial wage and wealth returns due to the possession of particular forms of debt. The opposite is true for Blacks, especially women, who are more likely to possess student loan, medical, and other predatory, debilitating forms of debt.[32] We add Afro-Latinxs within this racialized frame, in that we showed, through indicators such as wealth, income, education, poverty, unemployment, and occupational status, that economic conditions for Afro-Latinxs in the U.S. more closely resemble those of African Americans than of Latinxs in the general U.S. population.

Given the observed similarities between African Americans and Afro-Latinxs, arguably policies designed to improve the economic status of African Americans would be beneficial to Afro-Latinxs as well. We highlight some of these policies, which are unapologetically bold yet necessary in the current and persistently anti-Black climate, so as to inform social movements that seek to improve the material lives of all groups, especially Black Americans of all origins.

In chapter 1 we highlighted the finding that a significant portion of U.S. Afro-Latinxs possess African American parentage. We also affirmed that, despite more educational attainment as compared to other Latinxs, the Afro-Latinx economic experience in the U.S. suffers from the breadth of economic penalties that comes with the Black experience in the U.S. The common historical thread between Afro-Latinxs and African Americans is undoubtedly grounded in the institutions of slavery and subsequent oppressive systems, which, despite different colonial regimes (Spain/Portuguese and English/Dutch/French settler-colonialism), were crucial and determinant in shaping future wealth trajectories for Black Americans, including Afro-Latinxs.

We are aware of the longtime movements for reparations for African Americans, and understand the current limits and potential for political plausibility in the United States. We would be remiss, however, if we didn't extend our support and recommendation despite these obstacles. There is already considerable literature from Latin America that theorizes and documents attempts at reparation policies for Afro-Latinx and Indigenous (and intersecting) communities.[33] Some of the arguments are quite similar to arguments presented in the U.S. The work of William Darity Jr. and Kirsten Mullen makes a practical case for reparations for African American communities. They argue three central principles should be accomplished by a reparations program: acknowledgment, restitution, and closure.[34]

By default, those with direct U.S. slavery ancestry would be eligible for such a policy, but we concur with Darity Jr. and Mullen that we should consider a policy that extends beyond addressing solely the legacies of slavery. Policies and persistent racial terror post-slavery, including during the Jim Crow era and in more contemporary times (e.g., redlining, eminent domain, and mass incarceration), have been well-documented as mechanisms designed to strip and dispossess African Americans of wealth.[35] The question remains for U.S. Afro-Latinxs as to who would be eligible, what criteria would be set, and how does one address Afro-Latinxs who do not declare African American parentage but were subject to systemic wealth dispossession in their historical/home context in the Caribbean and Latin America. In other words, we must situate Afro-Latinx economic realities within a domestic and diasporic global frame, and support transnational movements that seek restitution in all anti-Black global spaces.[36]

We continue with structural policies that would address disparities documented above, especially income and wealth gaps. In previous chapters, we outlined the wealth position of U.S. Afro-Latinxs using proxy measures (given the absence of specific data), finding initial evidence that their overall wealth position is similar to that of the Black American community. One such policy proposal, based on the late African American historian Manning Marable's "baby bonds" proposal, seeks to rectify the well-documented wealth gap using redistributive means. It should be pointed out, however, that this proposal, expanded and popularized by economists William Darity Jr. and Darrick Hamilton, and supported by a burgeoning number of scholars, researchers, community activists, and legislators, is not intended to solve the persistent injustice that is the racial wealth gap.[37] It is simply one remedy that must be accompanied by attendant public policies with more systemic effects on the lives of communities of color—universal health care, a federal "job guarantee," debt-free education, ensured food security, universal housing, an end to mass incarceration, and many of the recommendations made by the Movement for Black Lives summarized previously.

A "Universal Wealth Account" would function as a federal bond assigned to an individual at birth to be accessed at the age of 18 for the purpose of supporting educational pursuits (in the absence of tuition-free higher education, which we support), buying a home, or starting a business.[38] The amount of the "baby bond" would depend on the family's net assets, or wealth, measured by the difference between one's debt and assets, and this benefit would be universal.[39] All families would be eligible, but due to the racialized distribution of wealth in the U.S., evident among the Afro-Latinx community, members of subaltern groups would likely receive larger sums. As we've noted, the average wealth position of Afro-Latinxs is similar to that of African Americans. Groups with more Afro-Latinx members also exhibit drastic wealth disparities as compared to other Latinxs and groups such as non-Latinx whites and Asians.

Another policy recommendation that has gained traction in public discourse is a "Jobs Guarantee," with roots in the work of Sadie Alexander, the nation's first Black woman economist, as well as the Franklin Delano Roosevelt (FDR) administration's full employment programs that included the Works Progress Administration (WPA) and the Civilian Conservation Corps (CCC).[40] As these popular public works programs dissipated, and employment prospects improved for most (white) Americans in a budding postwar economy, economist Nina Banks points out that Alexander remained a strong advocate for government-led full employment given persistent hiring discrimination and intentional exclusion of Black Americans from the fruits of economic growth.[41] Recalibrated during the civil rights movement and subsequently within the framework of the "Humphrey-Hawkins Act" of 1978 (all the while championed by Coretta Scott King until her death), potential for a job guarantee has been recently (politically) revitalized, with evidence of strong public support among African Americans, Latinxs, and other communities of color.[42] What makes this policy proposal different is that, unlike temporary job programs or racist workfare programs of the past, a job guarantee would be a permanent public option for living wage employment with no strings attached.[43] It would be different than traditional government-subsidized job training programs, and would move us away from approaches that assume what individuals need are improved labor market skills (including so-called "soft skills," the implication being that Blacks lack such skills, an absurd and racist notion). There are examples, like CETA (Comprehensive Employment and Training Act) of the 1970s, in which unemployment and support for public service/works were simultaneously addressed. CETA, however, has been criticized—it was intended to serve the "disadvantaged," but ended up, in some instances, subsidizing the nonprofit sector, with some funding going to elite organizations.[44]

For the Afro-Latinx community, such a bold policy would not only address higher levels of unemployment and poverty, but also "underemployment" and other forms of precarious work. As we highlighted in chapter 3, boasts by Donald Trump about historically low Black and Latinx unemployment rates obfuscated a trend he inherited since the end of the Great Recession. In addition, if the non-Latinx white unemployment rate were anywhere near that of Black or Latinx unemployment rates, we believe elite actors in government would consider it a national crisis and would act quickly. In addition, less discussed is the role of jobs that don't pay a livable wage. A job guarantee (JG) would mitigate or remove the threat of unemployment, bringing us to actual full employment, especially in disaffected communities. In sum, it could serve as a remedy for labor market discrimination experienced among Afro-Latinxs and the Black collectivity in the United States at large.

Other benefits of the JG are crucial, especially in the context of climate change. It could have full- or part-time options, be consistent with movements around the world to reduce the work week given existing high levels of worker productivity, and directly move the U.S. away from a carbon-based economy through a "just transition" via a comprehensive program such as a "Green New Deal." It could also allow people to be self-sufficient with a livable wage and dignified work, especially for communities of color with a disability, and the undocumented. It also has intersectional applicability, in that Afro-Latinx LGBTQ communities as well as the undocumented will benefit, given research that seeks to understand how LGBTQ people of color experience discrimination in the labor market as well as the criminal justice system.[45] Finally, the JG could also extend to the formerly incarcerated, given the disproportionate ethnic and racial makeup of those in U.S. prisons. While it is unclear how many Afro-Latinxs are incarcerated nationally (see chapter 5), the overwhelming presence of Blacks and Latinxs in the prison industrial complex (and localized evidence for "Black Hispanics") places U.S. Afro-Latinxs well within movements that seek not only criminal justice reform from policing to sentencing, but also dismantling (abolition) of our punitive, racialized institutions altogether.[46]

These are bold policy recommendations we prescribe given our findings. It is clear that Afro-Latinas are crowded into low-wage occupations—sectors of the economy less likely to offer paid family leave (see chapter 3), making it difficult to seek educational opportunities while balancing the challenges of parenthood as well as other caregiving responsibilities. Recently, support for expanded paid family leave and universal childcare policies were given prominent placement on Democratic presidential candidate platforms, in which their successful implementation would undoubtedly benefit Afro-Latinxs regardless of gender identity and family arrangement.[47] This has been joined by what we might call a domestic "debt jubilee" movement thanks to years of grassroots organizing from groups like the Debt Collective around the documented debilitating levels of student (and other forms of) debt we discussed.[48] As an example, the current revitalized movement toward debt-free college, with tuition-free models at public universities and "Historically Black Colleges and Universities" (HBCUs) being implemented at the state level (providing models for larger national proposals), would further alleviate the wealth and debt disparities we've documented. This would have a targeted, and proportionately positive, effect on Black, Latinx, Afro-Latinx and other communities of color, especially women, while providing non-exclusive paths to opportunity and economic well-being higher education is supposed to yield.[49]

There are other bold, transformative policies we have not discussed, but what we've offered must undoubtedly come with an end to fiscal austerity and neoliberal movements that seek to dismantle the public sector and resort to market-based solutions. As we consider the U.S. Afro-Latinx economic condition, we end by reiterating that government spending on transformative policies is less about scarcity and more about intentional policy choices. This means that single-payer health care, free and reduced-cost public transportation, universal housing, worker-owned enterprises, and other collective efforts contained in the above recommendations are not only realistic, with immediate and long-term impact, but would mitigate persistent market-based anti-Black discrimination in a variety of spheres.

NOTES

1. "Vision for Black Lives," Movement for Black Lives, 2016, https://m4bl.org/policy-platforms/.
2. Movement for Black Lives, "Vision for Black Lives."
3. The organization specifically states: "While this platform is focused on domestic policies, we know that patriarchy, exploitative capitalism, militarism, and white supremacy know no borders. We stand in solidarity with our international family against the ravages of global capitalism and anti-Black racism, human-made climate change, war, and exploitation. We also stand with descendants of African people all over the world in an ongoing call and struggle for reparations for the historic and continuing harms of colonialism and slavery." Movement for Black Lives, "A Vision for Black Lives," 4.
4. In expanding the narrative that BLM is simply a U.S.-specific movement, a recent piece highlighted the historical to present global connectivities, especially with Latin America. Bowen and colleagues write: "The Black Lives Matter movement is not a U.S. cultural export to Latin America and should not be treated as such, for the assertion that 'Black lives matter' is far from new in the Americas. From the maroon communities of Jamaica, Suriname, and Brazil to Black independence movements starting with the Haitian Revolution, Black peoples across the Americas have long articulated a demand that Black life, personhood, and autonomy be valued and respected. Today's movements are only the latest iteration in the long Black struggle for liberation." Larnies A. Bowen, Ayanna Legros, Tianna Paschel, Geísa Mattos, Kleaver Cruz, and Juliet Hooker, "A Hemispheric Approach to Contemporary Black Activism," NACLA, March 20, 2018, 1, https://nacla.org/news/2017/03/20/hemispheric-approach-contemporary-black-activism.
5. See discussion on "stratification economics" in chapters 1 and 2.
6. Darrick Hamilton and William A. Darity Jr., "Crowded Out? The Racial Composition of American Occupations," in *Researching Black Communities: A Methodological Guide*, ed. James S. Jackson et al. (University of Michigan Press, 2012), 60–78.

7. Patrick L. Mason, "Understanding Recent Empirical Evidence on Race and Labor Market Outcomes in the USA," *Review of Social Economy* 58, no. 3 (September 2000): 321, https://doi.org/10.1080/00346760050132355.

8. Mason, "Understanding Recent Empirical Evidence on Race and Labor Market Outcomes in the USA."

9. For a sociological critique of "statistical discrimination," see for example Stephen Steinberg in which he writes: "Employers who make their hiring decisions on the basis of what group a person belongs to, rather than on individual merits, are engaged in patent acts of prejudice." Stephen Steinberg, "Immigration, African Americans and Race," *New Politics* 10, no. 3 (Summer 2006): 2, http://nova.wpunj.edu/newpolitics/issue39/Steinberg39.htm.

10. Dennis J. Aigner and Glen G. Cain, "Statistical Theories of Discrimination in Labor Markets," *Industrial and Labor Relations Review* 30, no. 2 (January 1977): 176, doi:10.2307/2522871.

11. And as we outlined throughout the book, we applied "stratification economics" (SE) as an empirically grounded explanation of intergroup disparities, as it delves across disciplines to locate the structural reasons for persistent inequality. It also holds as constant that supposed group deficiencies, or self-sabotaging attitudes committed and recycled by subaltern groups, are not explanatory in aforementioned disparities. For more, William A. Darity Jr., Darrick Hamilton, and James B. Stewart, "A Tour de Force in Understanding Intergroup Inequality: An Introduction to Stratification Economics," *Review of Black Political Economy* 42, nos. 1–2 (2015): 1–6, doi:10.1007/s12114-014-9201-2; also see William Darity Jr., "The New (Incorrect) Harvard/Washington Consensus on Racial Inequality," *DuBois Review* 8, no. 2 (Fall 2011): 467–76, doi: 10.1017/S1742058X11000439.

12. We also share sociologists Louise Seamster and Victor Ray's illuminating analysis on research-based claims of racial progress, in that race is a central tenet and "master category" of social differentiation, with undeniable, causal, intentional disparate effect. Their analysis is crucial for "stratification economics," in that it should be viewed not as existing on the margins of economics or as alternative framework, but equally part of the "master narrative," a fundamental theoretical premise in explaining the economic disparities we documented in this book affecting Afro-Latinxs. They also provide a succinct sociological history of unfounded cultural arguments, as well as center the significance of settler-colonial projects and their present institutionalized manifestations (see our chapter 2 on wealth dispossesion), and point to limitations in Black agency as direct outcome of structural racism. Louise Seamster and Victor Ray, "Against Teleology in the Study of Race: Toward the Abolition of the Progress Paradigm," *Sociological Theory* 36, no. 4 (2018): 315–342, https://doi.org/10.1177/0735275118813614.

13. Darrick Hamilton and William A. Darity Jr., "The Political Economy of Education, Financial Literacy, and the Racial Wealth Gap (2017)," *Review* 99, no. 1 (2017): 59–76, 70, http://dx.doi.org/10.20955/r.2017.59-76.

14. See discussion in chapter 1. Also see William Darity Jr., Jason Dietrich, and Darrick Hamilton, "Bleach in the Rainbow: Latin Ethnicity and Preferences for

Whiteness," in *The Afro-Latin@ Reader*, ed. Miriam Jiménez Román and Juan Flores (Durham, NC: Duke University Press, 2010), 485–98.

15. We are referring here to a long-standing debate as to whether or not Latinos and Asian groups are "becoming white," given the propensity for newer immigrants to choose white or "some other race" over other racial categories, including "Black/African American." For a good discussion of the debate, see exchanges in *American Prospect* by Richard Alba, William Darity Jr., and others. Richard Alba, "The Likely Persistence of a White Majority," *Atlantic*, January 11, 2016; https://prospect.org/civil-rights/likely-persistence-white-majority/; William Darity Jr., "The Latino Flight to Whiteness," *Atlantic*, February 11, 2016, https://prospect.org/civil-rights/latino-flight-whiteness/; for methodological debate, also see William Darity Jr. and Tanya Golash-Boza (2008), who challenged use of the New Immigrant Survey, arguing that detecting discrimination through the study posed a difficulty for Latinx immigrants given that so many assign themselves a "white" status despite evidence of discrimination based on phenotype. However, they did find that there WAS strong evidence of discrimination against immigrants as a group, but that result was driven by its Latinx respondents—this means that regardless of how the group was self-identifying (anti-Black) coloristic discrimination was evident. Tanya Golash-Boza and William Darity Jr., "Latino Racial Choices: the effects of skin colour and discrimination on Latinos' and Latinas' racial self-identifications," *Ethnic and Racial Studies* 38, no. 5 (2008): 899–934, https://doi.org/10.1080/01419870701568858.

16. Tanya K. Hernández, "Afro-Latin@s and the Latin@ Workplace," in *The Afro-Latin@ Reader*, ed. Miriam Jiménez Román and Juan Flores (Duke University Press, 2010): 520–24. Also see Tanya K. Hernández, "Employment Discrimination in the Ethnically Diverse Workplace," 49 *Judges* J. 33 (2010), https://ir.lawnet.fordham.edu/faculty_scholarship/14.

17. Tanya K. Hernández, "Afro-Latin@s and the Latin@ Workplace," in *The Afro-Latin@ Reader*, ed. Miriam Jiménez Román and Juan Flores (Duke University Press, 2010), 520–24.

18. Lavariega Monforti and Sanchez used regression and descriptive analysis from a national survey (Kaiser/Pew Latino National Survey, 2002) to find that 84 percent of Latinos surveyed felt that intra-group discrimination (among Latinx peers) is a problem. Notably, they also argued this was more true for those "less integrated" in society, and for self-identified Black Latinxs! J. Lavariega Monforti and G. R. Sanchez, "The Politics of Perception: An Investigation of the Presence and Sources of Perceptions of Internal Discrimination Among Latinos," *Social Science Quarterly* 91 (2010): 245–265, doi:10.1111/j.1540-6237.2010.00691.x; also see as further examples of intra-group discrimination, Jasmine M. Haywood, "'Latino spaces have always been the most violent': Afro-Latino collegians' perceptions of colorism and Latino intragroup marginalization," *International Journal of Qualitative Studies in Education* 30, no. 8 (2017): 759–82, doi:10.1080/09518398.2017.1350298; Jasmine M. Haywood, "Anti-Black Latino racism in an era of Trumpismo," *International Journal of Qualitative Studies in Education* 30, no. 10 (2017): 957–64, doi: 10.1080/09518398.2017.1312613.

19. Tanya K. Hernández, "Afro-Latin@s and the Latin@ Workplace," in *The Afro-Latin@ Reader*, ed. Jiménez Román and Flores (Duke University Press, 2010), 521.

20. Juliana Menasce Horowitz, Anna Brown, and Kiana Cox, "Race in America, 2019," Pew Research Center, April 9, 2019.The survey used the Massey-Martin scale for skin tone classification, in which respondents are asked to visually identify their skin shade based on a left-to-right gradient scale representing lighter to darker hands. See discussion of findings and methodology at https://www.pewsocialtrends.org /2019/04/09/race-in-america-2019/#Hispanics-discrimination. For a similar survey, see Ana González-Barrera, "Hispanics with darker skin are more likely to experience discrmination than those with lighter skin," Pew Research Center, 2019, https:// www.pewresearch.org/fact-tank/2019/07/02/hispanics-with-darker-skin-are-more -likely-to-experience-discrimination-than-those-with-lighter-skin/. Also see Atiya Kai Stokes-Brown, "America's Shifting Color Line: Re-examining determinants of Latino Racial Self-Identification," *Social Science Quarterly* 93, no. 2 (2012): 309–32, dx.doi.org/10.1111/j.1540-6237.2012.00852.x.

21. Alan Aja, Stephan LeFebvre, Nancy López, Darrick Hamilton, and William Darity Jr., "Toward a Latino/a/x Stratification Economics," *Review of Black Political Economy* (Fall 2020).

22. Nancy López, "What's Your 'Street Race-Gender'? Why We Need Separate Questions on Hispanic Origin and Race for the 2020 Census," *RWJF* (blog), November 26, 2014, http://www.rwjf.org/en/blogs/human-capital-blog/2014/11/whats yourstreet.html. Also see Nancy López, Edward Vargas, Melina Juárez, Lisa Cacari-Stone, and Sonia Bettez, "What's Your 'Street Race'? Leveraging Multidimensional Measures of Race and Intersectionality for Examining Physical and Mental Health Status among Latinxs," *Sociology of Race and Ethnicity*, 2017, https://doi .org/10.1177/2332649217708798.

23. Nancy López, "What's Your 'Street Race-Gender'? Why We Need Separate Questions on Hispanic Origin and Race for the 2020 Census," *RWJF* (blog), November 26, 2014, 1, http://www.rwjf.org/en/blogs/human-capital-blog/2014/11/whats yourstreet.html.

24. Another possible idea is to include a specific question that would speak directly to Afro-Latinxs in a context that controls for varying social meanings of race. We could take methodological cue, for instance, from the upcoming Mexican Census 2020, which in a test-run for a question in a 2015 survey that sought to recognize Afro-Mexican identity, already uncovered 1.4 million Afro-Mexicans (however undercounted due to the influence of *mestizaje*, the initial count found that Afro-Mexicans are primarily concentrated in particular geographies long known for Afro-descendant presence but perpetually erased via official state-level counts. See for instance Sameer Rao, "Mexico Finally Recognizes Afro Mexicans in National Census," *Colorlines*, 2015, https://www.colorlines.com/articles/mexico-finally-recognizes-afro -mexicans-national-census. Rao reports the role of social movements (Afro-Mexican community activists and allies) in pressuring the state for the new question.

25. For more on the Afro-Latin@forum's work, as well as the "check both" census campaign, see here: http://www.afrolatinoforum.org/check-both-campaign.html. Also see Miriam Jiménez Román, "Check Both! Afro-Latin@s and the U.S. Census," *NACLA*, 2010. Available at: https://nacla.org/node/6816.

26. George Reid Andrews (2018) provides a succinct, recent update on the debates surrounding terminologies used in respective national censuses. For more background, see George Reid Andrews, "Afro Latin America by the Numbers: The Politics of the Census," *ReVista: Harvard Review of Latin America* (Winter 2018), https://revista.drclas.harvard.edu/; also see Edward Telles, *Pigmentocracies: Ethnicity, Race, and Color in Latin America* (University of North Carolina Press, 2014).

27. Carmen Phillips, "Why This Census of U.S. Afro-Latinos in Groundbreaking," *Remezcla*, July 17, 2018, https://remezcla.com/features/culture/census-us-afro -latinos-groundbreaking/. Also see www.blackcensus.org/es. Note: another example is a more recent national survey of "Hispanics" by Gustavo López and Ana González-Barrera of the Pew Research Center (n = 1,520), which specifically asked respondents if they consider themselves "Afro-Latino, Afro-Caribbean, or Afro-(Country of Origin), or not?" See our discussion chapter 1. Gustavo López and Ana Gonzalez-Barrera, "Afro-Latino: A Deeply Rooted Identity among U.S. Hispanics," Pew Research Center, March 1, 2016, https://www.pewresearch.org/fact-tank/2016/03/01/afro-latino-a -deeply-rooted-identity-among-u-s-hispanics/.

28. Patrick Mason (2004), for instance, used data from 1979 and 1989 and found that despite "Hispanic" tendencies to identify away from Blackness, such preferences would not protect them from race-based discrimination. Patrick Mason, "Annual income, hourly wages, and identity Among Mexican Americans and other Latinos," *Industrial Relations* 43, no. 4 (2004): 817–34, https://ssrn.com/abstract=591471. For more see Wendy Roth, "The Multiple Dimensions of Race," *Ethnic and Racial Studies* 39, no. 8 (2016): 1310–38, https://doi.org/10.1080/01419870.2016.1140793. Also see William Darity Jr., Jason Dietrich, and Darrick Hamilton, "Bleach in the Rainbow: Latin Ethnicity and Preference for Whiteness," *Transforming Anthropology* 13 (2005): 103–09, doi:10.1525/tran.2005.13.2.103.

29. Nancy López's (2014) concerns about the conflation of race and ethnicity for survey purposes stems from research in inter/intra-group health disparities, which finds similarities of treatment and outcomes between "Black-Hispanics" and "non-Hispanic Blacks." Calling for "more than one measure of race," the concept of "street race-gender" is defined as "the meanings ascribed to a conglomeration of markers of physical appearance, including but not limited to skin color, hair texture, facial features, among other characteristics and interacting with gender as a key concept for mapping and interrupting inequality. Nancy López, "What's Your 'Street Race-Gender'? Why We Need Separate Questions on Hispanic Origin and Race for the 2020 Census," *RWJF* (blog), November 26, 2014, 1, http://www.rwjf.org/en/blogs/human -capital-blog/2014/11/whatsyourstreet.html.

30. The late Devah Pager's work is crucial and essential. Her independent work (see Pager, 2008), and collaborative studies (Quillian et al., 2017) underscore the breadth of persistent hiring discrimination against Blacks and Latinxs (measured independently). In the latter piece, meta-analysis of hiring discrimination field experiments found that since 1989, whites experience on average 36 percent more "callbacks" than African Americans, and 24 percent more so than Latinos, yielding the observation of no change in hiring progress (at point of hire) for the former (and little evidence of decline among Latinos). Lincoln Quillian, Devah Pager, Ole Hexel, Arnfinn H. Midtbøen, "The persistence of racial discrimination in hiring," *Proceedings of the Na-*

tional Academy of Sciences 114, no. 41 (October 2017): 10870–75, doi: 10.1073/pnas
.1706255114; also see Devah Pager and Hana Shepherd, "The sociology of discrimination: Racial discrimination in employment, housing, credit, and consumer markets," *Annual Review of Sociol*ogy 34 (2008): 181–209, doi: 10.1146/annurev.soc.33
.040406.131740.

31. Darrick Hamilton, William A. Darity Jr., Anne Price, V. Sridharan, and Rebecca Tippett, "Umbrellas Don't Make It Rain: Why Studying and Working Hard
Isn't Enough for Black Americans," Samuel DuBois Cook Center on Social Equity
at Duke University, the New School, and Insight Center for Community Economic
Development, 2015, http://www.insightcced.org/uploads/CRWG/Umbrellas-Dont
-Make-It-Rain8.pdf; Janelle Jones and John Schmitt, "A College Degree is No Guarantee," Center for Economic and Policy Research, 2014, http://cepr.net/documents
/black-coll-grads-2014-05.pdf.

32. Jhumpa Bhattacharya et al. (2019) look at the race-gendered components of
wealth, especially among millennial women. On a policy front, they point to the role
of a lack of paid family leave as intersecting with single parenting and debt accumulation as a driver of inequality for Black women. Jhumpa Bhattacharya, Anne Price, and
Fenaba Addo, *Clipped Wings: Closing the Wealth Gap for Millennial Women* (Asset
Funders Network, Texas Women's Foundation, The New York Women's Foundation, 2019). Also see chapters 2 and 4 for discussion and references.

33. See for example Ana Luisa Aurajo, *Reparations for Slavery and the Slave
Trade: A Transnational and Comparative History* (Bloomsbury Academic, 2018).
We would be remiss if we didn't include Puerto Ricans here, as there is reparations
theory literature that calls for forms of restitution given its colonial status and extraction of its resources both under Spanish and U.S. rule, and as equally important, long-
term debilitating health effects as a result of U.S. military bombings. See Alan Aja,
Stephan Lefebvre, Reynaldo Ortíz-Minaya, Darrick Hamilton, and William Darity Jr.,
"Bold Policies for Puerto Rico: A Blueprint for Transformative, Justice-Centered Recovery," *Diálogo Interdisciplinary Studies Journal* 12, no. 2 (Fall 2018), doi: 10.1353
/dlg.2018.0023; Pedro Malavet, "Reparations Theory and Postcolonial Puerto Rico:
Some Preliminary Thoughts," 13 *Berkeley La Raza Law Journal* 387 (2002), http://
scholarship.law.ufl.edu/facultypub/210.

34. William Darity Jr. and Kirsten Mullen, *From Here to Equality: Reparations
for Black Americans in the 20th Century* (University of North Carolina Press, 2020).
Also see "For Reparations: A Conversation with William Darity, Jr." with Adam
Simpson and Carla Skandier, The Next Systems Project, 2017, https://thenextsystem
.org/for-reparations.

35. Mehrsa Baradaran, *The Color of Money: Black Banks and the Racial Wealth
Gap* (Cambridge, Massachusetts: Belknap Press: An Imprint of Harvard University
Press, 2017); Richard Rothstein, *The Color of Law: A Forgotten History of How Our
Government Segregated America*, First edition (New York: Liveright Publishing
Corporation, 2017).

36. We would like to note that reparations as household payments/transfers should
also be conjoined with larger individual to community level wealth building projects.
A reparation-based Marshall Plan, for instance, for our most devastated localities
where chronic structural neglect and unemployment are disproportionately felt by

Black, Latinx, native, and other communities (and/or amid threats of displacement by gentrification and/or climate change) is of utmost urgency. While this is highly underdeveloped on our part, we would be remiss if we did not mention it.

37. Darrick Hamilton and William A. Darity Jr., "Can 'Baby Bonds' Eliminate the Racial Wealth Gap in Putative Post-Racial America?," *Review of Black Political Economy* 37, nos. 3–4 (2010): 207–16, https://doi.org/10.1007/s12114 -010 9063-1.

38. Darrick Hamilton and William A. Darity Jr., "Can 'Baby Bonds' Eliminate the Racial Wealth Gap in Putative Post-Racial America?," *Review of Black Political Economy* 37, nos. 3–4 (2010): 207–16, https://doi.org/10.1007/s12114 -010 9063-1.

39. Darrick Hamilton, "Race, Wealth, and Intergenerational Poverty," *American Prospect*, 14, August 2009, https://prospect.org/article/race-wealth-and-inter generational-poverty.

40. See Mark Paul, William A. Darity Jr., and Darrick Hamilton, "The Federal Job Guarantee: A Policy to Achieve Full Employment," Center on Budget and Policy Priorities, March 9, 2018, https://www.cbpp.org/research/full-employment/the-federal -job-guarantee-a-policy-to-achieve-permanent-full-employment; Pavlina Tcherneva, *The Case for a Job Guarantee* (Polity Press, 2020); Nina Banks, "The Black Woman Economist Who Pioneered a Federal Jobs Guarantee," Institute for New Economic Thinking, February 22, 2019, https://www.ineteconomics.org/perspectives/blog/the -black-woman-economist-who-pioneered-a-federal-jobs-guarantee.

41. Nina Banks, "The Black Woman Economist Who Pioneered a Federal Jobs Guarantee," Institute for New Economic Thinking, February 22, 2019, https://www .ineteconomics.org/perspectives/blog/the-black-woman-economist-who-pioneered-a -federal-jobs-guarantee.

42. Jeanne Theoharis and David Stein point out that Scott King's vision, aside from full employment, was "broader than that: it encompassed a transformation of a warmaking society, a demand for genuine welfare rights and real measures of justice, as well as protected voting rights for black people." See Jeanne Theoharis and David Stein, "What Coretta Scott King Can Teach Democrats About a Job Guarantee," *Huffington Post*, May 23, 2018, https://www.huffpost.com/entry/opinion-stein-theoharis -coretta jobsguaranteen5b0471dee4b0784cd2af2bf6; also see analyses on multiple facets of urgency, social to environmental, for a federal job guarantee as argued by Pavlina Tcherneva, *The Case for a Job Guarantee* (Polity Press, 2020); also see Jesse Meyerson, "Five Economic Reforms Millenials Should be Fighting For," *Rolling Stone*, January 3, 2014, https://www.rollingstone.com/politics/politics-news/five-economic -reforms-millennials-should-be-fighting-for-102489/; Alan Aja, Raul Carrillo, and Rita Sandoval, "Why the Latinx Community Should Fight for a Job Guarantee," *Latino Rebels*, 2018, https://www.latinorebels.com/2018/05/09/why-the-latinx-com munity-should-fight-for-a-job-guarantee/; Kate Aronoff, "Yes, A Job Guarantee Could Create 'Boondoggles,' It also Might Save the Planet," May 1, 2018, https://inthese times.com/article/federal-jobs-guarantee-boondoggle-climate-bernie-sanders.

43. A prevailing narrative on the job guarantee suggests that it was rooted in capitalist status quo–like New Deal policies, and that the original intent was that it be a temporary program. Recent evidence uncovered on direct job creation by Steven

Attewell finds that it had a more radical, bold intent, seeking not just to combat un-employment but as part of a more comprehensive plan to attack poverty and inequal-ity in America. Steven Attewell, *People Must Live by Work: Direct Job Creation in America, from FDR to Reagan* (University of Pennsylvania Press, 2019).

44. Colleen Hooper, "Ballerinas on the Dole: Dance and the U.S. Comprehensive Employment Act (CETA), 1974–1982," *Dance Research Journal* 49, no. 3 (2017): 70–89, doi: https://doi.org/10.1017/S0149767717000365.

45. See for instance recent results of a poll by National Public Radio, Robert Wood Johnson Foundation, Harvard Chan School of Public Health that highlighted percep-tions of discrimination by LGBTQ people of color, which found greater degrees of "per-sonal discrimination" when applying for jobs as compared to white LGBTQ respon-dents. The poll findings can accessed at: https://www.npr.org/2017/11/25/564887796/for-lgbtq-people-of-color-discrimination-compounds. Limitations of the poll aside, self-reported data is that all "people of color" are grouped as aggregated due to low sample size challenges. Also see Deena Prichep, "For LGBTQ People of Color, Dis-crimination Compounds," National Public Radio, November 25, 2017, https://www.npr.org/2017/11/25/564887796/for-lgbtq-people-of-colordiscrimination-com-pounds; Black Futures Lab, "When the Rainbow is Not Enough: LGBT+ Voices in the 2018 Black Census," 2019, https://blackcensus.org/.

46. Alex Vitale's *The End of Policing* explains the racist origins of policing in the U.S., with specificity to their purpose to control non-white and poor communities (with excellent analysis on the "War on Drugs" and historic ways in which African Americans and Latinxs have been independently to collectively targeted at all levels of law enforcement to sentencing). His policy proposals, which would make polic-ing essentially obsolete, challenges current neoliberal reforms of the "carceral state" and argues for non-punitive approaches that include local/community level support programs, economic investment, and inclusive political representation. Alex Vitale, *The End of Policing* (Verso Books, 2017).

47. For a recent, succinct synopsis of state-level family leave proposals and their larger national implications, see Maya Rossin-Slater, "Easing the Burden: Why Paid Family Leave Policies are Gaining Steam," Institute for Economic Policy Research, Stanford University, 2018, https://siepr.stanford.edu/research/publications/paid-family-leave-policies.

48. For more on the Debt Collective's short-term aims to long-term goals toward debt cancellation, see here: https://debtcollective.org/.

49. During the 2019/20 primary election, presidential candidates Senators Eliza-beth Warren and Bernie Sanders offered unprecedented student debt cancellation policies. For more, see Katherine Mangan, "Warren's Free-College Plan Would Cancel Student Debt for Millions," *Chronicle of Higher Education*, 2019, https://www.chronicle.com/article/Warren-s-Free-College-Plan/246153. For comparative of their proposals, see Nick Hazelrigg, "Sanders vs. Warren on College Debt Relief," *Inside Higher Ed*, June 26, 2019, https://www.insidehighered.com/news/2019/06/25/sanders-outflanks-warren-proposal-universal-student-loan-debt-relief.

References

Addo, Fenaba. "The Perpetuation and Persistence of Racial Wealth Inequality." In *People of Color in the United States: Contemporary Issues in Education, Work, Communities, Health, and Immigration*, ed. P. B. Jackson, 343–49. ABC-CLIO Corporate, 2016.

Aigner, Dennis J., and Glen G. Cain. "Statistical Theories of Discrimination in Labor Markets." *Industrial and Labor Relations Review* 30, no. 2 (1977): 175–87, doi:10.2307/2522871.

Aja, Alan A. *Miami's Forgotten Cubans: Race, Racialization and the Local Afro-Cuban Experience*. London, United Kingdom: Palgrave Macmillan, 2016.

Aja, Alan A., Gretchen Beesing, Daniel Bustillo, Danielle Clealand, Mark Paul, Khaing Zaw, Anne E. Price, Darrick Hamilton, and William Darity Jr. "The Color of Wealth in Miami." A Joint Publication of the Kirwan Center on the Study of Race and Ethnicity (Ohio State University), Samuel DuBois Cook Center on Social Equity (Duke University), Insight Center for Community Economic Development (Oakland, California), 2019. http://kirwaninstitute.osu.edu/the-color-of-wealth-in-miami/.

Aja, Alan A., Daniel Bustillo, Darrick Hamilton, and William Darity Jr. "From a Tangle of Pathology to a Race-Fair America." *Dissent*, 2014. https://www.dissent magazine.org/article/from-a-tangle-of-pathology-to-a-race-fair-america.

Aja, Alan A., Raúl Carrillo, and Rita Sandoval. "Why the Latinx Community Should Fight for a Job Guarantee." *Latino Rebels*, May 9, 2018. https://www.latinorebels .com/2018/05/09/why-the-latinx-community-should-fight-for-a-job-guarantee/.

Aja, Alan A., William A. Darity Jr., and Darrick Hamilton. "How Cities Can Do Better than the Fight for $15." *Yes! Magazine*, October 6, 2017. https://www.yes magazine.org/economy/2017/10/06/how-cities-and-towns-can-do-better-than-the -fight-for-15/.

Aja, Alan A., Stephan Lefebvre, Nancy López, Darrick Hamilton, and William Darity Jr. "Toward a Latinx/a/o Stratification Economics." *Review of Black Political Economy*, forthcoming 2021.

Aja, Alan A., Stephan Lefebvre, Reynaldo Ortiz-Minaya, Darrick Hamilton, and William Darity Jr. "Bold Policies for Puerto Rico: A Blueprint for Transformative, Justice-Centered Recovery." *Dialogo Interdisciplinary Journal* 21, no. 2 (Fall 2018): 3–14. *Project MUSE*, doi:10.1353/dlg.2018.0023.

Akee, Randall, Maggie R. Jones, and Sonya R. Porter. "Race Matters: Income Shares, Income Inequality and Income Mobility for All U.S. Races." *Demography* 56, Issue 3 (2019): 999–1021. https://link.springer.com/article/10.1007%2Fs13524-019-00773-7.

Alba, Richard. "The Likely Persistence of a White Majority." *Atlantic*, January 11, 2016. https://prospect.org/civil-rights/likely-persistence-white-majority/.

Alba, Richard, and Victor Nee. *Remaking the American Mainstream: Assimilation and Contemporary Immigration*. Cambridge, MA: Harvard University Press, 2003.

Alcantara, Amanda. "Afro-Latinidad and Redefinining Resilience in the Latinx Community: A Speech." Dartmouth College, November 4, 2016. http://www.radical latina.com/2016/11/afro-latinidad-and-redefining_2.html.

Alexander, Michelle. *The New Jim Crow: Mass Incarceration in the Age of Color Blindness*. New York: New Press, 2012.

Allen, Vincent C., Christina LaChance, Britt Rios-Ellis, and Kimberly A. Kaphingst. "Issues in the Assessment of 'Race' Among Latinos: Implications for Race and Policy." *Hispanic Journal of Behavioral Sciences* 33, no. 4 (November 2011): 411–24. doi: 10.1177/0739986311422880.

Andrews, George Reid. "Afro-Latin America by the Numbers: The Politics of the Census." *ReVista: Harvard Review of Latin America*, Winter 2018. https://revista .drclas.harvard.edu/book/afro-latin-america-numbers-politics-census.

Appel, Hannah, Sa Whitley, and Caitlin Kline. "The Power of Debt: Identity and Collective Action in the Age of Finance." *Debt Collective*, 2019.

Aronoff, Kate. "Yes, A Job Guarantee Could Create 'Boondoggles,' It also Might Save the Planet." *In These Times*, May 1, 2018. https://inthesetimes.com/article /federal-jobs-guarantee-boondoggle-climate-bernie-sanders.

Asante-Muhamad, Dedrick, and Chuck Collins. "Inequality Crisis: Blacks and Latinos on the Road to Zero Wealth." *USA Today*, September 17, 2017. https://eu.usatoday .com/story/opinion/2017/09/13/inequality-crisis-blacks-and-latinos-on-road-zero -wealth-asante-muhammad-collins-column/659766001/.

Asante-Muhamad, Dedrick, Emanuel Nieves, Chuck Collins, and Josh Hoxie. "The Road to Zero Wealth: How the Racial Wealth Divide Is Hollowing Out America's Middle Class." *Prosperity Now*, September, 2017. https://prosperitynow.org /resources/road-zero-wealth.

Attewell, Steven. *People Must Live by Work: Direct Job Creation in America, from FDR to Reagan*. Philadelphia: University of Pennsylvania Press, 2019.

Aurajo, Ana Luisa. *Reparations for Slavery and the Slave Trade: A Transnational and Comparative History*. New York: Bloomsbury Academic, 2018.

Banks, Nina. "Black Women on the Verge: Revolutionary Transformation or Super-Exploitation? Missing Black Men and Its Impact on Black Women." Presentation at the 2nd Annual National Economic Association-American Society of Hispanic

Economists Freedom and Justice Conference, Howard University, Washington, DC, 2015.

————"Black women's labor market history reveals deep-seated race and gender discrimination." Economic Policy Institute's *Working Economics* blog, February 19, 2019. https://www.epi.org/blog/black-womens-labor-market-history-reveals-deep-seated-race-and-gender-discrimination/.

————"The Black Woman Economist Who Pioneered a Federal Jobs Guarantee." Institute for New Economic Thinking. February 22, 2019. https://www.ineteconomics.org/perspectives/blog/the-black-woman-economist-who-pioneered-a-federal-jobs-guarantee.

Baradaran, Mehrsa. *The Color of Money: Black Banks and the Racial Wealth Gap.* Cambridge, Massachusetts: Belknap Press: An Imprint of Harvard University Press, 2017.

Barajas, H. L., and J. L. Pierce. "The Signficance of Race and Gender in School Success Among Latinas and Latinos in College." *Gender & Society* 15, no. 6 (2001): 859–78. https://doi.org/10.1177/089124301015006005.

Baum, Sandy, and Patricia Steele. "Who Borrows Most? Bachelor's Degree Recipients with High Levels of Student Debt." College Board, Trends in Higher Education Series, 2010. https://trends.collegeboard.org/sites/default/les/trends-2010-who-borrows-most-brief.pdf.

Bayer, Patrick, Fernando Ferreira, and Stephen L. Ross. "What Drives Racial and Ethnic Differences in High Cost Mortgages? The role of high risk lenders." NBER Working Paper No. 22004, February 2016. http://www.nber.org/papers/w22004 DOI is 10.3386/w22004.

Becker, Gary S. *The Economics of Discrimination.* Second Edition. Chicago: University of Chicago Press, 1971.

Bentley-Edwards, Keisha L., Malik Chaka Edwards, Cynthia Neal Spence, William A. Darity Jr., Darrick Hamilton, and Jasson Perez. "How does it feel to be a problem? The Missing Kerner Commission Report." *RSF: The Russell Sage Foundation Journal of the Social Sciences* 4, no. 6 (September 2018): 20–40. DOI: https://doi.org/10.7758/RSF.2018.4.6.02.

Betancur, John. "Framing the Discussion of African American–Latino Relations: A Review and Analysis." In *Neither Enemies nor Friends*, edited by Suzanne Oboler and Anani Dzidzienyo, 159–72. London: Palgrave Macmillan, 2005.

Bhattacharya, Jhumpa, Anne E. Price, and Fenaba Addo. *Clipped Wings: Closing the Wealth Gap for Millennial Women.* Asset Funders Network, Texas Women's Foundation, The New York Women's Foundation, 2019.

Black Futures Lab. "When the Rainbow is Not Enough: LGBT+ Voices in the 2018 Black Census, 2019. https://blackcensus.org/.

Bonilla-Silva, Eduardo. "From bi-racial to tri-racial: Towards a new system of racial stratification in the USA." *Ethnic and Racial Studies* 27, no. 6 (2004): 931–50. DOI: 10.1080/0141987042000268530.

————. *Racism without Racists: Color-blind racism and the persistence of racial inequality in the United States.* Boulder: Rowman & Littlefield, 2nd edition, 2009.

————. "Rethinking Racism: Toward a Structural Interpretation." *American Socio-logical Review* 62, no. 3 (1997): 465–80. https://doi.org/10.2307/2657316.

————."We are all Americans! The Latin Americanization of racial stratification in the USA." *Race and Society* 5 (2002): 3–16. https://doi.org/10.1016/j.racsoc.2003.12.008.

Borrell, Luisa N., and Natalie D. Crawford. "Disparities in Self-Reported Hypertension in Hispanic Subgroups, Non-Hispanic Black and Non-Hispanic White Adults: The National Health Interview Survey." *Annals of epidemiology* 18, no. 10 (2008): 803–12. doi:10.1016/j.annepidem.2008.07.008.

Bowen, Larnies A., Ayanna Legros, Tianna Paschel, Geísa Mattos, Kleaver Cruz, and Juliet Hooker. "A Hemispheric Approach to Contemporary Black Activism." *NACLA*, March 20, 2018. https://nacla.org/news/2017/03/20/hemispheric-approach-contemporary-black-activism.

Broady, Kristen E., Curtis L. Todd, and William Darity Jr. "Passing and the Costs and Benefits of Appropriating Blackness," *Review of Black Political Economy* 45, Issue 2 (2018): 104–22. https://doi.org/10.1177/0034644618789182.

Brown, Anna, and Eileen Patten. "Statistical Portrait of Hispanics in the United States, 2012." Pew Research Center's Hispanic Trends Project, April 2014.

Burton, Linda M., Eduardo Bonilla-Silva, Victor Ray, Rose Buckelew, and Elizabeth Hordge Freeman. "Critical Race Theories, Colorism, and the Decade's Research on Families of Color." *Journal of Marriage and Family* 72, no. 3 (2010): 440–59. DOI:10.1111/j.1741-3737.2010.00712.x.

Cartagena, Juan. "Lost Votes, Lost Bodies, Lost Jobs: The Effect of Mass Incarceration on Latinx Civic Engagement." In *Behind Bars: Latinxs/as and Prison in the United States*, edited by Suzanne Oboler, 133–148. New York: Palgrave Macmillan, 2009.

Charron-Chénier, Raphael, and Louise Seamster. "(Good) Debt is an Asset." *Contexts* 17, no. 1 (2081): 88–90. https://doi.org/10.1177/1536504218767126

Chiteji, Ngina, and Darrick Hamilton. "Family Connections and the Black-White Wealth Gap Among Middle Class Families." *Review of Black Political Economy* 30, no. 1 (2002): 9–27. https://doi.org/10.1007/bf02808169.

Clealand, Danielle Pilar. *The Power of Race in Cuba: Racial Ideology and Black Consciousness during the Revolution.* New York: Oxford University Press, 2017.

Cobás, Jose A., Jorge Duany, and Joe R. Feagin, eds. *How the United States Racializes Latinos: White Hegemony and its Consequences.* London: Routledge Press, 2009.

Cohn, D'vera. "Race and the Census: The 'Negro' Controversy." Pew Research Center, January 21, 2010. https://www.pewsocialtrends.org/2010/01/21/race-and-the-census-the-negro-controversy/.

Connolly, N. D. B. *A World More Concrete: Real Estate and the Remaking of Jim Crow South Florida.* Chicago: University of Chicago Press, 2014.

Conrad, Cecilia A. "Changes in the Labor Market Status of Black Women, 1960–2000." In *African Americans in the U.S. Economy*, edited by Cecilia A. Conrad, John Whitehead, Patrick Mason, and James Stewart, 157–62. Lanham: Rowman & Littlefield Publishers, 2005.

Cordero-Guzmán, Héctor. "Characteristics of Participants in Puerto Rico's Nutritional Assistance Program (PAN) and their connections to the Labor Market." Working Paper, American Sociological Association annual conference proceedings, August 8, 2018.

Crenshaw, Kimberlé, "Mapping the Margins: Intersectionality, Identity Politics, and Violence Against Women of Color." *Stanford Law Review* 43, no. 6 (July 1991): 1241–99. https://doi.org/10.2307/1229039.

Cruz-Janzen, Marta I. "Latinegras: Desirable Women—Undesirable Mothers, Daughters, Sisters, and Wives." In *The Afro-Latin@ Reader: History and Culture in the United States*, edited by Miriam Jiménez Román and Juan Flores, 282–95. Durham: Duke University Press, 2010. DOI: 10.1353/fro.2001.0035.

Cuevas, Adolfo G., Beverly Aurajo Dawson, and David Williams. "Race and Skin Color in Latino Health: An Analytical Review." *American Journal of Public Health* 106, no. 12 (2016): 2131–36. https://www.ncbi.nlm.nih.gov/pmc/articles /PMC5104999/.

Darity Jr., William A. "Forty Acres and a Mule in the 21st Century." *Social Science Quarterly* 89, no. 3 (2008): 656–64. https://doi.org/10.1111/j.15406237 .2008.00555.x.

———. "Stratification Economics: The Role of Intergroup Inequality." *Journal of Economics and Finance* 29, no. 2 (Summer 2005): 144–53. https://doi .org/10.1007/bf02761550.

———. "The Human Capital Approach to Black-White Earnings Inequality: Some Unsettled Questions." *Journal of Human Resources* 17, no. 1 (1981): 72–93. https://doi.org/10.2307/145525.

———."The Latino Flight to Whiteness." *American Prospect*, 2016. http://prospect. org/article/latino-flight-whiteness.

———. "The New (Incorrect) Harvard/Washington Consensus on Racial Inequality." *DuBois Review* 8, no. 2 (Fall 2011): 467–76. DOI: 10.1017/S1742058X11000439.

Darity Jr., William A., Jason Dietrich, and Darrick Hamilton. "Bleach in the Rainbow: Latino Ethnicity and Preference for Whiteness." In *The Afro-Latin@ Reader: History and Culture in the United States*, edited by Miriam Jiménez Román and Juan Flores, 485–98. Durham: Duke University Press, 2010.

Darity Jr., William A., Jason Dietrich, and Darrick Hamilton. "Bleach in the Rainbow: Latin Ethnicity and Preference for Whiteness." *Transforming Anthropology* 13 (2005): 103–9. doi:10.1525/tran.2005.13.2.103.

Darity Jr., William A., Darrick Hamilton, and Jason Dietrich. "Passing on Blackness: Latinos, race, and earnings in the USA." *Applied Economics Letters* 9, no. 13 (2002): 847–53. DOI: 10.1080/13504850210149133.

Darity Jr., William A., Darrick Hamilton, Patrick Mason, Gregory Price, Alberto Davila, Marie T. Mora, and Sue Stockly. "Stratification Economics: A General Theory of Intergroup Inequality." In *Hidden Rules of Race: Barriers to an Inclusive Economy*," edited by Andrea Flynn, Dorian T. Warren, Felicia Wong, and Susan Holmberg, New York: Cambridge University Press, 2017, 35–51.

Darity Jr., William A., and Kirsten Mullen. *From Here to Equality: Reparations for Black Americans in the 20th Century*. Chapel Hill: University of North Carolina Press, 2020.

Darity Jr., William A., Jason Dietrich, and David K. Guilkey. "Persistent Advantage or Disadvantage? Evidence in Support of the Intergenerational Drag Hypothesis." *American Journal of Economics and Sociology* 60, no. 2 (2001): 435–70. Accessed October 7, 2020. http://www.jstor.org/stable/3487929.

Darity Jr., William A., Darrick Hamilton, Mark Paul, Anne Price, Alan Aja, Antonio Moore, Caterina Chiopris. "What we get wrong about Closing the Wealth Gap." DuBois Cook Center on Social Equity, Insight Center for Community Economic Development, 2018. https://socialequity.duke.edu/portfolio-item/what-we-get-wrong-about-closing-the-racial-wealth-gap/.

Darity Jr., William A., and Patrick L. Mason. "Evidence on Discrimination on Employment: Codes of Color, Codes of Gender." *Journal of Economic Perspectives* 12, no. 2 (Spring 1998). DOI: 10.1257/jep.12.2.63.

Darity Jr., William A., Patrick L. Mason, and James B. Stewart. "The Economics of Identity: The Origin and Persistence of Racial Identity Norms." *Journal of Economic Behavior & Organization* 60, no. 3 (2006): 283–305. https://doi.org/10.1016/j.jebo.2004.09.005.

Davíla, Alberto, Marie T. Mora and Sue K. Stockly. "Does Mestizaje Matter in the U.S.? Economic Stratification of Mexican Immigrants." *American Economic Review* 101, no. 3 (May 2011): 593–97. DOI: 10.1257/aer.101.3.593.

Dawson, Beverly Aruajo, and Laura Quiros. "The Effects of Racial Socialization on the Racial and Ethnic Identity Development of Latinas." *Journal of Latina/o Psychology* 2, no. 4 (2014): 200–13. https://doi.org/10.1080/10911359.2012.740342.

De La Cruz-Viesca, Melany, Zhenxiang Chen, Paul M. Ong, Darrick Hamilton, and William A. Darity Jr. "The Color of Wealth in Los Angeles." A joint publication of Cook Center for Social Equity, Duke University, the New School, the University of California, Los Angeles, Asian American Studies Center, and the Insight Center for Community Economic Development; published by Federal Reserve Bank of San Francisco, 2015. http://www.aasc.ucla.edu/besol/Color_of_Wealth_Report.pdf.

de Onís, Catalina (Kathleen), "What's in an 'x'?: An Exchange about the Politics of 'Latinx.'" *Chiricú Journal* 1, no. 2 (2017): 78–91. DOI: 10.2979/chiricu.1.2.07.

Denavas-Walt, Carmen, and Bernadette D. Proctor, "Income and Poverty in the United States: 2014," *U.S. Census Bureau*, September 2015.

Denton, Nancy A., and Douglas S. Massey. "Racial identity among Caribbean Hispanics: The effect of double minority status on residential segregation." *American Sociological Review* 54 (1989): 790–808. DOI: 10.2307/2117754.

Desmond, Matthew. *Evicted: Poverty and Profit in the American City*. New York: Broadway Books, 2017.

Diette, Timothy M., Arthur H. Goldsmith, Darrick Hamilton, and William Darity Jr. "Race, Unemployment, and Mental Health in the USA: What We Can Infer About the Psychological Cost of the Great Recession Across Racial Groups." *Journal of Economics, Race and Policy* 1, Issue 2–3 (2018): 75–91. https://doi.org/10.1007/s41996-018-0012-x.

Dixon, Heriberto. "The Cuban-American counterpoint: Black Cubans in the United States." *Dialect Anthropology* 13 (1988): 227–39. https://doi.org/10.1007/BF00253917.

Dunn, Marvin. *Black Miami in the 20th Century*. Gainesville: University of Florida Press, 2016, 1997.

Elliott, James R. "Referral Hiring and Ethnically Homogeneous Jobs: How Prevalent Is the Connection and for Whom?" *Social Science Research* 30, no. 3 (2001): 401–25. https://doi.org/10.1006/ssre.2001.0704.

Ennis, Sharon R., Merarys Ríos-Vargas, and Nora G. Albert. "The Hispanic Population: 2010." U.S. Census Bureau, 2011.

Esdaille, Milca. "The Afro-Latino Connection." *Black Enterprise*, 2004. https://www.blackenterprise.com/the-afro-latino-connection/2/.

Falcón, Angelo. "Latino Statistical Disobedience? Countering the Addition of the Citizenship Question in the 2020 Census," 2018. Ahttp://campaign.r20.constantcontact.com/render?m=1101040629095&ca=3c56b127-edc3-473f-83af-8992a897b967.

Famighetti, Christopher, and Darrick Hamilton. "The Great Recession, education, race and home ownership." *Working Economics* blog, Economic Policy Institute, 2019.https://www.epi.org/blog/the-great-recession-education-race-and-homeownership/.

Feagin, Joe R. *Systemic Racism: a Theory of Oppression*. New York: Routledge, 2006.

Fernández, Roberto M., Emilio J. Castilla, and Paul Moore. "Social Capital at Work: Networks and Employment at a Phone Center." *American Journal of Sociology* 105, no. 5 (2000): 1288–1356. https://doi.org/10.1086/210432.

Finkeldey, Jessica G., and Stephen Demuth. "Race/Ethnicity, Perceived Skin Color and the Likelihood of Adult Arrest." *Race and Justice Sage Journals* (2019). https://journals.sagepub.com/doi/10.1177/2153368719826269.

Flores, Antonio. "How the U.S. Hispanic Population is Changing." September 8, 2017. Pew Research Center Facttank. https://www.pewresearch.org/fact-tank/2017/09/18/how-the-u-s-hispanic-population-is-changing/.

Flores, Juan. "Triple-Consciousness? Afro-Latinos on the Color Line." *Wadabagei: A Journal of the Caribbean and Its Diaspora* 8, no. 1 (2005): 80–85.

"For Reparations: A Conversation with William Darity, Jr." With Adam Simpson and Carla Skandier, The Next Systems Project, 2017. https://thenextsystem.org/for-reparations.

Franqui-Rivera, Harry. *Soldiers of the Nation: Military Service and Modern Puerto Rico, 1868–1952*. Lincoln, NE: University of Nebraska Press, 2018.

Garcia, Lisette M., and Alan Bayer. "Variations in Latino Groups in US Post-Secondary Educational Attainment." *Research in Higher Education* 46, no. 5 (August 2005): 511–33. DOI: 10.1007/s11162-005-3363-5.

Gittleman, Maury, and Edward N. Wolff. "Racial and Ethnic Differences in Wealth." In *Race and Economic Opportunity in the Twenty-First Century, Chapter 2*, edited by Marlene Kim. London: Routledge, 2007. DOI:10.4324/9780203960783.

Golash-Boza, Tanya, and William Darity Jr. "Latino racial choices: the effects of skin colour and discrimination on Latinos' and Latinas' racial self-identifications." *Ethnic and Racial Studies* 31, no. 5 (2008): 899–934. DOI: 10.1080/01419870701568858.

Goldrick-Rab, Sara, Robert Kelchen, and Jason Houle. "The Color of Student Debt: Implications of Federal Loan Program Reforms for Black Students and Historically Black Colleges and Universities." Discussion paper, Wisconsin HOPE Lab, September 2, 2014. https://www.academia.edu/15492963/The_Color_of_Student _Debt_Implications_of_Federal_Loan_Program_Reforms_for_Black_Students _and_Historically_Black_Colleges_and_Universities.

Goldsmith, Arthur H., Darrick Hamilton, and William A. Darity Jr. "Shades of Discrimination: Skin Tone and Wages." *American Economic Review* 96, no. 2 (2006): 242–45. https://doi.org/10.1257/000282806777212152.

González, Juan. *Harvest of Empire: A History of Latinos in America.* New York: Penguin Books, 2001.

González-Barrera, Ana. "Hispanics with darker skin are more likely to experience discrmination than those with lighter skin." Pew Research Center, 2019. https:// www.pewresearch.org/fact-tank/2019/07/02/hispanics-with-darker-skin-are-more -likely-to-experience-discrimination-than-those-with-lighter-skin/.

Gosin, Monika. "A Bitter Diversion: Afro-Cuban immigrants, race and everyday life resistance." *Latino Studies* 15, no. 1 (2017): 4–28. https://link.springer.com /article/10.1057/s41276-017-0046-2.

———. *The Racial Politics of Division: Interethnic Struggles for Legitimacy in Multicultural Miami.* Ithaca: Cornell University Press, 2019.

———. "(Re)framing the Nation: the Afro-Cuban challenge to Black and Latino struggles for American identity." Dissertation, U.C. San Diego, 2009.

Granovetter, Mark. *Getting a Job: A Study of Contract and Careers.* Chicago: University of Chicago Press, 1995.

———. "The Impact of Social Structure on Economic Outcomes." *Journal of Economic Perspectives* 19 (2005): 33–50. doi:10.1257/0895330053147958.

Greenbaum, Susan. "Afro-Cubans in Tampa." In *The Afro-Latin@ Reader*, edited by Miriam Jiménez Román and Juan Flores, 51. Durham: Duke University Press, 2010.

———. *More than Black: Afro-Cubans in Tampa.* Gainesville: University of Florida Press, 2002.

Grosfoguel, Ramón. *Colonial Subjects: Puerto Ricans in a Global Perspective.* First edition ed. Berkeley: University of California Press, 2003.

Hamilton, Darrick. "A Federal Job Guarantee: A Step Toward Racial Justice." *Dissent* Magazine, November 9, 2015. https://www.dissentmagazine.org/online _articles/federal-job-guarantee-racial-justice-darrick-hamilton.

———. "Post-racial rhetoric, racial health disparities, and health disparity consequences of stigma, stress and racism." Washington Center for Equitable Growth, 2017. https://equitablegrowth.org/working-papers/racial-health-disparities/.

———. "Race, Wealth, and Intergenerational Poverty." *American Prospect*, August 14, 2009. https://prospect.org/article/race-wealth-and-intergenerational-poverty.

Hamilton, Darrick, and William A. Darity Jr. "Can 'Baby Bonds' Eliminate the Racial Wealth Gap in Putative Post-Racial America?" *Review of Black Political Economy* 37, nos. 3–4 (2010): 207–16. https://doi.org/10.1007/s12114-010 9063-1.

———. "Crowded Out? The Racial Composition of American Occupations." In *Researching Black Communities: A Methodological Guide*, edited by James S. Jackson et al., 60–78. Ann Arbor: University of Michigan Press, 2012.

———. "The Political Economy of Education, Financial Literacy, and the Racial Wealth Gap." *Federal Reserve Bank of St. Louis Review*, First Quarter, 99, no. 1 (2017): 59–76. http://dx.doi.org/10.20955/r.2017.59-76.

Hamilton, Darrick, William A. Darity Jr., Anne Price, Vishnu Sridharan, and Rebecca Tippett. "Umbrellas Don't Make It Rain: Why Studying and Working Hard Isn't Enough for Black Americans." Samuel DuBois Cook Center on Social Equity at Duke University, the New School, and Insight Center for Community Economic Development, 2015. http://www.insightcced.org/uploads/CRWG/Umbrellas-Dont -Make-It-Rain8.pdf.

Hamilton, Darrick, Arthur Goldsmith, and William A. Darity Jr. "Shedding 'Light' on Marriage: The Influence of Skin Shade on Marriage for Black Females." *Journal of Economic Behavior and Organizations* 72, no. 1 (2009): 30–50. https://doi.org /10.1016/j.jebo.2009.05.024.

Hawkins, Denise. "In Cuba, African Roots Run Deep, but It's a Lesson Students Aren't Learning in the Classroom." NBC News, September 1, 2017. https://www. nbcnews.com/news/nbcblk/cuba-african-roots-run-deep-it-s-lesson-students-aren -n767616.

Hay, Michelle. *I've Been Black in Two Countries, Black Cuban Views on Race in the U.S.* El Paso: LFB Scholarly Publishing, 2009.

Haywood, Jasmine M. "Anti-Black Latino racism in an era of Trumpismo." *International Journal of Qualitative Studies in Education*. 30, no. 10 (2017): 957–964. DOI: 10.1080/09518398.2017.1312613.

Hazelrigg, Nick. "Sanders vs. Warren on College Debt Relief." *Inside Higher Ed*, 2019. https://www.insidehighered.com/news/2019/06/25/sanders-outflanks-warren -proposal-universal-student-loan-debt-relief.

Hernández, Tanya K., "Afro-Latin@s and the Latin@ Workplace." In *The Afro-Latin@ Reader*, edited by Miriam Jiménez Román and Flores 520–24. Durham: Duke University Press.

———. "Employment Discrimination in the Ethnically Diverse Workplace." 49 *Judges J.* 33 (2010). https://ir.lawnet.fordham.edu/faculty_scholarship/14.

———. *Multiracials and Civil Rights: Mixed Race Stories of Discrimination*. New York: NYU Press, 2018.

Herring, Cedric, Verna M. Keith, and Hayward Derrick Horton, eds. *Skin Deep: How Race and Complexion Matter in the "Color-Blind" Era*. Urbana: University of Illinois Press, 2004.

Hogan, Howard. "Race Reporting Among Hispanics: Analysis of ACS Data." In *Frontiers of Applied Demography* edited by D.A. Swanson. The Frontiers of Applied Demography, Applied Demography Series 9, COI 10 (2017).1007/978-3-319 -43329-5_9.

Holder, Michelle. *African American Men and the Labor Market during the Great Recession*. New York: Palgrave Macmillan, 2017.

————. "Revisiting Bergmann's Occupational Crowding Model." *Review of Radical Political Economics* 50, no. 4 (2018): 683–90. https://doi.org/10.1177 /0486613418788406.

Holzer, Harry. "Informal Job Search and Black Youth Unemployment." *American Economic Review* 77 (1987): 446–52. DOI: 10.3386/w1860.

Hooper, Colleen. "Ballerinas on the Dole: Dance and the U.S. Comprehensive Employment Act (CETA), 1974–1982." *Dance Research Journal* 49, no. 3 (2017): 70–89. DOI: https://doi.org/10.1017/S0149767717000365.

"Housing Discrimination Against Racial and Ethnic Minorities." Executive Summary (June). Prepared for the U.S. Department of Housing and Urban Development, Washington DC, 2012. http://www.huduser.org/portal/Publications/pdf/HUD-514 _HDS2012_execsumm.pdf.

Howell, J., and E. Korver-Glenn. "Neighborhoods, Race, and the Twenty-first-century Housing Appraisal Industry." *Sociology of Race and Ethnicity*, 2018. DOI: 10.1177/2332649218755178.

Hoxie, Josh. "Blacks and Latinos will be broke in a few decades." *Fortune*, September 19, 2017. http://fortune.com/2017/09/19/racial-inequality-wealth-gap-america/.

Hugo López, Mark. "Hispanic Identity." Pew Research Center, 2013. http://www .pewhispanic.org/2013/10/22/3-hispanic-identity/.

Hunter, Margaret. "The Persistent Problem of Colorism: Skin Tone, Status and Wages." *Sociology Compass* 1, Issue 1 (July 2007). https://doi.org/10.1111/j.1751 -9020.2007.00006.x.

Jiménez Román, Miriam. "Check Both! Afro-Latin@s and the U.S. Census." NACLA, November 18, 2010. https://nacla.org/article/check-both-afro-latins-and-census.

Jiménez Román, Miriam, and Juan Flores, eds. *The Afro-Latin@ Reader*. Durham: Duke University Press, 2010. DOI: 10.1353/fro.2001.0035.

Jones, Janelle, and John Schmitt. "A College Degree Is No Guarantee." Center for Economic and Policy Research, 2014. http://cepr.net/documents/black-coll -grads-2014-05.pdf.

Jones, Janelle, John Schmitt, and Valerie Wilson. "50 Years after the Kerner Commission Report." Economic Policy Institute, February 26, 2018. https://www.epi.org /publication/50-years-after-the-kerner-commission/.

Jorge, Angela. "The Black Puerto Rican Woman in Contemporary American Society." In *The Afro-Latin@ Reader: History and Culture in the United States*, edited by Miriam Jiménez Román and Juan Flores, 269. Durham: Duke University Press, 2010. DOI: 10.1353/fro.2001.0035.

Kamarck, Elaine, and Christine Stenglein. "How many undocumented immigrants are in the United States and who are they?" Brookings Institution *"Voter Vitals" Report*, Washington, D.C, 2019. https://www.brookings.edu/policy2020/votervital /how-many-undocumented-immigrants-are-in-the-united-states-and-who-are-they/.

Katz, Michael B. *The Undeserving Poor: America's Enduring Confrontation with Poverty*. Second edition. Oxford: Oxford University Press, 2013.

Katznelson, Ira. *When Affirmative Action Was White: An Untold History of Racial Inequality in Twentieth-Century America.* New York: W.W. Norton & Co., 2005

Kaufman, Jennifer E., William T. Gallo, and Marianne C. Fahs."The contribution of dementia to the disparity in family wealth between black and non-black

Americans." *Ageing and Society*, August 2018. https://www.cambridge.org/core /journals/ageing-and-society/article/contribution-of-dementia-to-the-disparity-in -family-wealth-between-black-and-nonblack-americans/A401D90931B25C0CD 197CEFCA20CAC87.

Killewald, Alexandra, and Brielle Bryan. "Does Your Home Make You Wealthy?" *Russell Sage Foundation Journal of the Social Sciences* 2, no. 6 (2018): 110. DOI: 10.7758/rsf.2016.2.6.06.

Killewald, Alexandra, F. T. Pfeffer, and J. N. Schachner. "Wealth Inequality and Accumulation." *Annual Review of Sociology* 43, no. 1 (2017): 379–404. DOI: 10.1146 /annurev-soc-060116-053331.

Kochhar, Rakesh and Anthony Cilluffo. "How Wealth Inequality has changed in the U.S. since the Great Recession, by race, ethnicity and income." Pew Research Center, November 1, 2017. http://www.pewresearch.org/fact-tank/2017/11/01/how -wealth-inequality-has-changed-in-the-u-s-since-the-great-recession-by-race -ethnicity-and-income/.

Laó-Montes, Agustín. "Afro-Latinidades and the Diasporic Imaginary." *Iberoamericana* 5, no. 17 (2005): 117–30.

LaVeist-Ramos, Thomas Alexis, Jessica Galarraga, Roland J. Thorpe, Caryn N. Bell, and Chermeia J. Austin. "Are Black Hispanics Black or Hispanic? Exploring Disparities at the Intersection of Race and Ethnicity." *Journal of Epidemiology and Community Health* 66, no. 7 (2012): e21. http://dx.doi.org.proxyau.wrlc .org/10.1136/jech.2009.103879.

Lefebvre, Stephan. "U.S.-Latinx: Might Trump Prompt 'Statistical Disobedience'?" *AULA* blog, 2018. https://aulablog.net/2018/08/21/.

Lin, Nan. *Social Capital: A Theory of Social Structure and Action*. New York: Cambridge University Press, 2001.

Lipsitz, George. *The Possessive Investment in Whiteness: How White People Profit from Identity Politics*. Philadelphia: Temple University Press, 2006.

Logan, John R. "How Race Counts for Hispanic Americans." Lewis Mumford Center for Comparative Urban and Regional Research, University at Albany, 2003. DOI: 10.1177/0307920104040799.

———. "How Race Counts for Hispanic Americans." In *The Afro-Latin@ Reader: History and Culture in the United States*, edited by Miriam Jiménez Román and Juan Flores, 475–84. Durham: Duke University Press, 2010.

López, Antonio. *Unbecoming Blackness: The Diaspora Cultures of Afro-Cuban America*. New York: NYU Press, 2012.

López, Gustavo, and Ana Gonzalez-Barrera. "Afro-Latino: A Deeply Rooted Identity among U.S. Hispanics." Pew Research Center, March 1, 2016. https://www.pew research.org/fact-tank/2016/03/01/afro-latino-a-deeply-rooted-identity-among -u-s-hispanics/.

López, Nancy. "Contextualizing Lived Race-Gender and the Racialized-Gendered Social Determinants of Health." In *Mapping "Race": Critical Approaches to Health Disparities Research*, edited by Laura Gómez and Nancy López, 179–211. New Brunswick, NJ: Rutgers University Press, 2013.

———. "Killing two birds with one stone? Why we need two separate questions on race and ethnicity in the 2020 census and beyond." *Latino Studies* 11, no. 3 (2013b): 428–38. https://doi.org/10.1057/lst.2013.25.

———. "What's Your 'Street Race-Gender'? Why We Need Separate Questions on Hispanic Origin and Race for the 2020 Census." *RWJF* (blog). November 26, 2014. http://www.rwjf.org/en/blogs/human-capital-blog/2014/11/what_s_your_street .html.

López, Nancy, Edward Vargas, Melina Juárez, Lisa Cacari-Stone, and Sonia Bettez. "What's Your 'Street Race'? Leveraging Multidimensional Measures of Race and Intersectionality for Examining Physical and Mental Health Status among Latinxs." *Sociology of Race and Ethnicity*, 2017. https://doi.org/10.1177/2332649217708798.

Luthra, Renee Reichl, and Roger Waldinger. "Into the Mainstream? Labor Market Outcomes of Mexican Origin Workers." *International Labor Migration Review* 44, no. 4 (2010): 830–68. https://doi.org/10.1111/j.1747-7379.2010.00827.x.

Malavet, Pedro A. "Reparations Theory and Postcolonial Puerto Rico: Some Preliminary Thoughts." 13 *Berkeley La Raza Law Journal* (2002): 387. https://scholarship .law.ufl.edu/facultypub/210/.

Mangan, Katherine. "Warren's Free-College Plan Would Cancel Student Debt for Millions. *Chronicle of Higher Education*, April 22, 2019. https://www .chronicle.com/article/Warren-s-Free-College-Plan/246153.

Mangino, William. "The Negative Effects of Privilege on Educational Attainment: Gender, Race, Class, and the Bachelor's Degree." *Social Science Quarterly* 95, no. 3 (2014): 760–84. https://doi.org/10.1111/ssqu.12003.

———. "Why Do Whites and the Rich Have Less Need for Education?" *American Journal of Economics and Sociology* 71, no. 3 (2012): 562–602. https://doi. org/10.1111/j.1536-7150.2012.00823.x.

Martínez, Brandon P. "Housing Inequality: Racial Disparities in the Homeownership and Home Equity Patterns of Cuban-Americans." *Open Access Theses*, 2018, 712. https://scholarlyrepository.miami.edu/oa_theses/712.

Martínez, Brandon P., Nick Petersen, and George Wilson. "Pathways to Cuban-American Homeownership: A Case Study of Race Assimilation, and Ownership Dynamics." In *Latinos in the 21st Century: Their Voices and Lived Experiences*, edited by I. Álvarez and A. Vargas. New York: Nova Science Publishers, 2018.

Mason, Patrick. "Annual income, hourly wages, and identity Among Mexican Americans and other Latinos." *Industrial Relations* 43, no. 4 (2004): 817–34. https://ssrn .com/abstract=591471.

———. "Male Interracial Wage Differentials: Competing Explanations." *Cambridge Journal of Economics* 23, no. 3 (1999): 261–99.

———. "Race, Culture, and Skill: Interracial Wage Differences Among African Americans, Latinos, and Whites." *Review of Black Political Economy* 25, no. 3 (1997): 5–39. https://doi.org/10.1007/s12114-997-1001-5.

———. "The Janus Face of Race: Rhonda M. Williams on Orthodox Economic Schizophrenia." *Review of Black Political Economy* 29, no. 4 (2002): 63–75.

———. "Understanding Recent Empirical Evidence on Race and Labor Market Outcomes in the USA." *Review of Social Economy* 58, no. 3 (2000): 319–38. https:// doi.org/10.1080/00346760050132355.

Massey, Douglas S. "Residential Segregation is the Linchpin of Racial Stratification." *City and Community*, March 15, no. 1 (2016): 4–7. Accessed at: https://online library.wiley.com/doi/abs/10.1111/cico.12145.

———. "Segregation and Stratification: A Biosocial Perspective." *Du Bois Review*, 1, no. 1 (2004): 7–25. https://doi.org/10.1017/S1742058X04040032.

———. "The Racialization of Latinos in the United States." In *The Oxford Handbook of Ethnicity, Crime and Immigration*, 2014. http://www.oxfordhandbooks.com/view/10.1093/oxfordhb/9780199859016.001.0001/oxfordhb-978019985 9016-e-002.

Massey, Douglas, and Nancy Denton. *American Apartheid: Segregation and the Making of the Underclass*. Cambridge, MA: Harvard University Press, 1993.

———. "The Dimensions of Residential Segregation." *Social Forces* 67, no. 2 (December 1, 1988): 281–315. DOI: 10.2307/2579183.

——— "Hypersegregation in U.S. Metropolitan Areas: Black and Hispanic Segregation Along Five Dimensions." *Demography* 26, no. 3 (August 1989): 373–91. DOI: 10.2307/2061599.

Masud-Piloto, Félix. *From Welcomed Exiles to Illegal Immigrants: Cuban Migration to the U.S.* Lanham: Rowman & Littlefield, 1996.

———. "Nuestra Realidad: Historical Roots of Our Latino Identity." In *Beyond Comfort Zones in Multiculturalism: Confronting the Politics of Privilege*, edited by Sandra Jackson and José Solis, 53–60. Westport: Bergin and Garvey (1995).

McCabe, B. J. "Why Buy a Home? Race, Ethnicity, and Homeownership Preferences in the United States." *Sociology of Race and Ethnicity*, 2018. 2332649217753648. DOI: 10.1177/2332649217753648.

McCormick, Jennifer, and César Ayala. "Felicita 'La Prieta' Mendez (1916–1998) and the end of Latino school segregation in California." *CENTRO Journal* 19, no. 2 (Fall 2007).

McMillan-Cottom, Tressie. *Lower Ed: The Troubling Rise of For-Profit Colleges in the New Economy*. New York: New Press, 2017.

Menasce Horowitz, Juliana, Anna Brown, and Kiana Cox. "Race in America, 2019." Pew Research Center, April 9, 2019.

Meschede, Tatjana, Joanna Taylor, Alexis Mann, and Thomas Shapiro. "Family Achievement? How a College Degree Accumulates Wealth for Whites and Not for Blacks." *Federal Reserve Bank of St. Louis Review* 99, no. 1 (2017): 121–37. https://dx.doi.org/10.20955/r.2017.121-137.

Meyerson, Jesse. "Five Economic Reforms Millenials Should Be Fighting For." *Rolling Stone*, January 3, 2014. https://www.rollingstone.com/politics/politics-news/five-economic-reforms-millennials-should-be-fighting-for-102489/.

Mirabal, Nancy. "Melba Alvarado, El Club Cubano Inter-Americano, and the Creation of Afro-Cubanidades in New York City," In *The Afro-Latin@ Reader*, edited by Miriam Jiménez Román and Juan Flores. Durham: Duke University Press.

Modestin, Yvette. "An Afro-Latina's Quest for Inclusion," in *The Afro-Latin@ Reader: History and Culture in the United States*, ed. Miriam Jiménez Román and Juan Flores, 420. Durham, NC: Duke University Press, 2010.

Monforti, J., and G. R. Sanchez. "The Politics of Perception: An Investigation of the Presence and Sources of Perceptions of Internal Discrimination Among Latinos." *Social Science Quarterly* 91 (2010): 245–65. doi:10.1111/j.1540-6237 .2010.00691.x.

Motel, Seth, and Eileen Patten. "Hispanics of Puerto Rican Origin in the United States, 2010 (statistical profile)." Pew Research Center, Pew Research Hispanic Trends Project, 2012a. http://www.pewhispanic.org/2012/06/27/hispanics-of -puerto-rican-origin-in-the-united-states-2010/, 120–126.

———. "Statistical Portrait of Hispanics in the United States." Pew Research Center, Pew Research Hispanic Trends Project, 2014. http://www.pewhispanic .org/2014/04/29/statistical-portrait-of-hispanics-in-the-united-states-2012 /#persons-without-health-insurance-by-age-race-and-ethnicity-2012.

———. "The 10 Largest Hispanic Origin Groups: Characteristics, Rankings, Top Counties | Pew Research Center." Pew Research Center, 2012. http://www.pew hispanic.org/2012/06/27/the-10-largest-hispanic-origin-groups-characteristics -rankings-top-counties.

Muñoz, Ana Patricia, Marlene Kim, Mariko Chang, Regine O. Jackson, Darrick Hamilton, and William Darity Jr. *The Color of Wealth in Boston—Federal Reserve Bank of Boston.* Boston: Federal Reserve Bank of Boston, 2015. https://www .bostonfed.org/publications/one-time-pubs/color-of-wealth.aspx.

Nam, Yunju, Darrick Hamilton, William A. Darity Jr., and Anne E. Price. "Bootstraps Are for Black Kids: Race, Wealth, and the Impact of Intergenerational Transfers on Adult Outcomes." Insight Center for Community Economic Development, September 2015. http://www.insightcced.org/wpcontent/uploads/2015/07/Bootstraps-are -for-Black-Kids-Sept.pdf.

Neckerman, Kathryn M., and Joleen Kirschenman. "Hiring Strategies, Racial Bias and Inner City Workers." *Social Problems* 38, no. 4 (1991): 433–47. DOI: 10.2307/800563.

Newby, C. Alison, and Julie A. Dowling. "Black and Hispanic: The Racial Identification of Afro-Cuban Immigrants in the Southwest." *Sociological Perspectives* 50, no. 3 (2007): 343–66.

"Nine Charts about Wealth Inequality in America." Urban Institute. https://apps .urban.org/features/wealth-inequality-charts/ Updated June 2017.

North, Anna. "We asked all the 2020 candidates how they'd fix childcare: Here's what they said." *Vox*, July 5, 2019. https://www.vox.com/2019/5/22/18302875/2020 -election-democrats-child-care-kids-president.

Oboler, Suzanne, and A. Dzidzienyo, eds. *Neither Enemies nor Friends: Latinos, Blacks, Afro-Latinos.* London: Palgrave McMillan, 2005.

Oliver, Melvin, and Thomas Shapiro. *Black Wealth/White Wealth: A New Perspective on Racial Inequality* (2nd Ed). New York: Routledge, 2006.

Omi, Michael, and Howard Winant. *Racial Formation in the United States.* Third edition. New York: Routledge/Taylor & Francis Group, 2015.

Pager, Devah, and Hana Shepherd. "The sociology of discrimination: Racial discrimination in employment, housing, credit, and consumer markets." *Annual Review of Sociology* 34 (2008): 181–209. doi: 10.1146/annurev.soc.33.040406.131740.

Pager, Devah, and Bruce Western. "Race at Work: Realities of Race and Criminal Record in the NYC Job Market." Published report presented at NYC Commission on Human Rights Conference. Schomburg Center for Research in Black Culture, New York, NY, December 9, 2005.

Painter, Matthew A., Malcolm D. Holmes, and Jenna Bateman. "Skin Tone, Race/ Ethnicity, and Wealth Inequality among New Immigrants." *Social Forces* 94, no. 3 (2015): 1153–85. DOI: 10.1093/sf/sov094.

Painter, Matthew A., and Zhenchao Qia. "Wealth Inequality Among Immigrants: Consistent Racial/Ethnic Inequality in the United States." *Population Research and Policy Review* 35, no. 2 (2016): 147–75. DOI: 10.1007/s11113-016-9385-1.

Paul, Mark, William A. Darity Jr., and Darrick Hamilton. "The Federal Job Guarantee: A Policy to Achieve Full Employment." Center on Budget and Policy Priorities, March 9, 2018. https://www.cbpp.org/research/full-employment/the-federal-job -guarantee-a-policy-to-achieve-permanent-full-employment.

Paul, Mark, Khaing Zaw, Darrick Hamilton, and William A. Darity Jr. "Returns in the Labor Market: A Nuanced View of Penalties at the Intersection of Race and Gender." *Equitable Growth*, 2018. https://equitablegrowth.org/workingpapers/inter sectionality-labor-market/.

Perry, Andre M., Jonathan Rothwell, and David Harshbarger. "The Devaluation of Assets in Black neighborhoods: The case of residential property." Brookings Institute. November 27, 2018. https://www.brookings.edu/research/devaluation-of-assets-in -black-neighborhoods/.

Petersen, Nick, and Marisa Omori. "Unequal Treatment: Racial and Ethnic Disparities in Miami-Dade Criminal Justice." ACLU of Florida, Miami, Florida, 2018. 1–49. https://www.aclufl.org/en/publications/unequal-treatment-racial-and-ethnic -disparities-miami-dade-criminal-justice.

Phillips, Carmen. "Why This Census of U.S. Afro-Latinos is Ground-breaking." *Remezcla*, July 17, 2018. https://remezcla.com/features/culture/census-us-afro latinos-groundbreaking/.

Piketty, Thomas. *Capital in the 21st Century.* Cambridge: Harvard University Press, 2013.

Piketty, Thomas, and Emmanuel Saez. "Inequality in the Long Run." *Science* 344, 6186 (May 2014). DOI: 10.1126/science.1251936.

Piston, Spencer. "Lighter skinned minorities are more likely to support Republicans." *Washington Post*, 2014. https://www.washingtonpost.com/news/monkey cage/wp/2014/09/17/lighter-skinned-minorities-aremorelikelytosupportrepubli cans/?utm_term=.2ae6d4c2e2ec.

Power, Marilyn. "From Home Production to Wage Labor: Women as Reserve Army of Labor." *Review of Radical Political Economics* 15, no. 1 (Spring 1983): 71–91. https://doi.org/10.1177/048661348301500105.

Prichep, Deena. "For LGBTQ People of Color, Discrimination Compounds." National Public Radio, November 25, 2017. https://www.npr.org/2017/11/25 /564887796/for-lgbtq-people-of-color-discrimination-compounds.

Pujols, Jomaira Salas. "Black Latinos are almost Invisible in the Census. We Can Fix That." March 8. *Huffington Post*, March 8, 2018. https://www.huffpost.com /entry/opinion-salas-pujols-black-latinos-census_n_5aa03347e4b002df2c603a9f .

Pulido, Laura, and Manuel Pastor. "Where in the world is Juan? And what color is he? The Geography of Latina/o Racial Identity in Southern California." *American Quarterly* 65, no. 2 (June 2013). doi:10.1353/aq.2013.0020.

Qian, Zhenchao, Daniel T. Lichter, Dmitry Tumin, "Divergent Pathways to Assimilation? Local Marriage Markets and Intermarriage Among U.S. Hispanics," *Journal of Marriage and Family* 80, no. 1 (2017): 271–88. https://onlinelibrary .wiley.com/doi/full/10.1111/jomf.12423.

Quillian, Lincoln, Devah Pager, Ole Hexel, and Arnfinn H. Midtbøen. "The persistence of racial discrimination in hiring." *Proceedings of the National Academy of Sciences* 114, no. 41 (October 2017): 10870–75; DOI: 10.1073/pnas.1706255114.

Quiros, Laura, and Beverly Aurajo Dawson. "The Color Paradigm: The Impact of Colorism on the Racial Identity and Identification of Latinas." *Journal of Human Behavior in the Social Environment* 23, no. 3 (2013): 287–97. https://www .tandfonline.com/doi/abs/10.1080/10911359.2012.740342?src=recsys&journalCo de=whum20.

"Race Timeline: Has Race Always Been the Same?" PBS, http://www.pbs.org/race /003_RaceTimeline/003_01-timeline.htm.

Rao, Sameer. "Mexico Finally Recognizes Afro Mexicans in National Census." *Colorlines,* 2015. https://www.colorlines.com/articles/mexico-finally-recognizes -afro-mexicans-national-census.

Ray, Victor, and Louise Seamster. "Rethinking racial progress: a response to Wimmer." *Ethnic and Racial Studies* 39, no. 8 (2016): 1361–69. DOI: 10.1080 /01419870.2016.1151540.

Rivera, Maritza Quiñones. "From Trigueñita to Afro-Puerto Rican: Intersections of the Racialized, Gendered, and Sexualized Body in Puerto Rico and the U.S. Mainland." *Meridians* 7, no. 1 (2006): 162–82. https://doi.org/10.2979/MER .2006.7.1.162.

Rivera-Rideau, Petra R., Jennifer Jones, Tianna Paschel, eds. *Afro-Latin@s in Movement: Critical Approaches to Blackness and Transnationalism in the Americas,* Afro-Latin@ Diasporas Series, Palgrave Macmillan, 2016.

Rochin, Refugio I. "Latinos and Afro-Latino Legacy in the United States: History, Culture and Issues of Identity." *Professional Agricultural Workers Journal* 3, no. 2 (2016): https://econpapers.repec.org/article/agspawjal/236907.htm.

Rodriguez, Clara E., Michael H. Miyawaki, and Grigoris Argeros. "Latino Racial Reporting in the US: To Be or Not to Be." *Sociology Compass* 7, no. 6 (2013): 390–403. https://doi.org/10.1111/soc4.12032.

Rosales, Steven. "Fighting the Peace at Home: Mexican American Veterans and the 1944 GI Bill of Rights." *Pacific Historical Review* 80, no. 4 (2011): 597–627. https://doi.org/10.1525/phr.2011.80.4.597.

Rosenblum, Alexis, William Darity Jr., Angel L. Harris, and Tod G. Hamilton. "Looking Through the Shades: The Effect of Skin Color on Earnings by Region of Birth and Race for Immigrants to the United States." *Sociology of Race and Ethnicity* 2, no. 1 (2015). https://journals.sagepub.com/doi/abs/10.1177/2332649215600718.

Ross, Stephen L., and Margery Austin Turner. "Housing Discrimination in Metropolitan America: Explaining Changes between 1989 and 2000." *Social Problems* 52, no. 2 (2005): 152–80.

Rossin-Slater, Maya. "Easing the Burden: Why Paid Family Leave Policies are Gaining Steam," Stanford Institute for Economic Policy Research, 2019. https://siepr .stanford.edu/research/publications/paid-family-leave-policies.

Roth, Wendy. "The Multiple Dimensions of Race." *Ethnic and Racial Studies* 39, no. 8 (2016): 1310–38. https://doi.org/10.1080/01419870.2016.1140793.

Rothstein, Richard. *The Color of Law: A Forgotten History of How Our Government Segregated America*. First edition. New York: Liveright Publishing Corporation, 2017.

Rugh, Jacob S., and Douglas S Massey. "Segregation in Post-Civil Rights America: Stalled Integration or End of the Segregated Century?" *DuBois* 11 (2014): 202–32. https://doi.org/10.1017/s1742058x13000180.

Sáenz, Rogelío, and Maria Cristina Morales. *Latinos in the United States, Diversity and Change*, Cambridge, UK: John Wiley & Sons, 2015.

Sawyer, Mark Q. *Racial Politics in Post-Revolutionary Cuba.* New York: Cambridge University Press, 2005.

Seamster, Louise. "Black Debt, White Debt." *Contexts* 18, no. 1 (2019): 30–35. https://doi.org/10.1177/1536504219830674.

Seamster, Louise, and Raphael Charron-Chenier. "Predatory Inclusion and Education Debt: Rethinking the Racial Wealth Gap." *Social Currents*, 2017. https://doi.org /10.1177/2329496516686620.

Seamster, Louise, and Victor Ray. "Against Teleology in the Study of Race: Toward the Abolition of the Progress Paradigm." *Sociological Theory* 36, no. 4 (2018): 315–42. https://doi.org/10.1177/0735275118813614.

Shapiro, Thomas M. "Race, Home Ownership and Wealth," *Journal of Law and Policy* 20 (2006). DOI: 10.3233/JEM-2006-0279.

Shapiro, T., T. Meschede, and S. Osoro. *The Roots of the Widening Racial Wealth Gap: Explaining the Black-White Economic Divide*. Institute for Assets & Social Policy, 2013.

Sharon, Lee, and Sonya Tafoya. "Special issue on The United States Census at the Dawn of the 21st Century." *Journal of Economic and Social Measurement* 31, no. 3–4 (2006): 233–52. DOI: 10.3233/JEM-2006-0279.

Steinberg, Stephen. *The Ethnic Myth; Race, Ethnicity and Class in America*. Boston, MA: Beacon Press, 1981.

———. "Immigration, African Americans and Race Discourse," *New Politics* 10, no. 3 (Summer 2005).

———. *Race Relations: A Critique*. Stanford University Press, 2007.

———. *Turning Back: The Retreat from Racial Justice in American Thought and Policy*, Beacon Press, 1995, 2001.

Stokes-Brown, Atiya Kai. "America's Shifting Color Line: Reexamining Determinants of Latino Racial Self-Identification." *Social Science Quarterly* 93, no. 2 (June 2012). https://onlinelibrary.wiley.com/doi/full/10.1111/j.1540-6237.2012.00852.x.

Tafoya, Sonya M. "Shades of belonging: Latinos and Racial Identity." Pew Hispanic Center, Pew Research Center, Washington, DC, 2004.https://www.pew research.org/hispanic/2004/12/06/shades-of-belonging/.

Taylor, Keeanga-Yamahtta. "Against Black Homeownership." *Boston Review*, November 19, 2019. http://bostonreview.net/race/keeanga-yamahtta-taylor-against -black-homeownership.

———. *Race for Profit: How Banks and the Real Estate Industry Undermined Home Ownership*. Chapel Hill: University of North Carolina Press, 2019.

Tcherneva, Pavlina R. *Beyond full employment: employer of last resort as an institution for change* (Working Paper No. 732) [PDF le]. Levy Economics Institute, 2012. http://www.levyinstitute.org/pubs/wp_732.pdf.

———. *The Case for a Job Guarantee*. Wiley Press, 2020.

Telles, Edward. "Latinos, Race and the U.S. Census," *The ANNALS of the American Academy of Political and Social Science*," April 25, 2018. https://journals.sagepub .com/doi/abs/10.1177/0002716218766463?journalCode=anna.

Telles, Edward. *Pigmentocracies: Ethnicity, race, and color in Latin America*. UNC Press, 2014.

Telles, Edward, and Stanley Bailey. "Understanding Latin American Beliefs about Racial Inequality," *American Journal of Sociology* 118, no. 6 (May, 2013): 1559–95. DOI: 10.1086/670268.

Telles, Edward, Mark Q. Sawyer, and Gaspar Rivera-Salgado. *Just Neighbors? Research on African American and Latino Relations in the United States*. Russell Sage Foundation, 2011. https://doi.org/10.1177/0094306113491549zz.

Theoharis, Jeanne, and David Stein. "What Coretta Scott King Can Teach Democrats About a Job Guarantee." *Huffington Post*, May 23, 2018. https://www.huffpost .com/entry/opinion-stein-theoharis-coretta-jobs-guarantee_n_5b0471dee4b0784c d2af2bf6.

Tippett, Rebecca, Avis Jones-DeWeever, Maya Rockeymoore, Darrick Hamilton, William Darity Jr. *Beyond Broke: Why Closing the Racial Wealth Gap Is a Priority for National Economic Security*. Durham, NC: Duke Center for Global Policy Solutions, 2014.http://globalpolicysolutions.org/wpcontent/uploads/2014/04 /Beyond_Broke_FINAL.pdf.

Tórres, Andy. *Between Melting Pot and Mosaic: African Americans and Puerto Ricans in the New York Political Economy*. Philadelphia: Temple University Press, 1995.

Treschan, Lazar. "Latino Youth in New York City: School, Work and Income Trends for New York's Largest Group of Young People." Community Service Society Policy Brief. October, 2010.

Turner, M. A., R. Santos, D. Levy, D. Wissoker, C. Arandia, R. Pitingolo. Housing Discrimination Against Racial and Ethnic Minorities 2012. Executive Summary (June). Prepared for the U.S. Department of Housing and Urban Development, Washington DC, 2013. http://www.huduser.org/portal/Publications/pdf/HUD-514 _HDS2012_execsumm.pdf.

Valdés, Mimi. 2011. "Black and Latina in Hollywood." *Essence*, October 2011.

Valdés, Vanessa K. *Diasporic Blackness: The Life and Times of Arturo Schomberg.* Albany: SUNY Press, 2017.

Vargas, Nicholas. "Latina/o Whitening? Which Latina/os Self-classify as White and Report Being Perceived as White by Other Americans?" *Du Bois Review: Social Science Research on Race* 12, no. 1 (2015): 119–36.

Vargas, Nicholas, and Kevin Stainback. "Documented Contested Racial Identities Among Self-Identified Latina/os, Asians, Blacks and Whites." *American Behavioral Scientist* 60, no. 4 (2016): 442–64. http://doi.org/10.1177/0002764215613396.

"Vision for Black Lives." Movement for Black Lives. 2016. https://m4bl.org/policy-platforms/.

Vitale, Alex. *The End of Policing.* New York: Verso Books, 2017.

Wade, Peter. *Race and Ethnicity in Latin America.* 2nd edition. London, United Kingdom: Pluto Press, 2010.

Waldinger, Roger. "The Making of an Immigrant Niche." *International Migration Review* 28, Issue 1 (1994): 3–29. DOI: 10.2307/2547023.

Waldinger, Roger, and MI Lichter. *How the Other Half Works: Immigration and the Social Organization of Labor.* Berkeley: University of California Press, 2003.

Walker, Nancy, Michael Senger, Francisco A. Villaruél, and Angela Arboleda. *Lost Opportunities: The Reality of Latinos in the U.S. Criminal Justice System.* Washington, DC: National Council of La Raza, 2004.

Western, Bruce. "The Impact of Incarceration on Wage Mobility and Inequality." *American Sociological Review* 67 (2002): 526–46.

Whalen, Carmen Teresa. "Sweatshops Here and There: The Garment Industry, Latinas, and Labor Migrations." *International Labor and Working Class History* 61 (Spring, 2002): 45–68. DOI: https://doi.org/10.1017/S0147547902000054.

White, Gillian B. "Why Blacks and Hispanics Have Such Expensive Mortgages." *Atlantic*, February 26, 2016. https://www.theatlantic.com/business/archive/2016/02/blacks-hispanics-mortgages/471024/.

Whitten, Norman, and Arlene Torres, eds. *Blackness in Latin America & the Caribbean*, Vol. 1. Bloomington: Indiana University Press, 1998.

Wilson, Valerie. "Before the State of the Union, a Fact Check on Black Unemployment." *Working Economics* blog, Economic Policy Institute, February 1, 2019. https://www.epi.org/blog/before-the-state-of-the-union-a-fact-check-on-blackunemploy ment/.

Wolfers, Justin, David Leonhardt, and Kevin Quealy. "1.5 Million Missing Black Men." *New York Times*, April 21, 2015. http://www.nytimes.com/interactive/2015/04/20/upshot/missing-black-men.html?_r=0.

Wray, L. Randall. "Job guarantee." In *International Encyclopedia of the Social Sciences*, 2nd ed., William A. Darity Jr., 204–6. Detroit, MI: Gale Macmillan, 2008.

Zaw, Khaing, Darrick Hamilton, and William A. Darity Jr. "Race, wealth and incarceration: Results From the National Longitudinal Survey of Youth." *Race and Social Problems* 8, no. 1 (2016): 103–55. https://psycnet.apa.org/record/2016 08694-001.

Index

About the Authors

Michelle Holder is Associate Professor of Economics at John Jay College, City University of New York. Prior to joining the John Jay faculty, she worked professionally as an economist for a decade in both the nonprofit and government sectors. Her research focuses on the Black community and women in the American labor market, and her economic policy reports have been covered by the *New York Times,* the *Wall Street Journal*, the *New York Amsterdam News*, and *El Diario*. She has also appeared on, or been quoted in, media outlets such as CNN, the *Washington Post*, NPR, *The New Yorker*, and PBS. Michelle is currently a Senior Fellow with the Schwartz Center for Economic Policy Analysis (SCEPA) at the New School for Social Research in NYC. Her first book *African American Men and the Labor Market during the Great Recession* was released from Palgrave Macmillan in 2017. Michelle's educational background includes master's and doctoral degrees in economics from the New School for Social Research, and a bachelor's degree in economics from Fordham University.

Alan A. Aja is Professor in the Department of Puerto Rican and Latino Studies at Brooklyn College (City University of New York). He has published in a range of scholarly and public outlets with focus on the racial wealth gap, intergroup disparities, economic stratification, public policy, social movements, economic democracy, and sustainability. His publications include the book *Miami's Forgotten Cubans: Race, Racialization and the Local Afro-Cuban Experience* (Palgrave Macmillan, 2016) and independent and collaborative pieces in the *Boston Review, Rolling Stone, Teen Vogue, Education Week, The Nation, Dissent, American Prospect, Latino Rebels,* and the *Washington Post*. Prior to joining Brooklyn College, Aja worked as a labor organizer in Austin and El Paso, Texas. Aja's educational background includes a doctoral degree from the New School for Social Research in NYC, a master's degree in Sustainable International Development from Brandeis University, and a bachelor's degree in Sociology and Communication from the University of Kentucky.